Just Vibrations

Just Vibrations

The Purpose of Sounding Good

✦ ✦ ✦

WILLIAM CHENG

University of Michigan Press
Ann Arbor

Published in the United States of America by the
University of Michigan Press
Manufactured in the United States of America
♾ Printed on acid-free paper

2019   2018   2017   2016   4   3   2   1

A CIP catalog record for this book is available from the British Library.

Library of Congress Cataloging-in-Publication Data

Names: Cheng, William, 1985– author.
Title: Just vibrations : the purpose of sounding good / William Cheng.
Description: Ann Arbor : University of Michigan Press, [2016] | Includes
   bibliographical references and index.
Identifiers: LCCN 2016017738| ISBN 9780472073252 (hardcover : alk.
   paper) | ISBN 9780472053254 (pbk. : alk. paper) | ISBN 9780472122356
   (e-book)
Subjects: LCSH: Musicology—Moral and ethical aspects. | Musicologists—
   United States. | Cheng, William, 1985– | Chronic pain—Patients. | Gay
   musicologists—United States. | Music—Moral and ethical aspects.
Classification: LCC ML3797 .C54 2016 | DDC 780.72—dc23
LC record available at https://lccn.loc.gov/2016017738

DOI: http://dx.doi.org/10.3998/ump.14078046.0001.001
ISBN 978-0-472-90056-5 (open access e-book)

for Chris

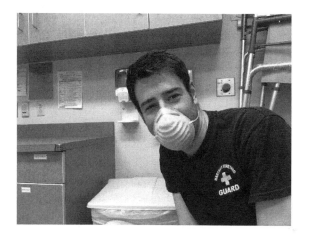

here—significantly, smiling
Mt. Auburn Hospital in Cambridge, MA
2 June 2014

Then with both hands [Milo] made a great circular sweep in the air and watched with delight as all the musicians began to play at once. The cellos made the hills glow red, and the leaves and grass were tipped with a soft pale green as the violins began their song. . . . As Milo frantically conducted, the sky changed slowly from blue to tan and then to a rich magenta red. Flurries of light-green snow began to fall, and the leaves on the trees and bushes turned a vivid orange. All the flowers suddenly appeared black. . . . Seven times the sun rose and almost as quickly disappeared as the colors kept changing. In just a few minutes a whole week had gone by. At last the exhausted Milo, afraid to call for help and on the verge of tears, dropped his hands to his sides. The orchestra stopped.

—Norton Juster, *The Phantom Tollbooth* (1961)

About the Cover Art

✦ ✦ ✦

Jess Landau is a fine artist and photographer whose work involves themes of culture, community, personality development, and human desires for interpersonal connection. In 2014, she received her BFA in photography and art therapy from the University of the Arts in Philadelphia.

The cover art shows a portrait printed on the inner surface of an eggshell (using liquid emulsion, a chemical applied in alternative darkroom printing). It comes from a series called Growth, which Landau created in an effort to heal after suddenly losing a childhood friend to suicide. Handling the eggshell during the photographic printing process exemplified the time needed to appreciate present moments, along with the importance of reflecting on life's fragility. Her website is www.jesslandau.com.

Open Access and Alt-Text

✦ ✦ ✦

Just Vibrations has been published in both print and Open Access. The goal of digital OA is to reach as many readers as possible, especially those who might otherwise be unable to afford or access this text. By harmonizing the book's medium and message (of care, outreach, accessibility), OA offers an electronic file that accommodates convenient text searches, text-to-voice dictation, and transportability via e-readers. For readers with additional visual needs, Alt-Text is available in the digital version for all illustrations in this book. Alt-Text verbally describes images so that readers can access their content.

OA for *Just Vibrations* has been made possible through the generosity of Harvard University's William F. Milton Fund, the Dartmouth Open-Access Publishing Equity Fund, and the University of Michigan Press.

Acknowledgments

✦ ✦ ✦

For all the care devoted to this manuscript, the acknowledgments remains a section where things won't sound good enough. Appreciative words can't do justice to my enduring gratitude for the people without whom the book wouldn't exist.

Susan Brison, Richard Leppert, and Alexander Rehding imparted the vital spirit I needed to trace this project from beginning to end. At the University of Michigan Press, editor Mary Francis trusted in the book early on and presciently knew what it could become long before its fulfillment. For insightful copyediting and smooth production at the Press, I thank Richard Isomaki, Marcia LaBrenz, and Christopher Dreyer. Two anonymous reviewers went to remarkable lengths to recommend diverse improvements.

Revisions benefited from a workshop at the Leslie Humanities Center of Dartmouth College, with participants Aimee Bahng, Andrew Dell'Antonio, Brianne Gallagher, Rosemarie Garland-Thomson, Christian Haines, Graziella Parati, and Steve Swayne. Steve and other Dartmouth music faculty—Michael Casey, Kui Dong, Ashley Fure, Ted Levin, Melinda O'Neal, Sally Pinkas, and Spencer Topel—made me feel unfalteringly welcome and empowered me to do the work I most believed in. Having the freedom to write a book like this was an immense privilege that I won't take for granted. A year's leave via the Harvard Society of Fellows afforded me much-needed headspace during the final stretch. Jess

Landau lent her gorgeous art for the cover. Susan McClary generously took the time to pen a profound and vibrant foreword.

I'm grateful for all friends who read the manuscript, gave care, or otherwise patiently handed me building blocks of prose. Alas, the appearance of names below in list form belies the uniqueness of people's individual, crucial contributions: Chloe Angyal, Michael Bakan, Karol Berger, Michaela Bronstein, Avery Brown, Scott Burnham, Suzanne Cusick, Ryan Dohoney, Rowan Dorin, Noah Feldman, Marta Figlerowicz, Charles Hiroshi Garrett, Roger Mathew Grant, Thomas Grey, Heather Hadlock, Lydia Hamessley, Kyle Kaplan, Mark Katz, Eva Kim, Christine Larson, Frank Lehman, Neil Lerner, Hannah Lewis, Fred Maus, Felicia Miyakawa, Roger Moseley, Anthony Newcomb, Emily Richmond Pollock, Elaine Scarry, Kay Kaufman Shelemay, Anthony Sheppard, Cassie Stoddard, Joseph Straus, Elizabeth Teisberg, Scott Wallace, Emily Wilbourne, Eunice Wong, and Rosalind Wong. I'm also fortunate to have shared portions of this work during colloquiums and classroom discussions at Dartmouth College, Northwestern University, Harvard University, Cornell University, Clark University, New York University, University of Oregon, and Eastman School of Music, where students and faculty provided encouragement and critiques. For late-stage conversations, eagle eyes, and helping hands, I thank Naomi André, Mike Backman, Gregory Barz, Samantha Bassler, Anna Maria Busse Berger, Lauren Berlant, Monique Bourdage, Samantha Candon, Dale Chapman, Paula Durbin-Westby, Yesim Erdmann, Roger Freitas, Samuel Golter, Stephanie Jensen-Moulton, Jeannette Jones, Loren Kajikawa, Kelly Katz, Catherine LaTouche, Peter McMurray, Katherine Meizel, Diana Morse, Stephan Pennington, Marcus Pyle, Maureen Ragan, Matthew Leslie Santana, Amartya Sen, Anne Shreffler, and Jonathan Sterne.

Final and always thanks go to Chris Schepici, my parents, and family, whose love makes life good.

Brief excerpts from *Just Vibrations* appeared in recent articles for *Slate, Huffington Post, Washington Post,* and *Musicology Now.*

Contents

✦ ✦ ✦

Foreword

Humanizing the Humanities

✦ ✦ ✦

Susan McClary
Case Western Reserve University

Many people choose to specialize in the humanities because they promise a life of the mind, a labor that involves reading poetry, gazing at paint-
ings, listening to music. With the humanities growing ever more embattled in today's institutions of higher learning, our advocates often claim
that immersion in cultural media makes our students better people:
more open to empathy, more fully acquainted with and tolerant of multiple points of view. If only world leaders would take time out to attend to
da Vinci or Schubert or Proust; then, we'd like to imagine, there might
be universal peace. A worthy goal, of course. But to what extent do the
humanities (as practiced in our universities) actually foster the ideals to
which we give voice?

I recall vividly the first time I noticed a turning point in literary studies. I was serving as a member of the doctoral committee for a candidate
in an English department, and I admired her close readings of Derrida,
de Man, and Deleuze. But I kept thinking that this must be a prolegom-
enon to an analysis of a novel or a poem—an analysis that never material-
ized. At the dissertation defense, I asked the candidate to demonstrate

her points with respect to an actual work. She was shocked that I would expect such a thing. When pressed further, she could not offer a single title within her stated area of specialization.

And I feared that young musicologists would eventually jump on this bandwagon of French theory and obfuscating prose. The urge to do so may be all the more tempting for those who were spooked by undergraduate classes that focused on the labeling of chords. Resisting now the analysis of what they dismissed cavalierly as "the music itself" could become a moral high ground. Never mind that relatively few scholars can understand the gnarliest prose styles of critical theory; this lack of popular comprehension only renders the writer more smug, and, alas, worthy of greater adulation. Certain humanists effectively seal themselves off with hermetic language and competition for impenetrability.

The so-called New Musicology is sometimes blamed for spreading these trends from other disciplines into music studies. To be sure, some of us did introduce Adorno, Foucault, and the like into the field. But much like the hapless Australians who imported rabbits only to have those lagomorphs take over their environment, so we occasionally witness theory usurping our publications. If I might raise a word of justification, musicologists such as Lawrence Kramer, Rose Rosengard Subotnik, and myself first turned to cultural theory in order to break through the thick wall of aesthetic autonomy that musicology had erected around its subject matter. Creatures of the 1960s, we had witnessed popular music's power to transform genders, sexualities, race relations, and the political status quo. Our goal was not to exchange the jargon of music theory for that of deconstruction.

Will Cheng's *Just Vibrations* holds a mirror up to musicology and other humanities disciplines, inviting scholars who focus on the arts to take stock. As a young gay man, he never had to fight those tawdry battles over gender and sexuality that wrenched the field in the 1990s; as an individual who experiences severe chronic pain, he did not have to invent the field of disability studies. Thanks to Philip Brett, Joseph Straus, and other pioneers, he seems to have inherited a musicology perfectly suited to his needs.

And yet for all the strides we have made in the last two decades, Cheng demonstrates that we still fall short of meeting our goals. Is there room for caring, he asks, in what can sometimes manifest as a dog-eat-dog academy? Does the hermeneutics of suspicion discourage restorative approaches to our research? To what extent do we flaunt prohibitive prose as a defense mechanism against insecurity and fears of seeming soft?

If the Nazis taught us anything, it is that one may listen to Mozart and still act in barbaric ways. Today's musicians are not likely to offend so egregiously—though the television series *Mozart in the Jungle* reveals that classical music does not guarantee good behavior. And at conferences of the American Musicological Society, some of the most confrontational sessions still resemble blood sport.

Perhaps we can aspire to the grace and balance we experience when we listen to music. Perhaps we can bring that beauty and humaneness into our relationships with our colleagues and students. Rodney King asked, "Can we all get along?" Will Cheng brings that question back to those of us who purport to identify with music. He challenges us to infuse the humanities with the ideals we profess to uphold.

Introduction

Dare We Care?

✦ ✦ ✦

Running Games

In the spring of sixth grade, my friend Philip and I spent our lunch breaks running from a clan of corrupt ninjas. It was a dangerous time to be a student at Annie B. Jamieson Elementary in Vancouver, British Columbia. Ninjas were relentless, and since they blended so smoothly into the shadows, none of our other classmates believed they existed. Good thing Philip and I could fend for ourselves: we knew the ideal hiding spots, stayed swift on our feet, melded into crowds, and communicated over walkie-talkies in secret code (more or less Mandarin, given that the ninjas were reputedly French-Canadian). The affair concluded melodramatically one rainy recess at the monkey bars, with Philip dying in my arms while a flock of our peers looked on with genuine concern. Yet by the next day, everything returned to normal. Philip came back from the dead, and the ninjas vanished, as ninjas do.

In childhood, we played many games. Some games weren't simply adversarial, but driven further by the imagination of clear and present dangers: cops and robbers, Bloody Mary in the mirror, the nominally dehumanized *It* of tag—always posing a sense of virtual villainy afoot. Play-fighting was par for the course; as animals boisterously show, it's helpful should real threats ever strike.[1] So we hid from the Seeker as

2 · JUST VIBRATIONS

if our lives depended on it, scarpered when Mr. Wolf howled for dinner, and leaped across the nice furniture in the house because the floor
seethed with lava. In adult life, even the most serious activities continue
to be deemed game-like, from relationships and elections to drone operations and the war on drugs. As grownups, we remain experts at inventing and obsessing over bogeymen—no longer actual monsters under the
bed (though superstitions can persist), but in the form of criminals, politicians, corporations, and ideologies. In the absence of immediate concerns, we might nonetheless go rooting out causes for outrage, jumping
on social media pages to join the deluge of righteous protest that sweeps
the Internet. From cradle to grave, we imagine dragons. They bring the
world alive, fueling the fiery power grabs of daily existence.

Even when engaged as harmless games, the summoning of big bad
adversaries channels a feeling of paranoia. Around the same time Philip
and I were making a public display battling ninjas, I began stumbling
privately toward a murky awareness of my gay identity. With neither the
proper vocabulary nor maturity to process my emotions, I had only an
inkling that something about me wasn't right, wasn't normal. Accompa-
nying this impression was an equally vague anxiety about being found
out. I couldn't yet put my finger on what I was trying to hide, but whatever it was, I knew I wanted to keep it under wraps. Each day of an otherwise privileged upbringing was attended by a pulsing dread about
how the secret might burst. Through a slip of the tongue? An off-pitch
inflection or a limp twirl of the hand? A misdirected glance in the locker
room? With dilated pupils?

In angst, I found sanctuary in two activities—playing piano and playing video games. With piano, the demands were simple: eighty-eight keys,
make them sing. Video games were straightforward as well: a handful of
buttons, beat the boss. Of particular comfort was the clarity of rules and
goals. The flow of play afforded meditative escape into a protracted present. Aside from worries about the next cadence or the next castle, time
fell away. Like many queer or questioning youths, I lived in cloudy fear
of futurity, with scary tomorrows emptied of heterosexual prospects and
cozy conformity. Getting in the groove of a Chopin waltz or *Mario Kart*
was akin to hitting Pause on life, freezing the countdown to the outing
sure to come. At worst, the hazards of playing piano were wrong notes,
memory slips, and my teacher's rebukes when I swayed too dramatically
on the bench in precocious efforts to appear profound. Video games
proved even more forthcoming in their concrete presentations of pitfalls
and enemies. Although these pixelated obstacles were virtual, they—like

French-Canadian ninjas—sometimes felt more tangible than the dangers out there in the physical world, and infinitely more vanquishable than whatever demons rattled here in my psyche.

A pair of opposing metaphors from Chinese lore sums up the world's queer and playful indeterminacies: paper tigers, things that seem more powerful than they really are; and hidden dragons, things that are more powerful than they initially seem.[2] Paper tigers, spawned from paranoid imaginations, crumple like origami under investigative pressure. They are the spooky shadows cast by household objects, the freaky noises of branches scraping against the window, the flimsy strawmen invoked in polemics, and anything else we treat as threats until we acknowledge (with sheepish relief, maybe slight disenchantment) that they are not very threatening at all. Hidden dragons, by contrast, are underestimated forces, perchance dangers, that elude attention and care: environmental menaces (secondhand smoke, greenhouse gas emissions), medical misdiagnoses (severe health conditions masked by run-of-the-mill symptoms), hurtful words (leaving deep, latent cuts), and thorns that sting with extra savagery by virtue of rosy ruse.[3] People disagree widely, of course, on what perils are real or false, urgent or trivial. This truism alone accounts for plenty of society's ails. Opinions can diverge based on political partisanship, religious belief, philosophical dogma, and cultural affinity.

If any consensus exists, it's that life is a dangerous game. No guarantees of extra lives or take-backs or do-overs. But even in a world overrun by red herrings and silent killers, we sometimes go looking for still *more* trouble, conjuring foes and obstacles where none existed. We might do this out of boredom, mischievous impulses, or efforts to distract ourselves from other problems at hand. Threats, by definition, bear directly on our happiness and survival. On this front, we have every reason to keep our priorities straight. Frequently, however, people show that they're not above queering such priorities. On an unpredictable basis, we switch up our views of the booby-trapped universe, resist social mandates of what and whom we're meant to fear and fight, dance away from paths of least resistance, and play fast and loose with dictums of self-preservation.

Paranoid impulses lurk in the recesses of academia. Years ago, Eve Kosofsky Sedgwick came up with the term *paranoid reading* to describe the mainstream strategies of modern critical scholarship.[4] Academics, according to Sedgwick, are trained to write in a manner that preemptively repels potential knocks against their work. With abundant qualifiers, quotes, caveats, and precautionary self-disparagement, the savvy scholar anticipates and suppresses others' grievances before they can be aired. Building on the ideas of Melanie Klein, Sedgwick found problems with these bids for power and, even more so, with aspirations to omnipotence.[5] As Heather Love puts it, paranoid readings involve "familiar academic protocols like maintaining critical distance, outsmarting (and other forms of one-upmanship), refusing to be surprised (or if you are, then not letting on), believing the hierarchy, becoming boss."[6] Paranoid work desires authority. Driven by negative affects and a "hermeneutics of suspicion," such scholarship aims to outfox, to enact power, and to produce results beyond reproach (figure I.1).[7] It embodies a form of "strong theory"[8] that is expository, generalizable, and glaringly ambitious, "disavowing its affective motive and force, and masquerading as the very stuff of truth."[9] By actively mining for the threats in the world, practitioners of paranoid readings rarely fail to unearth the truths that they are chasing. With seductive rhetoric and logic, they produce self-satisfying critiques, which in turn affirm, after the fact, that no one can ever be paranoid enough. Examples of paranoid reading sound like what many academics today would simply consider *good* scholarship. And this is the point: paranoid registers have become so common that they now pass as self-evident and normal. To attempt otherwise can come off as weak or weird. "In a world where no one need be delusional to find evidence of systemic oppression," sighed Sedgwick, "to theorize out of anything *but* a paranoid critical stance has come to seem naïve, pious, or complaisant."[10]

Because paranoid readings work to stave off unfavorable judgment, they encourage a polyvocal writing style, one that mixes the author's voice and values into an echo chamber of what others have said (citations and footnotes galore), what others would say (using impersonal pronouns such as the royal *we* or the universal *one*), and what others will say (anticipated criticisms). With rapid-fire delivery of points and counterpoints, this rhetoric performs a flashy fugue that spins out the authorial subject and its answers into multiple guises. In the paranoid mode, polyphony is key and complexity is king. Its fugue reverberates through a fun house of mirrors, a daunting setup that enables the writer-illusionist to keep the true self a moving target, leaving interlocutors guessing. A hermeneutics of suspicion plays peekaboo with signifiers and their vanishing traces, a dour game of semiotic cat and mouse. As Rita Felski points out, suspicious reading "is a language game in quite a literal sense of 'game.' As such, it combines rules and expectations with the possibility of unexpected moves and inventive calculations, enabling a form of care-

Figure I.1. Bill Watterson, *Homicidal Psycho Jungle Cat: A Calvin and Hobbes Collection* (1994). It is revealing (and probably no coincidence) that Calvin's proposed title refers to gender (a jab at the perceived denseness of, among other critical ventures, early '90s feminist theory).

fully controlled play."[11] Trained as a musicologist, I've learned to play this game by parsing musical texts and moments through analysis, archival research, and fieldwork. Music scholars' recent efforts to privilege sensation and performance have upped the ante, pushing for contemplation of ephemeral events, excitable bodies, and unruly choreographies.[12] Although music comes with "broad shoulders" capable of supporting variable interpretations, riding around on these shoulders never feels all that steady.[13] As impressive as any critical effort might be, there's always more ground to cover, more notes to catch.

But as we scramble for authority—as we race for erudite discoveries and prestige—should we pause to check our moral pulse as well as the pulse of respective academic fields? Amid paranoid readings and dialectical games, what and whom are we really running for, running to, and running from? How do real and imagined monsters (critics, fears, failures) nip at our heels and dictate our courses? Can we ever afford to slow down? As we seek professional strength and safety, what important things might we be leaving in the dust? In the face of modern information and illusions, how can we renegotiate the means and purposes of careful labor, intellectual inquiry, and living soundly?

Yes, It Is!

Leading up to the 2009 conference for Feminist Theory and Music, Lydia Hamessley shared this memory:

The genesis of the first FTM can be traced to the American Musicological Society annual meeting in Baltimore, MD in 1988. At that conference, there was an unprecedented critical mass of panels and papers that focused on "women in music." . . . At a Committee on the Status of Women meeting, Rosemary Killam rose in anger when a male audience member (I absolutely cannot remember who it was) suggested that it wasn't his problem if his female students couldn't work late in the library because they feared walking across campus late at night. "Oh yes, it is, sir; yes, it is!" she shouted.[14]

What institutional and intellectual alibis could lead a scholar (or any person) to voice a disregard for students' safety? We can try to guess where this male audience member believed his priorities lay: in musicology, in the study of music—its beauty, import, intricacies. Music served as an out, enabling him to run from extracurricular care.

Maybe this man didn't mean what he said. No doubt, we all say bad things and lamentably sound off from time to time. Maybe he regretted his words and quickly reformed his views. Most of us would agree, after all, that a professor does bear responsibilities for students' well-being. It's common sense and basic decency, an implicit clause in the job contract.[15] Actually, it's more than just a clause: arguably, it's the moral bottom line. Students, not least women walking alone at night, have legitimate reasons to be on guard against incident of rape and violence. In September 2015, the Association of American Universities published results of a massive survey on sexual assault. Across twenty-seven universities, "the incidence of sexual assault and sexual misconduct due to physical force, threats of physical force, or incapacitation among female undergraduate student respondents was 23.1 percent, including 10.8 percent who experienced penetration."[16] Although some writers have since criticized this survey for its methodologies and possible inaccuracies, the disseminated results have helped boost awareness and action across campuses.[17] Skeptics are entitled to continue quibbling about the infamous one-in-five or one-in-four statistic (the percentage of female college students who allegedly experience sexual assault), but at a certain point, the hairsplitting starts to sound apologist. Numerically, any study contains margins of error. The point is that ethically—when it comes to our collective obligations to address these injuries—the margin of error should be zero.

Let's pose the question of scholarly priorities in a more challenging way. Is musicology *about* the safety of a female music student?[18] No, it isn't, if we define musicology starkly as the study of music. But *yes, it is,* if we envision musicology as all the activities, care, and caregiving of people who identify as members of the musicology community. In a post-Obama *yes-we-can* era, Killam's *yes, it is!* can serve anew as a disciplinary rallying cry. Beyond overtly activist work, what if we regularly upheld care not just as a bonus activity or a by-product of scholarship? In a world where injuries run rampant, what if care *is* the point?[19]

Riffing on Marshall McLuhan and Andy Warhol, Phil Ford has characterized the discipline of musicology as "anything you can get away with."[20] By this, he means that rather than categorically insisting on what topics do or do not fall under musicology, let's conceive of musicology as whatever self-identified musicologists choose to do. Disciplinary boundaries incessantly shift and shimmer anyway—so why not justify their flexibility via people's diverse, quirky interests? "The primary pleasure that scholarship offers is the chance to encounter other minds and thereby expand one's own," Ford muses. "The full range of other minds constitutes the true horizon that bounds the humanist; nothing human should be alien to us."[21] But if musicology is anything we can get away *with*, a caveat is that the discipline must simultaneously encompass everything we cannot afford to run away *from*—care, compassion, and interpersonal concerns that don't always sound scholarly as such. In other words, the purpose of disciplinary belonging isn't to get away with your choice of labor, so as merely to survive. The purpose is to thrive and to enable others to do so in turn.[22] For scholars fortunate enough to land on tenure tracks or obtain positions of influence, doesn't the task of caring become even more pressing? Cynthia Wu declares that we shouldn't "forget about the original purpose of tenure—to protect academic freedom."[23] Yet Wu also implores us not to forget the *duties* of academic freedom—namely, to advocate for people who do not possess such freedom and its privileges. Tenure, Jennifer Ruth believes, "enable[s] you to endure unpopularity for something bigger than yourself."[24] Academic freedom, then, isn't a license to be carefree. It's an *opportunity* to care widely, assertively, and generously.

Ford points to Susan McClary as an example of a scholar who endured unpopularity for her trailblazing overtures in feminist musicology. McClary's initial adversity can remind us to "appreciate the license her work gave to all of us coming up behind her. She took a lot of crap—the critical response to *Feminine Endings* was perhaps the most epic bout of mansplaining in the history of musicology—but she . . . did it with style, *and she got away with it.*"[25] The flair of McClary's prose, Ford emphasizes, went a long way in boosting the influence and controversies of *Feminine Endings*. As academics know, writing and speaking proficiently can carry enormous cachet. Sounding good grabs attention. It gets people to care.

With this in mind, *Just Vibrations* asks a small question with big answers: what is the purpose of sounding good? Rhetorically, sounding good entails writing and speaking in a seemingly intelligent manner, which can impress people, win arguments, and elevate one's status. Paranoid criticism, as described by Sedgwick, exemplifies some of these dazzling tactics. An ability to reason artfully and communicate efficiently reaps rewards.[26] Even in our most banal exchanges, we're constantly navigating tricky tides of verbal and sonic propriety. Recognizing the importance of language to our self-presentation, we choose words and sounds that minimize our risks of being shamed or shot down. Fear of sounding bad, sounding off, or sounding wrong can deter expression altogether. If you write eloquently enough, will your paper get accepted by a top-ranked journal? If you speak normatively enough during a phone interview, can you pass as straight, able-bodied, white, and American, potentially improving your chances? If you sing melodiously enough, will your amateur YouTube recordings go viral? History has shown how mighty pens and silver tongues—just ink on a page, just vibrations in the air—can move mountains and make leaders. In this regard, sounding good is a means of doing well in society, if by *well* we mean claiming positions of power.

My proposal, simply put, is this: what if the primary purpose of sounding good isn't to do well, but to do good? In competitive economies, doing well tends to mean pulling ahead of others. Doing good would involve reaching out and reaching back, lending help to those in need, and seeking opportunities for care and repair. Repair is a crucial word here. Its many significations include physical reassembly, bodily rehabilitation, restorative justice, monetary reparation, and disaster relief.[27] But repair also attaches to crass synonyms of *fix* and *cure*, notions easily co-opted by a capitalist ethos of purportedly healthy competition and its reinvestments in inequality, resilience, and normativity.[28] In *Just Vibrations*, I'm interested in the ethical tensions within repair's connotations, and specifically in reparative horizons where speech acts and other sonic matter converge. Literate societies put huge stock in rhetorical ability—yet for reasons of alterity, disability, or disenfranchisement, some people do not speak well (by societal conventions), some are admonished for speaking too much (oversharing and making noise), some do not speak frequently (due to, say, shyness), some speak unusually (slowly, or with a stutter, or via conspicuous technological assistance), some do not speak at all (from injury or trauma), and some speak but nevertheless go unheard.[29] By the same token, some people hear (neuro)typically, whereas others hear less (by normative standards), hear differently (Deaf Gain), or hear too much (sensory overload, hyperacusis). None of these conditions should be grounds for depriving individuals of compassion and connection. Try to recall a time in your life when you found yourself speechless or supernoisy, whether from joyous news or devastating injuries, from a gorgeous sight or a terrible deed. Amid crushing silence or the din of shouts—at the apex of emotion—you felt, as the saying goes, *beside yourself*. As such, sounding good likely also felt *beside the point*, as you stayed mute or snorted or sobbed or hollered. Yet these are often the precise moments when we most desire companionship, consolation, and leeway. Beyond questions of words and feelings, *Just Vibrations* reimagines the viability of solidarity and optimism through our pressures to sound good and hear good in daily life, where *sounding* and *hearing* signify more capaciously than as the literal faculties of able minds and bodies.

An easy target for a societal dearth of care is neoliberalism, which insists on self-reliance over dependency, on cutthroat competition over mutual welfare.[30] Akemi Nishida notes how "productivity, or *hyper-productivity*, is an expectation and desire within academia under neoliberalism."[31] Despite a nominally shared root, people who identify as social liberals tend to scorn neoliberals' values of privatization and self-interest. But as for larger questions of who speaks and who gets heard, liberalism has its own shortcomings. "Liberalism invokes a notion of political participation in which one makes one's voice heard," points out Eva Feder Kittay. "It depends on a conception of the person as independent, rational, and capable of self-sufficiency."[32] Kittay has written extensively about her daughter Sesha, who lives with congenital cerebral palsy. Sesha cannot read, talk, or walk. Within liberal and neoliberal frameworks, her condition renders her a misfit in terms of autonomy and personhood. This is where care comes in. As Kittay avows, care "is a labor, an attitude, and a virtue. As labor, it is the work of maintaining ourselves and others when we are in a condition of need. It is most noticed in its absence, most needed when it can be least reciprocated."[33] Care is a labor of love.[34] Sesha loves and is loved. She loves people and she loves listening to music. Kittay remarks that "music is [Sesha's] life and Beethoven her best friend. At our home, listening to the *Emperor Concerto*, she gazes out the window enthralled, occasionally turning to us with a twinkle in her eye when she anticipates some really good parts."[35] Although Sesha may never be able to verbalize her enjoyment of Beethoven, her feelings feel evident for those who care to watch and listen.

As a musicologist, I've sometimes heard colleagues from other disciplines tell me how lucky I am to spend my days (they assume) listening to and thinking about music. Studying music, these envious comments imply, must be a labor of love. I've been led to wonder, therefore, whether musical skills ever enable or prime us to listen better to *people* and to take up love's labors more broadly. Do musicians and musicologists—having undergone so much ear-training—possess any specialized aural capabilities or inclinations when it comes not just to music, but also to human interlocutors (how they sound, what they say, and unvoiced concerns)? People and musical pieces are obviously different entities, yet people routinely identify *with* music and identify *as* musical, sounding out subjectivities through melodies, lyrics, and bodies. Without painting an exceptionalist portrait of musicianship, is it possible that people who work with music for a living can lead by example in agendas of interpersonal care and communication? Could we go beyond modest understandings of empathy as a complement to musicality, and venture empathy *as* a resonant form of musicality? If part of musicianship can involve listening for better worlds, then musicology has the potential to initiate various progressive currents in ethics and critical thinking. To be clear, this isn't saying that music makes us good people. It's saying that certain aural positions may hold profound uses outside the music classroom, and that as much as anyone else, musicians and music scholars already recognize the immense challenges and rewards of listening creatively and caringly.[36]

Care is, per John Rawls, a matter of fairness and a matter of justice.[37] And justice, asserts Amartya Sen, can accommodate both reason and emotion.[38] My caution here, however, has to do exactly with how societies privilege certain expressions of reason and emotion above others. If some people seem to lack rational faculties and rhetorical virtuosity, where do their voices fit in the chorus of just debate? Pain, impairment, intoxication, desire, and despair can all thwart our efforts to feel and appear reasonable. From time to time, lapses in judgment make us sound unintelligent, politically incorrect, or cold. To this end, my stance jibes with a memorable insight from the legal activist Bryan Stevenson, who works with the poor and the incarcerated: "*Each of us is more than the worst thing we've ever done.*"[39] To this, I would add that each of us is potentially better than the worst things we've ever said. Sadly, society and news media don't operate under this assumption. Think of how swiftly celebrities who utter prejudicial slurs (Mel Gibson, Isaiah Washington, Paula Deen) fall from grace, or how easily singers who sound off (Milli Vanilli, Ashlee Simpson, Amy Winehouse) get booed off the stage. Vindictive societies can enchain people far longer than necessary. Within the discipline of musicology, recall the male audience member quoted by Lydia Hamessley, or the numerous scholars who responded in misogynist fashion to feminist and queer musicology. Our baser instinct is to immortalize these individuals as villains: once a jerk, always a jerk; once a sexist, always a sexist. But Stevenson's merciful words would encourage us to believe that people can change, not least because people are more than what they once said.

Yet nor do I believe each of us is definable solely by the *best* thing we've ever said or done. We don't get to rest on laurels, so long as the world needs work. Yes, abundant impediments can erode our resolve to bring care into the equation: self-interest; lack of motivation; believing we're up against lost causes; and anxieties of being called a sanctimonious crusader. These deterrents don't release us from reparative work. A profusion of obstacles means, if anything, that we must work that much harder.[40]

Besides the foundations of musicology writ large, this book builds on a triad of critical muses: affect theory, care ethics (refracted through disability studies and ideas of dependence), and queer theory. *Affect* continues to elude easy definition, but Kathleen Stewart captures one shade of it beautifully. Ordinary affects, Stewart says, are "things that happen. They happen in impulses, sensations, expectations, daydreams, encounters, and habits of relating, in strategies and their failures, in forms of persuasion, contagion, and compulsion, in modes of attention, attachment, and agency."[41] Focusing on affect means seriously considering feelings, pleasurable as well as painful. For my aims, hermeneutics and sensation enter into a lively tango, toeing into slippery spaces for rich discussions of sound and selfhood. Affective concerns resonate with *care ethics* in that both prioritize embodied encounters and the precarities of lived experience. Care ethics, in turn, maintains strong attachments to feminist inquiries. It is no coincidence that Hamessley's anecdote, which raises questions about the care of female graduate students, pertains to the origins of the conferences for Feminist Theory and Music (now entering its twenty-fifth year).[42] A call for care, as productive as it sounds, comes historically loaded because of societal and cultural presumptions about who is or is not responsible for giving care. Women, more so than men, are expected to undertake care work and to *make* it work irrespective of professional obligations. Although some early proponents of feminist care ethics have argued that women are especially suited for caregiving,[43] critics have rebuked these arguments as essentialist, parochial, and perpetuating female slave morality.[44]

Insofar as care continues to be unjustly gendered, raced, classed, and allocated, I'm inclined to push care discourses out of their comfort zone and, in particular, to think of care as a *queer* matter. Calls for care can *sound queer* because they remain alien to straight-and-narrow mandates of professional life and capitalist systems.[45] Care can benefit from greater scrutiny, yet it remains weirdly radical, a sentimental outlier against normative critical impulses.[46] Although queer theory has a reputation for being angsty and abstract, optimistic and caring accounts are possible.[47] One of my favorite vignettes of queerness comes from José Esteban Muñoz: "Some will say that all we have are the pleasures of this moment, but we must never settle for that minimal transport; we must dream and enact new and better pleasures, other ways of being in the world, and ultimately new worlds. Queerness is a longing that propels us onward, beyond romances of the negative and toiling in the present. Queerness is that thing that lets us feel that this world is not enough, that indeed something is missing."[48] By this account, to perform queer *and* caring work is to recognize that things aren't always what they seem and that things don't have to stay the way they are. Queerness, more than an invitation for againstness, entails a sort of playfulness, a commitment to testing and transgressing boundaries in hopes of creatively thriving anew. One chapter in *Just Vibrations* deals overtly with LGBTQ subjects, yet queer inquiry at large serves to spark the book's vast imaginations of livability and living on.

You, Reader

I still remember what it felt like to lose a tenure-track job in 1982, when the Reagan recession drove the college where I worked into bankruptcy, and what it felt like to live for ten years the grindingly hard life of ad hoc, marginal and marginalizing labor as a journeyman adjunct faculty member, what it felt like to teach at three institutions in a single day, preparing lectures in my head as I drove from place to place. But I do not want to patronize you, my un- and under-employed colleagues, nor do I want to slip into some patronizing, falsely

empathetic stance, some version of "I feel your pain" or "just hang on!" I
remember too well how similar remarks would fill me with rage when I was young.
—Suzanne Cusick[49]

Momentum is building—not fast enough, but building all the same. The 2015 annual meeting of the American Musicological Society in Louisville, Kentucky, hosted more papers on accessibility, disability, labor, and public scholarship than ever before in AMS conference history. The program contained, however, a dire glitch. Among the most vital sessions was one called "Feminist Musicology and Contingent Labor," featuring people who spoke at once powerfully and vulnerably about the challenges of justice, fairness, and parenthood in adjunct teaching and professional pursuits.[50] The large room contained at least 150 chairs but, over the course of the session, drew no more than twenty audience members, including just three men (by my estimate). The low attendance owed unmistakably to the fact that this session took place at exactly the same time as the standing-room-only event of the LGBTQ Study Group, "A Serious Effort Not to Think Straight: Suzanne Cusick in Dialogue with Emily Wilbourne," which likewise grappled with themes of love, care, and reform. Although the organizers and participants of both panels had previously pleaded with AMS officials to move the sessions to separate time slots, the appeals were denied. Without casting blame at administrators or coordinators (who hold the difficult and unenviable task of putting together a huge program), a cruel irony lay in how this scheduling conflict reproduced the precise issues of competition and scarcity that these two exceptional sessions aimed to address.

Questions of care and outreach have lately assembled under the umbrella initiatives of accessible musicology and public musicology, both of which push scholars to teach and learn from people outside the academy. Public musicology's label is recent, but the practice is not.[51] Agendas of justice, social change, and environmentalism have radiated through many of musicology's siblings and study groups, from music education and music therapy to ecomusicology and applied ethnomusicology. By all appearances, public musicology has been happening for a while.[52] And how could it not, given this wired era of social media and rapid informational exchange? Borrowing from Nicholas Cook: we are all public musicologists now.[53] The only question is what kinds of scholars we choose to be and how to lead by example. Public scholarship, for what it's worth, cannot flourish in the paranoid mode. Scholarship qualifies as publicly salient only if it accommodates critiques *by* the public. It has to be accessible and comprehensible, open to praise and pushback from more than specialists alone. Addressing academics who aspire to public discourse, Mark Greif puts it this way: "Intellectuals: You—we— are the public. . . . The public must not be anyone less smart and striving than you are, right now. It's probably best that the imagined public even resemble the person you would like to be rather than who you are."[54] Intellectual diligence can coexist with social relevance. Public scholarship means speaking up without talking down.

I dedicate *Just Vibrations* foremost to people concerned with reparative work, advocacy, and the distant yet colorful horizons of intellectual and interpersonal responsibility. Certain case studies will sound familiar primarily to music scholars, but the project aims to reach anyone invested in the intersections of care and criticism. The book is for the tenured Distinguished Professor who feels professionally secure enough to take on risky endeavors with relative freedom; and for not-yet-tenured junior colleagues or graduate students who tread nervously through minefields of institutional norms, expectations, and politics. The book is for overworked, underpaid adjunct instructors who are multiply marginalized by bureaucracies, material scarcities, and the shrinking prospects of equitable employment; and for alternative academics who have ventured outside the ivory tower and wish to destigmatize the choices of alt-ac labor.[55] I don't presume to speak on behalf of anyone who does not wish it. I speak to you, the reader, and hope to have an eventual opportunity to speak *with* you about our points of agreement and disagreement.[56]

In this spirit, *Just Vibrations* listens for voices across diverse sources and mediums—not solely peer-reviewed print scholarship (still upheld as a gold standard in academia), but also trade books, queer memoirs, illness narratives, polemical blog posts, personal anecdotes, emotional email correspondences, and anonymous pleas for care on Internet forums. Without claiming to equate or democratize these disparate registers of expression, I unsettle conventional wisdoms about what sorts of publications are deemed more versus less valuable. One purpose is to let voices chime with each other. The result, though not always harmonious, can help destabilize the systemic dominance of so-called strong theory and writing. I want *Just Vibrations* to start a conversation. It isn't—shouldn't be—the last word.

Following Sedgwick's gambit in *Epistemology of the Closet*, I lay bare three interlaced axioms for my book.[57] First, that each of us has the potential to resonate molecularly, socially, and ethically with others.[58]

Second, that by attending to how our convictions, relations, and actions ripple through public spaces, we can achieve a sense of how we matter and what matters most. And third, that sounds—things we say, music we make, noises we hear, pressures we feel—are too often and too facilely conceived as just (*mere*) vibrations, at times to the detriment of agendas that are just (*fair, good, conscionable*). Presumably ephemeral and invisible, sound's offensive usages may escape commensurate prosecution and rectification, whether it's the threatening words of bullies (waved off as pure threats versus sticks and stones) or the deafening force of police squads' Long Range Acoustic Devices, deployed increasingly these days to quell protests. Music in particular, with its cultural connotations of leisure and pleasure, occasionally skirts moral scrutiny and serious intervention, even in such extreme cases as government-sanctioned music torture.[59] Yet unjust, unethical vibrations can emotionally, physically rub us the wrong way and thus awaken us to action. Joachim-Ernst Berendt conceives of loud and disturbing sounds as such: the English word *alarm*, he points out, comes from the Italian *allarme*, "which in turn leads to *all'arme*, a call to arms. When we hear noise, we are constantly— but unconsciously—'called to arms.' We become alarmed."[60] Alarms can drive us to care, convene, and act. By auditing our bodies' reactions big and small, we gain options of mobilizing against injurious manifestations of music, sound, noise, speech, and silence.

Chapter 1 traces the harrowing circumstances that moved me to undertake this project. Some years back, the onset of a chronic pain condition rendered me speechless for long spells at a time. Housebound and heavily medicated, I found myself unable to converse soundly, much less write properly. Pain swallowed language. My dialogues, internal and external, sounded fractured and feeble to my ears and, I assumed, to the ears of others. As an academic, I had taken rhetorical ability for granted. Its sudden recession left me adrift, unsure of my place in the world. Despite doctors' use of stethoscopes, ultrasounds, MRIs, and other impressive equipment, I sometimes felt like I, the patient, wasn't actually being heard. My intention behind these personal reflections isn't to present an overcoming narrative. What I offer, rather, is a total disclosure of the situational and affective motives behind this book's reparative slant. The goal isn't to peddle *inspiration*, but to proffer insights that may come to us on the brink of *expiration*, when we feel curtains closing on lyrics left unsung.[61]

Chapter 2 lends an ear to the powers and problems of sounding good in scholarly domains. Academic employment, promotions, and prestige hinge on writing and speaking well. Paranoid readings showcase critical athleticism, playing awesome tennis with theses and antitheses, facts and counterfactuals. But such semantic sports can harden into habit. In recent years, scholars have proposed *low*, *thin*, and *weak* critical modes as alternatives to the traditional rubrics of *high*, *thick*, and *strong*. Irrespective of the scholarly practice in question, we can do good by reflecting on which truths matter most to us and to others. For all the care shown in academic production, we cannot neglect the care due to our peers. Reflections on early backlash against feminist and queer musicology bring echoes of Rosemary Killam's *yes, it is!* and attendant feelings of responsibility. By applying pressure to concepts of aesthetic autonomy, academic freedom, and human agency, I aim to renovate the ivory tower's architecture so as to shelter those who most need it.

Chapter 3 takes a queer turn toward the endangered currency of hope in our modern critical and social transactions. The archives of LGBTQ scholarship to date indicate that shame is topically sexy, full of secrets and affective turmoil. Pride, by contrast, is too plain, too easy. Queer theory seems gay-married to paranoid imperatives—but why? Drawing on Guerrilla Queer Bar, the It Gets Better Project, David Halperin's peculiar visit to the AMS LGBTQ Study Group, and old debates about classical composers' sexualities, I probe the dilemmas of shame, resiliency, and survival from childhood to adulthood. Among the most profound open secrets is that paranoia can breed more paranoia, and pain more pain. Breaking this vicious cycle requires a firmer grasp on the slippery reins of hope. It means opting out of the cultures of humiliation that pervade twenty-four-hour news cycles, social media, and spectacles of failure. Without promises of happily ever after, questions linger as to what attitudes and actions might offer some happiness and care, here and now.

Chapter 4 insists that reparative attitudes toward soundscapes can serve as barometers of better worlds. I stress-test this hypothesis by applying it to acoustic offenses that run the gamut: from tiny bleeps and clangs of urban noise pollution (exceedingly ordinary) to the American government's use of music for torture (extraordinary, though not as rare as the dearth of public awareness would suggest). Practices of paranoid listening have proliferated alongside modes of paranoid reading. How we choose to think about the perpetration and tolerance of noise can lead us down ethical avenues of ruin or repair. I propose a vested awareness of how we might survive and thrive differently with the occasional hard reset on rote orientations toward scholarship, self, and sound. So many opportunities exist for us to vibe empathically with those around us, even those who are emphatically *not* us.

At its heart, *Just Vibrations* is a voluminous thought experiment that brings a motley of musical, cultural, philosophical, pedagogical, and queer wisdoms to bear on modernity's bitter truths and candied lies. The book charts a precarious escape route out of these suspicious games, sounding off against the power plays within and beyond music and musicology. From childhood onward, we get caught up in contests, facing real and imagined threats in daily routines. In academia, paranoid readings keep an iron grip on critical discourse. And in life as a whole, we rarely call time-outs or stage interventions for our mutually enabled dependencies on naysaying. But do alternatives to adversariality exist? If so, how can they resonate through the ways we write, identify, teach, learn, collaborate, perform, and love? What futures burst open when we temper our flares of chronic suspicion with cooling bouts of reparative belief, willful vulnerability, and childlike optimism? Looking to move against the grain, I try to do as I say—that is, to cultivate a tone that descants above the droning hums (and *hmms* . . .) of paranoid imperatives. This book strives not for paranoid readings' comprehensiveness or monumentality, but rather for impact and accessibility. The goal is prose that eschews the prosaic, opting instead to be conciliatory, flighty, upbeat: not blithe, but playful; not naive, yet radically wishful. By harmonizing rhetorical registers that are at once grave and gay—by setting the stark realities of the *here and now* against the important games of *as if* and *what if*—I feel my way through the noise, sounding out despair and pity and joy and pride. Tracking the pressures of dulcet and dissonant existence can ultimately work to illuminate our currencies of caring for a world that, in its morally bankrupt moments, seems to care so little for us.

A Note on Scenes from Childhood

Stories of youths flow freely through this book because they lend both weight and levity to explorations of optimism, imagination, and peril. Children do not, as a rule, sound good by societal standards: infants bawl on planes, kids say the darndest things, and moody teens clam up. Yet I cannot see a way to delve into a reparative project without diving for the trove of insights offered by youths as they mature, rebel, and resolve. My model isn't some archetypal Freudian child, but rather a figure along the lines of Jack Halberstam's description:

If, for the child, language is a playground where meaning is contingent, illusionary, motile, impermanent, and constantly shifting to keep up with the data flows that course across their inchoate consciousnesses, then maybe adults should improvise more, pick up terms, words, lexicons from children who, in many ways, live the world differently than we do, live it more closely, live it more intensely, and, sometimes, live it more critically.[62]

Childhood can be a queer, sometimes terrible, experience.[63] Bullies, puberty, and tragic realities haunt kids coming of age. Gay youths (even more so, transgender youths and LGBTQ youths of color) continue to get left out in the cold, facing homelessness and violence at high rates. This makes childhood all the more central in urgent conversations about care and the need for good.

So before pushing forward, here's one more glance back.

During my time at Annie B. Jamieson Elementary, students were required each year to bring earthquake preparedness kits, which teachers would collect and deposit in enormous steel boxes that sat on the playground. The idea was that if an earthquake trapped everyone within the school perimeter, students would find comfort in the kits' personalized objects. All kits needed to include at least four items: emergency rations (typically candy bars), a flashlight, a game (such as a deck of cards), and a sealed envelope containing a loving letter from parents or guardians. The precautionary measure was merited by a lot of talk—which continues to this day—about Vancouver being overdue for an enormous quake (the Big One).

Needless to say, these preemptively reparative measures made the students paranoid. My friends and I spent time imagining how the world could literally crack open any day. At the end of each earthquake-free year, our kits were returned to us and we got to eat the stale candy inside, play our games, and read affectionate letters. Year after year, my parents kept it short and sweet with the same note:

We love you! Don't worry, be happy . . . bye-bye.

The vaguely morbid farewell was my parents' English-as-second-language way of signing off (拜拜, the loanword of the English *bye-bye*, is more commonly used by Mandarin-speakers than the actual native term for farewell). In third grade, a friend teased me about my parents' silly choice of words. He called the letter *fobby* (the slang adjective for fresh-off-the-boat) and *Engrish.* I concurred with nervous laughter. Years later, I would come across an essay by Amy Tan in which she confessed her shame at having previously referred to her mother's English as "broken," which connotes a speech in need of repair, something that is "damaged and needed to be fixed, as if it lacked a certain wholeness and soundness."[64] Tan's shame informed my own as I came to regret ever having belittled my parents' language.

Because the point is that I still remember the earthquake letter. I happened to memorize its words because, as comically terse as they may be, the key sentiments are all there, idiomatic fault lines be damned:

Love! Optimism, happiness . . . closure.

My translation; or, things that matter in the end.

And so what if the syntax came broken, as long as I caught the falling pieces and held them close after all these years?

They sounded good to me.

CHAPTER 1

Aching for Repair

✦ ✦ ✦

Laugh, and the world laughs with you;
Weep, and you weep alone;
For the sad old earth must borrow its mirth,
But has trouble enough of its own.

                        . . .

There is room in the halls of pleasure
For a large and lordly train,
But one by one we must all file on
Through the narrow aisles of pain.
                    —Beginning and ending of "Solitude,"
                    a poem by Ella Wheeler Wilcox (1883)

Everything's Good

On a June afternoon in 2014, I lay in bed, body screaming and brain ablaze. Ears buzzing, I barely heard the phone ring. Someone from the physician's office was calling to report multiple red flags on my recent blood panel. I was told to go to the emergency room right away. My partner picked me up, and on our short ride to Mt. Auburn Hospital, I braced myself for the worst. I feared the doctors would tell me my system was shutting down. But I was just as afraid they'd say I looked fine enough and then send me away to continue a half-life of mysterious chronic pain. By this point, I had gone months scarcely able to eat or sleep or get out of bed, much less work or play piano or socialize. The week before the ER visit, I had passed out twice from pain, the first time landing on my back, the second time smacking my head against a desk on the way down.

After an electrocardiogram, blood draw, and physical exam at Mt. Auburn, an affable doctor delivered the verdict that I desired and dreaded: no emergency. Besides signs of malnourishment and fatigue, he said, my condition wasn't critical. Everything looked good. I could tell from his smile that he thought he was giving excellent news—surely a rare commodity in the ER—so I forced a croak of thanks. That night, as I tried to celebrate staying alive, I watched reruns of sitcoms in hopes that the occasional joke might tease an involuntary laugh out of me, against all odds. No such luck. I heard canned tracks of people laughing without me and saw cool comedies unfolding in spite of me. But the noise was still better than my body's abject vibes. Around this time, I was sobbing more than all of Julianne Moore's roles combined, though my breakdowns weren't nearly as pretty. Anytime I cried, I couldn't tell if I was yearning for a life before this pain, irretrievable; the present gauntlet of pain, intolerable; or some future relief, unimaginable. Tears ran together anyway, just vapor in the end.

Daydream in Thunder

It all began a year earlier, the summer of 2013—a searing feeling that spread across the abdomen and under the ribs, like a stomachache that never let up, with or without food, day or night. A constant companion, the pain wrenched me awake in the morning and beat me into uneasy slumber each evening. Medications, herbs, and dietary changes had no effect. A workup of endoscopies, ultrasounds, CTs, and MRIs turned up nothing. With each clean exam, doctors congratulated me, exclaiming I should be relieved that I didn't have ulcers or celiac disease or esophageal cancer. I sensed my body shutting down in slow motion and my mind coming apart, yet experts and charts and numbers and hard evidence—everything I trusted (as a scholar, as a person)—were saying I was okay. Nothing felt more real than the pain, but I started doubting its reality all the same. For once in my life, I wasn't seeking normal. I didn't want to pass in society or pass medical tests with flying colors. Although I recognized my tremendous privilege of having access to healthcare, this acknowledgment didn't mitigate the worst moments, when implosive pain would collapse any belief in bearable, much less privileged, existence.

Gastroenterologists didn't know where to start. They were perplexed as to why acid-inhibiting drugs were ineffective and why the gentlest palpations of my abdomen caused me to flinch greatly. Light contact—hugs from friends, a fitted shirt, or even dangling wires of Apple earbuds—fired twinges across the torso. One doctor concluded that I was overly sensitive to pain and sent me away with a vague diagnosis of functional dyspepsia. Thus began my resigned migration from internal medicine to pain clinics, from specialists I hoped could solve the problem to those who worked damage control.

Waiting rooms at pain clinics were hushed places. First rule of the clinics: no talking in the clinics. Sounds may disturb. Newcomers would quickly grasp that words weren't welcome. Patients snuck glances at one another but never held a gaze for long. Perhaps we feared that, with eye contact, we would see too much of one another's pain as well as the sorry reflections of our own. The only breaks in silence came from the greetings of nurses who fetched us one by one. They'd say to a patient, "How are you today?" and more often than not, the patient would mutter, "Good." A pleasantry, an empty exchange. Just vibrations, sounds of *good* without much truth.

Once inside the physician's room, questions didn't get any easier. Inquiries such as "Where does it hurt?" led me to gesture toward my abdomen, but if I wanted to be more comprehensive, I would've also mentioned my seized-up back, my locked hips, my throbbing head—just . . . inside. "Pain is a symphony," points out Atul Gawande, "a complex response that includes not just a distinct sensation but also motor activity, a change in emotion, a focusing of attention, a brand-new memory."[1] It's easy yet wrong to assume that most people with chronic pain experience the totality of their pain in one localized area of the body. Cascades of pain can lead to physical inactivity, tension, depression, alienation, loss of appetite, and side effects of medication, taking compounded tolls. A symphony; or rather, cacophony.

Sometimes, talking did help. I began meeting weekly with a cognitive behavioral therapist, Heidi, who imparted mindfulness techniques and encouraged me to keep a diary of my pain levels and feelings throughout the day. The result has been a sixty-page-and-counting document of pain scores (0 to 10) and strings of broken prose erring on the side of sad. Two things Heidi said have stayed with me. First, without feeding me promises that it gets better, she told me I "can still live a beautiful life" even with chronic, idiopathic pain. But during actual moments of excruciation, reclaiming beauty struck me as an impossibility: I felt wretched (emaciated, dejected, antisocial); believed I sounded bad (inarticulate, curt, defeated); and, even though I would go on walks along the Charles River and will myself to take in beauty everywhere, I usually ended up coveting all this resplendence as the pageantry of an alternate universe fairer than my own. Heidi's second insight: "Any pain is endurable if you know it's temporary." All pain is, of course, temporary in that death promises release. The question is whether there's *life* after pain.

I spent the next year in a daze, sleepwalking through entire seasons, now just yawning gaps in my memory. On the worst days, I didn't leave my apartment or eat or speak. On the best days, I wore a taut mask and forced myself outdoors. My ears rang inexplicably like church bells on the fritz. My vision came smeared with scrawls of floating dots and graffiti. Unable to focus or sit still, I found it difficult to read, much less write. Among prescribed medications, the drug gabapentin caused aphasia, leading me to grope for basic words like *curtains* or *polo shirt*. Syllables would sit on my tongue, then dissolve. Emails took an eternity to craft, and in live conversations, my speech was full of holes. Elaine Scarry's thesis in *The Body in Pain*—about the opposition between pain and creation, and about pain's language-destroying and world-shrinking effects—rang true in my case.[2] I ceased *producing* and was no longer invested in *making* anything of myself. My priority wasn't moving up and advancing my career, but simply going on. And instead of worrying about what scholarly legacy I could leave behind, I fantasized about leaving . . . period. Ideas of nonexistence lost their bite. A few depressive episodes earlier in life had been attended by angst about mortality, despite an otherwise healthy body. Yet with health now failing for real, death's threats sounded hollow.

Suffering blackouts, hallucinations, and nightmares, I could feel my tether to reality starting to fray. In the spring of 2014, I had published a book about music and video games, with case studies devoted to explorations of porous boundaries between the real and the virtual. But none of this knowledge kept me grounded. Fancy deconstructions of the real-virtual binary didn't ease my plight, nor did my familiarity with pertinent literature. In the clutches of pain, I couldn't translate critical insights into palpable doses of relief and resilience. Pretty prose floundered against ugly feelings. Social models of disability didn't contain instructions on how to cope.[3] Compassionate theories of pain's inexpressibility didn't remedy my loss for words. Knowing that others had gone through ordeals similar to (or far worse than) my own didn't make me feel less lonely. I became profoundly, sometimes ragefully, envious of people around me who looked pain-free, from a smiling barista to the hardcore cyclists braving Boston traffic. But I also began thinking about how even people who looked indomitably happy and able-bodied might be enduring pain all the same. Around this time, I tried picking up on others' chronic pain, the vibes of friends and strangers who may keep agony shut up in stoic facades. Small clues here and there: subtly raised shoulders, a grimace under a grin, sentences punctuated by breathy cadences. Maybe I was just projecting my problems onto others. But I couldn't help suspecting some of us shared memberships to a secret club of afflicted bodies, even if we all returned to our own homes at the end of each day to wither and burn, alone.

Alone at home, then, I sought answers on the Internet. Online message boards for chronic pain were inspiring and disheartening in equal measure. People related devastating stories and cried for care (figure 1.1). Many messages were rife with grammatical errors and misspellings and non sequiturs and ellipses. But these posts weren't incoherent. Rather, they were painfully coherent, a surplus of expression in typos and caesuras. Entering these forums was like walking into a thunderstorm: no triage, just a booming world of hurt. The gist of every post was the same. People were exclaiming (as they say in cell phone commercials): *Can you hear me now?* Now—right away, please. Pleas shouted into the ether in hopes of fetching echoes. On rare occasions, someone would come bearing happy news (that the pain's under control, or a cause has been found) and receive an outpouring of congratulations. Usually, this fortunate person would then vanish from the forums, never to be heard from again. And who could blame them? Go, fly, live. Maybe some day everyone will join you.

One bad night, I was in bed scrolling through an online support group when I came across a post, dated two years back, by a man who listed a phone number. He was experiencing complex pain syndromes, his insurance was maxed out, and his doctors had pretty much given up. He couldn't take it anymore. If someone could reach out, he said, please call, please care. As if by reflex, I picked up my phone and punched in the number. Before pressing dial, I paused: what if he remained sick, and I could only console him with clichés? Much of my own internal dialogue was a merry-go-round of "No pain, no . . . ," "What doesn't kill me . . . ," "Blessing in . . . ," "Look on the bright . . . ," and other fragmentary mottos punctuating the rhythms of hard days. Or what if he were *well*, and he made me feel queer for calling a stranger's number and disturbing a peaceful family dinner? Risking mild embarrassment, I dialed the number.

The phone didn't even ring once. Instead, I got an automated mes-

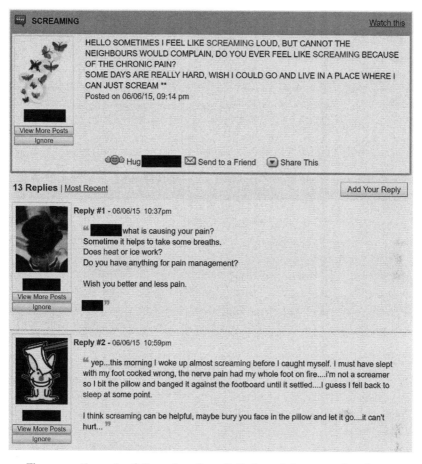

Figure 1.1. Example of discussions from *Daily Strength* forum on chronic pain

sage saying that the number was no longer in service. I hung up, fearing the worst.

Anterior Motives

Music is something I teach and talk and write about every day, [but] pain is not. I dwell in pain, subsisting in silence, in hopes that no one will notice and think less of me—expect less of me—or, by far the worst, take pity on me, while being thankful they are not me.

—M. Celia Cain, a music professor who lives with fibromyalgia[4]

Making a case for reparative readings, Eve Kosofsky Sedgwick declared that the "vocabulary for articulating any reader's reparative motive toward a text or a culture has long been so sappy, aestheticizing, defensive, anti-intellectual, or reactionary that it's no wonder few critics are willing to describe their acquaintance with such motives."[5] Strange, isn't it? For isn't motive crucial? Economists regularly home in on the incentives driving human choices and social behaviors, and legal trials forcefully weigh intent in cases of life and death. So it is curious that I drafted much of *Just Vibrations* without including the present chapter and reflecting on how I came to be interested in reparative work. I had allowed my own circumstances to go missing from the puzzle. The sentiments laid out in these pages originated from times when I most desired rehabilitation, yet was least able to imagine its fruition. I rebooted a mild writing regimen in late summer of 2014. I wasn't completely better (not by a long shot), but with the aid of medications and visits to the Beth Israel, Brigham, and Dartmouth-Hitchcock pain clinics, I gradually became able to sit still for twenty-minute intervals. I would write at the computer for as long as I could, trying to make up for lost time, then lie down to catch my breath; sit up, then go flat; and on this cycle went.

I share this ongoing episode of my life out of neither self-congratulatory transparency nor a wish to claim exemptions in readers' judgments of the book at hand. I share these stories because, in my mind, what follows makes little sense without a sense of self at the center.[6] In fact, with myself in these lines, I hope readers will feel free to scrutinize the book more, not less. Some writers, to be sure, still believe that academic and first-person narratives don't mix well. Feminist and queer theorists repeatedly run into accusations of narcissism, of overmixing the personal and the political.[7] Disability scholars who admit their own hardships are likewise charged with indulging in "moi-criticism," appealing to emotions (and scoring so-called sympathy points) rather than to the intellect.[8] My own writing has tended toward an interplay of moods and styles, merging anecdotal, journalistic, and academic registers that at once embody fractured feelings and reparative ambitions. Given academics' valorization of experimental art (rife for interpretation and politicization), I've long found it odd that much of academic writing itself shies away from experimental rhetoric.[9] A fear may be that, were unusual writing to proliferate, some academics could undeservedly claim bad writing as something that sounds good, or pass off ungrammatical fragments as brilliantly neurodiverse and neurodivergent.[10] Critical writing is the scholar's safe haven, an expressive vehicle beholding but not beholden to art's radical standards. Rita Felski puts it this way: "Critique often thinks of itself as a weightless, disembodied dance of the intellect—as something that is outside, against, at odds with prevailing norms and patterns of thought."[11] In this quote, "critique" is positioned as the sentence subject (a wink from Felski), capable of "[thinking] of itself." Such syntax riffs on how people attribute agency and exceptional status to critique. The myth is that good scholarship can stand on its own merits, good ideas speak for themselves, and a good paper practically writes itself.[12] But surely scholarship *about* art or about anything else is no more autonomous than art itself. Pretending otherwise risks leaving human interests out of the equation.

For months, I refrained from divulging my illness—my human interest—to peers in academia because I feared they would see and treat me differently. The first professional commitment from which I withdrew was an essay for *The Oxford Handbook of Music and Disability Studies*, and one of its editors, Joseph Straus, was the first colleague to whom I disclosed my pain.[13] Joe replied graciously, closing his email with this advice: "I hope you will take the time you need to get better. Nothing else really matters anyway."[14] Until this point, I had relayed my problems only to my partner and a few close friends. I even held out on telling— and, I assumed, causing unnecessary stress for—my parents until a week before my first surgery (a gallbladder removal that, in retrospect, targeted not only a red herring but subsequently worsened the pain by far). As I resumed professional duties over time, I role-played as someone of sound mind and body, getting through conferences and job interviews with a mix of painkillers and pure adrenaline. I came close to tears at random moments on these occasions, but each time, would compose myself, usually by dashing into the nearest restroom stall. I wasn't yet ready to stumble out of this closet of illness, worrying that people would consider me broken.[15] But some colleagues eventually perceived something was up anyway, asking if I was okay and pointing out that I looked low-energy or not quite like myself. This bred a whole extra set of insecurities. If people were noticing I didn't look well or sound good, would they start speculating about my condition? Would they judge my work with heightened suspicion or, alternatively, handle it with kid gloves? Would my terse replies and weak smiles signal aloofness, haughtiness, even inebriation? Would declining invitations to happy hours or conference receptions brand me as rude and reclusive?

Pain was a queer experience unto itself. My everyday rituals involved negotiations between passing and coming out, between self-effacement and self-advocacy, between craving and rejecting concrete labels. Abject yet immanent, pain unmoored my perspectives on futurity and finitude. Hopeful and hopeless feelings took turns preying on the purview of who I was and who I could be again. Pain necessitated a performative lifestyle, the undertaking of physical, physiognomic, and verbal choreographies that could either keep people in the dark or let them in on the secret. One problem was that I had no clear diagnosis and didn't know how to describe myself anyway. No external violence had been done to me, and I hadn't suffered a trauma per se. I briefly discussed disability leave with my department chair and dean, but didn't comfortably identify as disabled. Perhaps I didn't feel entitled or courageous enough. And what if the pain disappeared one day as suddenly as it came? With doctors scratching their heads, with tests coming out clean, what if the pain was truly in my mind (as opposed to what)? Or, on the contrary, what if I was downplaying the pain and therefore not receiving sufficient aid? I remember leaving certain physicians' offices scolding myself for not speaking up as vigorously as I could have on my own behalf. During one visit to a pain clinic, the nurse who took my vitals asked me how much pain I was experiencing on a scale from 0 to 10, with 10 being the worst. I first said 6, then quickly changed my mind and mumbled, "Wait . . . actually, 8." The nurse grinned and told me she had to write down the first number because it represented my gut instinct (my gut, as if it could think straight). I considered pleading with her to update the number and convey greater urgency to the physician. But I ended up just nodding and smiling.

Over endless consultations with gastroenterologists, anesthesiologists, surgeons, nutritionists, and acupuncturists, my ability to describe pain hardly improved. I was easily stumped by routine questionnaires asking whether the pain was *sharp* or *dull, shooting* or *throbbing*. One visceral irony lay in how despite the amazing medical technologies of imaging and auscultation, I didn't always feel seen or heard. Although stethoscopes let physicians eavesdrop on my heartbeats, these rituals of "hydraulic hermeneutics" couldn't substitute for my own illness narrative.[16] Physical exams of palpation and percussion (tapping my abdomen, checking for masses) treated my cavities and organs as vibrating instruments, but couldn't glean the agony induced by, among other things, precisely these forcible tests. Among the most dissonant experiences arose during MRI scans, which bombarded my supine figure with brassy noises of magnetic fields and oscillating coils; inside the tube, the sounds were harsh, yet, in my imagination, every *beep* served a purpose, working to sketch my scars and prove my pain. Even as MRIs homed in on my atoms, I longed to retain a sense of self apart from whatever results emerged. Physicians' tests positioned me as a resonant vessel, an object poised to confess structural flaws. The exams alone could not, however, say much about who I was—who I hoped to be—as a person, a musician, and a writer.

Piano and Prose: Impasse

During the time I took a hiatus from research, I also stopped playing piano, and as of 2016, I have yet to resume. In years past, I had given regular recitals, including a series of performances in graduate school called *Improvisations on Themes from the Audience*. These performances began with audience members recommending themes (anything from Bach to Beyoncé), which I would work into real-time mashups according to classical idioms of the eighteenth and nineteenth centuries. I loved the interactivity, the freedom, the danger. Austere etiquettes of Western art traditions flew out the window as people shouted out "Flight of the Bumblebee" or "Bohemian Rhapsody" or "that theme from *Star Wars* . . . no, the *other* one!" During a performance, I could reciprocally hear the audience's hearing of my playing because people would chuckle upon recognizing variegated melodies. At the same time, I tried to make listeners feel heard by weaving their recommendations into the recital's musical fabric. Ten fingers, numerous voices. To be clear, I don't think my improvisations always sounded good. I would hit weird notes or fudge up the pacing or linger too long on a single theme or overdo clichéd circles of fifths. But it was my favorite way to play, a way that felt electric and alive.

With the onset of illness, it became painful to sit on a hard bench and difficult to concentrate. My hands turned disobedient and my runthroughs of even easy repertoire became disorderly. Passagework sounded broken, yet not in a beautifully salvageable way. There was nothing romantic or *poète maudit* about playing through physical anguish. As much as I would've hoped to find some transcendental inspiration in pain, it hasn't panned out. No overcoming narrative, no supercrip courage.[17] But it wasn't for lack of trying. Some people, after all, have better luck when it comes to finding distraction or even respite in musical activity. In his book *Anatomy of an Illness*, Norman Cousins recalled his astonishing encounter with the conductor and cellist Pablo Casals in 1966, a few weeks before this musician's ninetieth birthday. At the time,

Casals had developed difficulty breathing and walking and dressing him-self. "His hands were swollen and his fingers were clenched," Cousins remembered.[18] But one day before breakfast, Casals headed to his piano. According to Cousins:

> I was not prepared for the miracle that was about to happen. The fingers slowly unlocked and reached toward the keys like the buds of a plant toward the sunlight. His back straightened. He seemed to breathe more freely. Now his fingers settled on the keys. Then came the opening bars of Bach's *Wohltemperierte Klavier*, played with great sensitivity and control. I had forgotten that Don Pablo had achieved proficiency on several musical instruments before he took up the cello. He hummed as he played, then said that Bach spoke to him here—and he placed his hand over his heart. Then he plunged into a Brahms concerto and his fingers, now agile and powerful, raced across the keyboard with dazzling speed. His entire body seemed fused with the music; it was no longer stiff and shrunken but supple and graceful and completely freed of its arthritic coils.[19]

No matter how accurate or embellished this description may be, suffice it to say that I haven't been capable of showing such virtuosic transfor-mation during pain. My inability to translate suffering into artistry has in fact made me doubt how much I care about music—a queer thing for a musicologist to wonder. If I loved music enough, shouldn't music some-times *be* enough to comfort and care for me?[20] Or, to frame this as the three-word inquiry people ask about difficult relationships: *Is love enough?* As my body and worldview came undone, it wasn't a huge stretch for me to start questioning my relationship to music. Playing music didn't serve as a magical security blanket, and listening to it couldn't help me sleep. Music wasn't exceptional. It was just one more thing excised from daily activities, one more broken luxury in a life falling silent.

My sense of inadequacy extended from the playing of piano to the perusal of books. In the summer of 2014, on the better days when I could focus enough to get some reading done, I opted for a mix of queer memoirs (for enjoyment) and critical theory (to stay abreast of academic literature).[21] In many ways, the two genres couldn't be more different. Memoirs come across as vulnerable and transparent, while critical the-ory can border on domineering and opaque. Authors of memoirs often sound out reparative measures, recounting life's challenges in search of meaning and closure, whereas critical theorists traffic in paranoid discourse, deferring meaning and closure via deconstruction. It was around this time that I began exploring ideas of resonance, the physical and metaphorical vibes at work in interactions between selves and surroundings. The writings of French philosopher Jean-Luc Nancy left a mark on me, though not in the traditional sense. Consider the following excerpts from Nancy's *Listening* (*À l'écoute*):

> To be listening is thus to enter into tension and to be on the lookout for a relation to self; *not*, it should be emphasized, a relationship to "me" (the supposedly given subject), or to the "self" of the other (the speaker, the musician, also supposedly given, with his subjectivity), but to the *relationship in self*, so to speak, as it forms a "self" or a "to itself" in general, and if something like that ever does reach the end of its formation.[22]

And, a few pages later:

> We should linger here for a long time while on rhythm: it is nothing other than the time of time, the vibration of time itself in the stroke of a present that presents it by separating it from itself. . . . Thus, rhythm separates the succession of the linearity of the sequence or length of time: it bends time to give it to time itself, and it is in this way that it folds and unfolds a "self."[23]

Self, "self," *self*, itself, "to itself," *in self*. With my own sense of self eroded by pain and painkillers, I had a hard time wrapping my mind around these passages, which I ended up highlighting in green and annotating with question marks. Nancy's writing struck a nerve, and as I now write this, over a year later, I think I've figured out why. To be clear: rather than gloss here what I take Nancy's words to *mean*, what follows is my attempt to describe my own feelings toward these words. Granted, people don't usually elaborate on the emotions elicited by others' scholarly writing. The aesthetic objects of critique (music, poetry, photography), maybe; but critique itself—less so. We do, in other words, commonly talk about what we think someone like Nancy is trying to say and what his theories let us say in turn. We don't talk about how Nancy makes us feel. Enlightened? Obtuse? Irritable? Under the generous canopy of critical inquiry, there should be room for discussions about the affects elicited by, not least of all, affect studies and phenomenology.[24]

Nancy boasts a monumental oeuvre and has plenty of admirers. But as I scanned and rescanned his definitions of listening and rhythm, I stayed stumped. Here was Nancy, showing off language resembling nested math equations, operating with what sounded like second-order and third-order logics—and here I was, out of order, making do with a shortened attention span and diminished retention. I could have coolly dismissed Nancy's writing as sophistry and shaken my head sagely at its esoteric pretense. I could have chosen to laugh at the impenetrable rhetoric and shared it on Facebook with a humorous tag (#obscurantism). Instead, I wept as I read: teardrops hit paper and made neon watercolors out of the highlights. Affliction had whittled down my patience for mind games and wordplay. Latching onto these few lines of text was arbitrary, even irrational. I know I reacted with disproportionate sadness and shame toward Nancy's abstract musings. Perhaps I fixated on this mental impasse as evidence of my futile endeavors to steady my intellect and repair my body. The hard words stood for all the things that no longer came easy: producing good work, eating good food, enjoying a pain-free summer car ride to the Cape with windows down and radio up. The smudged ink before me coalesced into a snapshot of my muddled psyche. It represented the end of my line, telling me this was as far as I will go.

My queer failure to understand Nancy may offer its own humble revelations. I think of Noam Chomsky, who, among others, has admonished postmodern theorists for polysyllabic posturing. These theorists, Chomsky says, envy (and seek to mimic) the complex, rarified work of physicists and mathematicians.[25] Revisiting the two *Listening* excerpts, however, it seems as if Nancy envies not only science but also music. Look at his language. It's arguably more musical *in itself* than it is *about* music itself. The prose delights in repetitions with minor variations and coy inversions, echoing with assonance all the while. And as with music, Nancy's words can accommodate sprawling interpretations. Recall that a trait of paranoid criticism is, according to Sedgwick, its attempt to ward off others' faultfinding efforts. One way to accomplish this involves comprehensive topical coverage and displays of erudition. Another way is to write in a manner that defies comprehension altogether. High theory's golden logic states that if you don't get it, you're not smart enough; if people can't see the emperor's new clothes, quip the sly weavers, it's because they're unfit for their posts.[26] As much as I'd like to feel as confident as the vocal child who denudes the emperor, there's always the fear that *I'm* the one who's lacking acuity, that I alone am the one who cannot see.

Assumptions about the intangibility and ephemerality of sound enable us to talk about it in abstruse, ambivalent ways. Discursively, this is freeing. Sociopolitically, this can be problematic, as such abstractions may be partly responsible for how sonic offenses go unaddressed. To me, Nancy's language is unclear. But does it also verge on unethical? Lest we doubt his elitism, consider how Nancy regards musicology and its Others: "If someone listens to music without knowing anything about it—as we say of those who have no knowledge of musicology—without being capable of interpreting it, is it possible that he is actually listening to it, rather than being reduced to hearing [*entendre*] it?"[27] How many people subscribe to this characterization of musicology? Is it strange that an author so invested in ideas of listening would write in a manner comprehensible to so few?

At the time, getting worked up over a morsel of cloudy philosophy may have been a poor use of my dwindling energy and scant moments of lucidity. Yet these passages by Nancy exemplified much of what I've found troublesome about academic operations and social hierarchies at large: worlds divided into the haves and have-nots—those who have purported knowledge of music and those who don't, those who just *get it* and those who cannot. A reparative reading of Nancy would give him the benefit of the doubt, refraining from accusing him of condescension. But more to the point, what is the purpose of sounding smart and writing well? Amid the imperatives of knowledge, aptitude, and eloquence, where do compassion and care fit in?

Senseless

I remember the day a doctor offered a correct diagnosis for my condition. He was a gastroenterologist, yet his diagnosis was not gastroenterological. After listening to my description of symptoms and previous treatments, he informed me that perhaps there was pain in my abdominal *wall*—the layers of skin, muscle, and fat surrounding the stomach and nearby organs. It goes by the name of abdominal cutaneous nerve entrapment syndrome (ACNES), or just abdominal wall neuropathy for short. As the doctor explained this, things started to click: why endoscopies came out clean, why changes in diet made little difference, why antacids were ineffective, and why I would yelp uncontrollably upon palpation of my abdomen. A quick online search brought up several medical articles pointing to ACNES as a frequently overlooked problem when it comes to idiopathic abdominal pain. It can be brought on or exacerbated by specific incidents or injuries, but often, people with the condition are seemingly just born this way.[28]

Once ACNES was raised as a possibility, all health practitioners who were involved recognized that we were dealing with neuropathy rather than gastritis or cholecystitis or pancreatitis. But for over a year, I had already presumed the malady to be digestive in nature, something deep within. I had developed an eating disorder through the systematic elimination of foods from my diet, becoming anemic in the process. I had grown to fear mealtimes, especially on social occasions. Lastly, I had lived with an assumption that my threshold for pain was unusually low, given that even soft contact with my abdomen would cause me to wince.[29] In essence, I had learned to feel weak. But my complaints now sounded justified, for with neuropathy, my peripheral nerves were transmitting needless pain signals to the spine and the brain. The problem didn't stem from organ failure. The problem was pain itself.

In a January 1939 interview, Winston Churchill spoke about the need for democracy and free press in the face of totalitarian threat. "Criticism may not be agreeable, but it is necessary," said Churchill. "It fulfills the same function as pain in the human body; it calls attention to the development of an unhealthy state of things."[30] Preserving people's rights to criticize their government keeps powers in check. Pain receptors alert us to injury, telling us to take our hands off a hot stove. In short, pain serves the body in the way that criticism serves the body politic. Norman Cousins, who lived with and recovered from chronic pain, shared Churchill's sentiments: "Pain is part of the body's magic. It is the way the body transmits a sign to the brain that something is wrong."[31]

But suppose that your nerves fire unnecessarily and pathologically, as in the case of neuropathy. Suppose the only wrong thing telegraphed by this pain is pain. Neuropathy is a body crying wolf, paranoia overdrive. Misfiring synapses yell *Watch out!* on a loop, raising alarms about phantom threats when in fact these nerves are their own worst enemies. The pain is useless and has, now and again, made me feel useless in turn. It's easy to call pain magical or inspirational or a badge of honor.[32] It's harder to appreciate such silver linings when you're still caught in the storm.

Suppose, contrary to Churchill's analogy, that certain practices of criticism likewise stem from socialized rituals rather than thoughtful decisions and reparative aims. Neuropathy involves pain for pain's sake; do paranoid readings, among other discursive practices, showcase criticism for criticism's sake? Suppose we, in daily interpersonal and academic activities, introduce more injurious stimuli into the world than

Figure 1.2. A sculpture called *Hope and Confidence* in one of the waiting rooms at the Dartmouth-Hitchcock Medical Center. Placed here in 1991, it was created by the American sculptor and plastic surgeon Dr. Burt Brent as a gift for his mentor Dr. Radford C. Tanzer. Do you see two hands of a single person, clenched together pleadingly and hopefully? Or do you see the respective hands of two people (say, patient and doctor) coming together in a gesture of care and outreach?

needed, for the sake of . . . what? Pursuit of truth? Authority? Thrill of competition? Do we ever get so busy trying to sound good and do well that we forget to care for others? Has naysaying become a reflex rather than a choice, a tendency hardwired into neural pathways? If so, would we even know it?

To date, I can't say what has or has not definitively come out of my pain, because I have not yet come out *from* it. I remain in it, it in me. I still visit pain clinics, receiving consultations, injections, and radiofrequency ablations. I underwent an anterior abdominal neurectomy at the end of 2015 with only minor relief. More surgeries loom. Pain is my shadow, forcing me to check my mood and stamina every time before booking a trip, teaching a class, or agreeing to coffee with a friend. On dark days, I stay at home, unavailed, letting hours dissipate, fantasizing about what I would trade to make the pain go away, barricading myself in the bargaining stage of grief, the futile stopover between anger and depression. On bright days, I write avidly, laugh loudly, and love better, wishing for each minute to linger a little longer.

As I've gradually shared drafts of this book, one shining spot is how many friends have reciprocally shared their own personal tales. Walls came down, sound barriers shattered. Across these emotional exchanges, a valuable affective commodity began to stir: confidence. Not confidence as in resilient authority or self-assurance, but confidence as in *confidentiality*—a readiness to trust, to empathize, and to be vulnerable in the company of another (figure 1.2). As I continue to wonder whether I can be unbroken, what 0–10 pain level tomorrow brings, and how I can make it through a conference next month, the sentimental vibes in these honest conversations have felt refreshingly truthful. They have confirmed my suspicion that it's possible to tread alternate paths of critique and care. For the moment, what I care about most is seeking a reparative lifestyle for myself and for those closest to me, as long as I'm able.

CHAPTER 2

Sing the Ivory Tower Blues

✦ ✦ ✦

I know of no rule which holds so true as that we are always paid for our suspicion by finding what we suspect.

—Henry David Thoreau[1]

Do you see now why it feels so good to be a critical mind? Why critique, this most ambiguous pharmakon, has become such a potent euphoric drug? You are always right!

—Bruno Latour[2]

Suspicious Times

In hard times, suspicion is always in style. It's a survival tactic, a way of life that lets us anticipate and avert bad surprises. At the most mundane, suspicion comes through in an arched eyebrow or a glance over the shoulder. Taken to extremes, it balloons into clinical paranoia and conspiracy mongering. With digital technology, our everyday means of deception and fabrication have multiplied, giving consumers persistent cause to wonder whether a broadcast is truly live, whether Beyoncé lip-synched the national anthem, whether leaked nude photos of Jennifer Lawrence are the real deal, and whether any of these matters are worth one's time to begin with. In the wake of Edward Snowden and whistleblown scandals, citizenries have plenty of reasons to keep up their guards and watch what they say. Fears of falling skies feel justified, grounded in the realities of climate change, unending wars on terror, and a global buildup of nuclear weapons capable of annihilating the planet many times over (overkill in the most literal sense).[3] News cycles paradoxically broadcast constant states of emergency—threats and catastrophes, just a channel or click away. Browse WebMD or watch *House* long enough and you will start believing you have the rarest of diseases. Cynics and hypochondriacs lack no vindication.

Even (or especially) in moments when we do feel safe—in precious instances when the world seems transparent and uneventful—we might manufacture dissent, stirring up drama for drama's sake: by engaging the made-up foes of games; fanning flame wars on Internet forums; impishly spreading rumors at school or by the water cooler; nitpicking at the tiny faults in near-perfect relationships; fashioning self-fulfilling omens; or otherwise making waves where waters were once calm. Nowadays, observes Bruno Latour, "The smoke of the event has not yet finished settling before dozens of conspiracy theories begin revising the official account, adding even more ruins to the ruins, adding even more smoke to the smoke."[4] Latour terms this "instant revisionism," a social mesh of immediate feedback, pushback, and blowback.[5] Deborah Tannen calls it "argument culture," the perpetuation of a "pervasive warlike atmosphere that makes us approach public dialogue, and just about anything we need to accomplish, as if it were a fight."[6] Yet even when we are the makers of mischief, it's tempting to see ourselves as embattled protagonists, to fixate on personal impediments and play up antagonistic presence. *Me against the world* is the mantra of the modern (neo)liberal individual, the spirit by which we console and congratulate ourselves as the scrappy heroes of spectacular adventures.

Academics frequently view their work and workplace as institutions under budgetary and ideological siege.[7] Hardly a day goes by without multiple articles in the *Chronicle of Higher Education* reporting the financial gutting of universities. Anti-intellectualism evokes barbarians rattling the gates of the ivory tower, but adversariality also rages within the tower itself: notwithstanding the conventions and collegiality of mutual citation, scholars learn not just to write, but to write *against*—to uproot status quo, fill in lacunae, and change up the game.[8] Musicologists, toiling on the fringes of academia's better-known fields, may find particular cause to believe they have something to prove. Music's reputation as an object of leisure—frivolous, recreational, merely pleasurable—has shaped the development and discontents of musicology since its inception.[9] The discipline's unsung status stands to enervate as well as energize its students, inspiring vigorous allegations against visual biases and the tuned-out sensorium. Prefatory tsk-tsks about ocularcentrism have become a reliable gambit, a way to open up discourses for sounds in need of bended ears.[10] Revisionist critiques, at their most fruitful, build dialectical momentum and foster constructive dialogue. In less productive cases, this rhetoric can descend into knee-jerk contrarianism and mudslinging. Big-name academics tend to generate high-profile rivalries. Each discipline has its Godzillas and Mothras, the clarion giants whose radioactive words edify, entertain, or perturb the younger colleagues who might not feel personally or professionally safe enough to enter the fray. There's the adage that academic politics are so vicious because the stakes are so low.[11] This saying is not only anti-intellectualist in its accusation but also infantilizing in its tone. It likens scholars to children who play at war, who feel free to engage in bombastic verbiage precisely because the procedures and consequences are thought to be virtual, a lot of simulated sound and fury, signifying nothing.[12]

Big Talk

What transformation would need to occur before those who pursue academic discourse can be "heard" (which I take to mean "respected"), not in spite of our mental disabilities, but with and through them?

—Margaret Price[13]

Against the monopoly of virtuosic paranoid readings, it's not easy to devise or trust alternate modes of scholarly production. Academics may find little incentive to rock the boat in the first place. One possibility lies, however, in what Sedgwick calls reparative reading—a way of approaching texts, events, and people with refreshing surges of positive affect. In one of her articles on music and torture, Suzanne Cusick glosses and builds on the reparative as follows:

The paranoid, [Sedgwick] showed, believes in the efficacy of knowledge, exposure and demystification. By contrast, the critical practices that result from the reparative position aim toward "a sustained *seeking of pleasure.*" Reparative critical practices produce weak theory with only locally applicable explanatory power, and they are easy to dismiss (from a paranoid position) as "merely aesthetic" or "merely reformist." And yet, Sedgwick concludes, the reparative is "no less realistic, no less attached to a project of survival, and neither less nor more delusional or fantasmatic" than the paranoid. Unlike the paranoid, however, it leads us toward moments when joy (not "gotcha!") can be a guarantor of truth, when practices that are weak, sappy or anti-intellectual may bespeak the spiritually and psychologically healthy reclamation of sustaining pleasure from a world that may not have intended to sustain us.[14]

The reparative is unflinchingly reflexive and reflective, unafraid to linger on the naked reasons for why and how we produce critical work. "Faced with the depressing realization that people are fragile and the world hostile," remarks Ellis Hanson, "a reparative reading focuses not on the exposure of political outrages that we already know about but rather on the process of reconstructing a sustainable life in their wake."[15] On its face, this mode of reading can come across as preachy and gooey. For doesn't sentimentality belong to greeting cards, romantic comedies, after-school specials, and cutesy banter between lovers? There's no crying in criticism; cynicism is safer, stronger.[16] The reparative's plea of *Can't we all just get along?* is answered by the paranoid's *Maybe . . . but why risk it?* and *Better safe than sorry!* Sounding strong feels good. Paranoid rhetoric stakes out authority and quashes opposition. Lauren Berlant reminds us that the "intellectual referent of the word 'smart' derives from its root in physical pain. Smartness is what hurts, or to say that something smarts is to say that it hurts—it's sharp, it stings, and it's ruthless. It is as though to be smart is to pose a threat of impending acuteness (L. *acutus*—sharp)."[17] Sharp tongues and rapier wits make powerful tools for combating others and shielding oneself.

Everyday acts of writing and speaking compel us to harness the voices of peers, mentors, and interlocutors who leave their marks on our linguistic habits and intellectual conscience. Paranoid motives amplify these voices to forge them into armor: that's not quite what I said, that's not *quite* what I said, that's not quite what *I* said, and so on. One irony is that the paranoid's myth-busting "strong theory" tends to rely on open-ended, wavering words and syntax: "seems," "might," "maybe," "one could say," "simultaneously A and not A," and other guarded constructions. Contrast this with reparative readings, which dare to be fallible and thus don't shy away from "is," "in fact," "I believe that," and affirmative language that leaves the writer open to contradiction. To embrace "weak theory," then, takes some strength as well, a willingness to risk being wrong—and being wronged.

Weak theory has close ties to "low theory," which Jack Halberstam posits as "theoretical knowledge that works at many levels at once . . . one of these modes of transmission that revels in the detours, twists, and turns through knowing and confusion, and that seeks not to explain but to involve."[18] Low theory, in Halberstam's formulation, isn't indebted to interpretative cohesion. It can appear protean and even scattered. Carolyn Abbate uses similar terminology in comparing "low hermeneutics" and "soft hermeneutics," a distinction that "separates a musical hermeneutics craving the blessing of history or the dead and seeing immanent supra-audible content in musical artifacts from the past (low) from that which acknowledges such content as a product born in messy collisions between interpreting subject and musical object (soft)."[19] Abbate goes on, all the same, to expose this differentiation as illusory. "In fact," she cautions, "soft hermeneutics inevitably becomes low as well; hermeneutics' fundamental gesture is determining and summoning authority, not leaving open or withdrawing."[20] In recent years, scholars have also begun seeking alternatives to anthropologist Clifford Geertz's influential ideal of "thick description," which favors ethnographic disclosures of meaning and depth.[21] Whereas thick description follows, as John Jackson Jr. notes, a seductive "totalizing ethos" that "imagines itself able to amass more and more factual information," the principles of "thin description" locate value in dialogues, surface behaviors, and "a way of knowing that privileges continued nonknowing."[22]

Weak, soft, low, thin—terms often pejoratively writ, connoting something fluffy or flimsy or sissy. As antidotes to paranoid readings, however, they take on antinormative forces of their own, performing disobedience and offering queer possibilities. Reparative work, after all, doesn't shoot for perfect compromise or intellectual homogeneity. Its goal isn't the elision of difference or the suspension of critical faculties, but rather a recognition that such faculties may prove meaningful even when they prioritize (rather than blackball) peace and pleasure. Reparative scholarship acknowledges that the transactions of power in rhetorical exchanges have potential to harm and to heal. Its aspirations go beyond the merely constitutive, the act of putting things and selves back together again. Its greater aims are creative and creational, making promises and moments anew.

Shortcomings of repair lie in the stark implausibility of its own lofty promises. It's impossible to behave reparatively around the clock and unfeasible to write only ever in the reparative mode. Sedgwick's own reparative calls contain paranoid traces of insecurity, despondence, and even *gotcha!*—feelings that undoubtedly show up in *Just Vibrations* and in all of our writing. "So many of us feel compelled to answer Sedgwick's call to reparation, which cracks us out of academic business as usual and promises good things both for Sedgwick and for us," says Heather Love. "But I also think we need to answer the call to paranoia and aggression. Sedgwick taught me to let the affect in, but it's clear that by doing so I won't only be letting the sunshine in."[23] Not only sunshine, but also shadows and chills: the point, perhaps, is to *allow* feelings in and out, to make room for affective archives at the hearths where we tell stories. Just because repair isn't promptly achievable shouldn't deter us from desiring its fulfillment. In efforts to do well and to do good, people can hold paranoia and repair in perpetual tension, recognizing that neither means (or feels like) much without the other.

Paranoid motives, whether born out of play or panic, boil down to power. Inhabiting a world believed to be overbearing and antipathetic, paranoiacs work to claim knowledge over fates and surroundings. And if paranoid readings prize control above all (seizing critical authority to prove, persuade, and even punish), then the reparative has the task of defetishizing control as a de facto positive value. This agenda can sound counterintuitive—for what does scholarship showcase if not intellectual control over subject matter? As a start, the reparative could acknowledge the improprieties and vices that the pursuit of power might entail; reflect on the ethics and politics of rhetorical norms; and decenter the tacit enviability of *ability* by shifting focus to adjunct rubrics of accessibility and accommodation.[24] It's satisfying to play master of a situation, but there's also wisdom, humanity, and even joy in surrendering to swirls of circumstances beyond our command.[25] Whether we're dealing with an improv recital, an online multiplayer game, BDSM, or a conference Q & A gone off the rails, life's out-of-control moments pose humbling reminders that we can't always stay in charge.

A reparative discourse would pick up negation as an option rather than as an obligation.[26] In his controversial 2003 book, *Decentering Music,* Kevin Korsyn painted a dire portrait of contemporary musical research. He likened the institution of musicology to the Tower of Babel:

> The situation [in musicology] recalls the biblical story of the attempt to build a tower that would touch the heavens. God frustrates this scheme by sowing linguistic confusion. . . . We can easily imagine how the exasperated builders might have turned to violence when their companions answered them in gibberish. Something similar has

happened to music, although the violence is rhetorical rather than physical. Members of opposing groups seem to be speaking different languages or playing different language games. . . . As voices become increasingly shrill, the hope of building a community, of joining a common enterprise, lies in ruins.[27]

If we can "easily imagine" that violence would arise simply from Babel's "linguistic confusion," then might we be giving people too little credit?[28] If being answered in "gibberish" is cause for turbulence, it may owe to a paranoia about being mocked or disrespected in foreign tongues, about being insulted without even knowing it. If the Tower lies in disrepair, the solution comes with learning to get along not despite but precisely because of human biodiversity and its ethical possibilities.[29] "The hope of harmony in the contemporary world," writes Amartya Sen, "lies to a great extent in a clearer understanding of the pluralities of human identity, and in the appreciation that they cut across each other and work against a sharp separation along one single hardened line of impenetrable division."[30] It goes without saying that people who sound different, or who do not express themselves well, or who do not (or cannot) speak at all—or talk only in *weak* or *soft* or *low* or *thin* or *queer* lingo—are not automatic candidates for exclusion or injury, and no less deserving of care.[31]

A shared language, in any case, doesn't accomplish much if uttered in sour tones. Prospects of repair depend as much on what we say as on how we say it. It doesn't take a musicologist to point out how intonation can make all the difference. It doesn't take a poststructuralist theorist of voice to observe how verbal inflections and modulations exceed and excite semantic content. Even over the phone, we (think we) can discern good or ill will in a voice, and hear a smile in how it gently sweetens the speech flowing through. Maybe some of us have traveled to countries where we didn't speak the native language, yet encountered the rare vendor or passerby who sang some pleasantry of such warmth that we felt the uncanny confidence of believing we knew not just the kind intentions behind the words, but exactly what those words were *saying*. Same goes for a colleague whose work we don't fully understand, or whose work doesn't fit our preconceptions of what is or is not valuable. Incomprehension doesn't justify instant dismissal or cynicism, much less rhetorical violence. If Babel is our reality, the challenge involves acting and speaking in manners that won't give others—*especially* those with whom communications seem difficult—reasons to feel shame.

A Case for Lento?

A bickering Babel evokes noises of people talking fast—maybe talking *at* and *past* one another, neglecting to listen and to learn. But tone aside, our daily communications also run up against expectations of tempo: how quickly we're supposed to talk, how efficiently we deliver information, and the idiosyncratic pacing that enables us to sound well spoken. At the beginning of this book, I asked what we're running from, running to, and running for. Some answers so far show that we run from monstrous failures, run toward success, and hopefully at times, run for something other than just our own pride and preservation. Hard to deny is that we're indeed constantly running. In an era of social media and flash-in-the-pan phenomena, there's little time for slow.

Over the last decade, however, a far-reaching philosophy called the Slow Movement has gained popular traction. It encompasses everything from slow food (versus fast food) and slow dating (versus speed dating and swipe-happy Tinder) to slow reading (savoring words, countering the hypermediated bombardment of modern information) and slow travel (enjoying leisurely journeys rather than rushing to destinations).[32] Advocates for slow scholarship and slow writing point to the potential harms in academia's breakneck mentalities: "Slowing down involves resisting neoliberal regimes of harried time by working with care while also *caring for ourselves and others*. A feminist mode of slow scholarship works for deep reflexive thought, engaged research, joy in writing and working with concepts and ideas driven by our passions."[33] Nevertheless, universities encourage competition, efficiency, and self-reliance.[34] Neoliberalism, in higher education and elsewhere, tends to operate via "linear time—an end-product driven time."[35] Its implicit questions to laborers are *What do you have to say for yourself?* and *How soon can you do as you say?*

Scholars and activists have lately used the term "crip time" to describe the temporal pressures and accommodations pertaining to disability in particular. Margaret Price emphasizes that crip time alludes to more than simply giving people extra time to complete tasks. At academic conferences, for example, "Adhering to crip time might mean permitting more than fifteen minutes between sessions; it might mean recognizing that people will arrive at various intervals, and designing sessions accordingly; and it might also mean recognizing that audience members are processing language at various rates and adjusting the pace of conversation."[36] The larger message here is a call for flexibility and for the destigmatization of slowness. People with phonic tics might seemingly speak *out of turn*, interrupting a conversation or disrupting a presentation. People who stutter could likewise be accused of speaking *out of time*, that is, out of sync with normative pace and taking too long to convey a thought. Unsympathetic listeners would fault speech impairments for erecting communication barriers, causing delays, and holding up queues. A crip-activist perspective would instead draw attention to how societies are too quick to privilege speediness and semantic economy. Business, academia, and everyday situations show prejudice against redundancy, roundabout rhetoric, and circular reasoning. Slow is bad. Repetitiveness is bad. By contrast, clear informational trajectories and efficient delivery sound good.

To crip (or to queer) normative attitudes toward time and teleology is foremost to ask why fluency holds so much sway, how disfluencies can be accommodated, and what the capital of time (*time is money*) says about human values and priorities. One problem is that not everyone can afford to slow down. Institutional, financial, and emotional penalties might await people who dare to lag behind others. "Self-help slow experts can advise us to improve our own lives by going slower," points out Luke Martell. "But this is not too far away from university managers who respond to stress and overload by pushing it away from the institution and structures on to individuals, by proposing solutions such as stress counselling or time-management training."[37] Put another way, a lone musician cannot just take a *ritardando* if the orchestra is going *a tempo* (or *presto*). Doing so would earn the wrath of the maestro and peers, with consequences sure to follow.

Norms of speed can lead some researchers and instructors to feel not merely slow by comparison, but veritably *stuck*—trapped on a treadmill powered by unrealistic expectations. In a recent spate of "quit lit," people have described how and why they left academia. Debra Erickson, observing these writers' analogies of confinement, notes how academia "has been unfavorably compared to many things: a cult, a bad boyfriend, fraternity-style hazing, or indentured servitude. In all of those analogs, victims are bound to perpetrators in such a way that the victims believe they have chosen to stay in dysfunctional relationships, when in reality they have been manipulated or coerced into them."[38] Within ensnaring relationships, care is lacking, yet leaving is hard. People on the cusp of escape are often ironically urged to *slow down* and wait it out, to take time and hold off on rash decisions. Exit barriers include peer pressure, anxieties about sunk costs, the lure of part-time (yet glass-ceilinged) instruction, and an inability to envision or obtain satisfying alternatives to academic work.

Another significant deterrent—more sentimental than circumstantial—may be someone's genuine love for scholarly work.[39] Academics learn to care for one of academia's most obvious goals: the fostering of learning. But is there really such a thing as *just* learning for learning's sake? Are cravings for knowledge always self-justified? Do paths to truth ever come with unforeseen tolls?

Truth and Care

I see misplaced notions of aesthetic autonomy—misplaced Romanticism— impeding the writing of history. . . . It is all too obvious by now that teaching people that their love of Schubert makes them better people teaches them nothing more than self-regard, and inspires attitudes that are the very opposite of humane. There are—there must be—better reasons to cherish art.

—Richard Taruskin[40]

A dream come true, stay true to yourself, tell the truth and shame the devil—by most measures and idioms, truth is good, a sign of something veridical and verifiable. Scholars seek truth, even if the word or idea itself is taboo (too taut, too arrogant): instead of insisting our claims to be true as such, we call them timely, relevant, or interesting. Ambivalence feels responsible and, for all its virtuosity, sounds humble. With admissions that certain truths may be unattainable or inexpressible, we submit narratives that work to enhance or revise collective wisdoms.[41]

Pursuits of truth have dark sides. Agendas of truthers (pushing 9/11 conspiracy theories), birthers (demanding Barack Obama's birth certificate), and deathers (insisting Osama bin Laden is alive) tend to upset the mainstream populace. On more personal levels, disclosures can be disgraceful and uncomfortable—for why else would the game Truth or Dare pose a quandary? We're not always ready to acknowledge or share facts about ourselves, and we tell white lies to spare others' feelings. Moral and legal maxims say that truth can set us free, but, as Susan Brison reflects, there is also "something deadening about the requirement for truth."[42] A judicial process may demand a victim to restate ad nauseam the horrifying truths about a trauma she would rather forget. Attempts to get the truth out of a suspected criminal might lead interrogators to use and justify injurious techniques. Forcing loved ones to verbalize the truths about their doubts and discontents can sink good relation-ships without good cause. Truth, when mandated or coerced, isn't freely given, and therefore not necessarily freeing.

If paranoid readings thirst for truth, reparative readings find satia-tion elsewhere. For all of truth's virtues, we can conceive of things no less important: love, for one; beauty, too. If we believe, as John Keats wrote, that beauty is truth, and truth beauty, then there's no conflict of interest here. We might sense ineffable truths about the beauties we behold. A beautiful object invites replication, compelling us to draw it, photograph it, describe it, remix it, and retweet it in order to share it with more and more people who may in turn come to appreciate that, yes, this is beautiful, something about it rings true.[43] Beauty, moreover, can complicate and illuminate our sense of self. It can move us to action, hopefully to do good. "It may even be the case," muses Elaine Scarry, "that far from damaging our capacity to attend to problems of injus-tice, [beauty] instead intensifies the pressure we feel to repair existing injuries."[44] Scarry offers this hypothesis to counter the presumption that "beauty, by preoccupying our attention, distracts attention from wrong social arrangements."[45] Yet there are cases in which, at least on the sur-face, a fixation on beautiful objects seems partially responsible for the beholder's neglect of justice and care. Recall the AMS audience member who, in Lydia Hamessley's anecdote, stood up and proclaimed that the safety of female graduate students was not his problem. Is it possible he said this out of a belief that his concerns lay primarily in musicological truths and musical beauties?

Concepts of music's aesthetic autonomy—that musical pieces can claim value apart from societal, political, and personal concerns—have in recent years become passé, synonymous with fuddy-duddy insularity and intellectual conservatism. In the 1990s, music's alleged autonomy floundered against the rise of feminist and queer provocations. Predict-ably, some people refused to get onboard these new trains of thought. Among the most notorious polemics came from Pieter van den Toorn, who criticized Susan McClary's musical hermeneutics of gender and sex as advancing "ulterior motives" and "naked self-interest."[46] Van den Toorn, doubtful of women's "self-proclaimed oppressed status," insist-ed that "arguments about sex and music are largely a form of propa-ganda, an attempt to advertise blanket claims of special disadvantage and oppression which, in contemporary life in the West generally, are dubious and farfetched."[47] Van den Toorn's tirade crescendoed toward an invective that feminists' allegations of injustice and injury amounted to self-victimizing bids for sympathetic attention. For all his keen ear-training as a music theorist, Van den Toorn heard the emphatic calls of feminism but didn't think to listen for its silences (the discontents *not* voiced, the charges not filed, the muted wounds of women facing discrimination, battery, rape). With entire articles and books devoted to caesuras, Kundry, and *4'33"*, musicologists of all people know that silence speaks volumes. In a response to Van den Toorn, Ruth Solie asserted that we're not dealing with rhetorical exercises or games of make-believe: "A reader might be tempted to seek refuge in amusement at the exactitude with which [Van den Toorn's] rhetoric enacts the very rage and aggression he says he's unfairly accused of. But there is no such refuge: on this side of the curtain it's not an academic exercise. A female is raped every six minutes in this country. . . . Amidst the routine inequities and accepted aggressions of that culture, my welfare remains precarious, and so does the welfare of the students I teach—who are also women. If this is 'naked self-interest,' so be it."[48] Although this skirmish took place a quarter-century ago, its frictions remain relevant. A misogynist (or a one-in-five denier) would tell Solie that her reply cries rape, that such an appeal to real-world violations is a cheap trick in the courts of academia, a trump card to shut men up. But crises of sexual assault do continue to strike universities nationwide. Bonnie Gordon, writing about *Rolling Stone*'s controversial 2014 report of an alleged gang rape at the University of Virginia, observes that there can be "very visceral reasons" for teaching courses on music and gender.[49] By critically reading rape in history and in musical texts, students acquire versatile "tools to identify the structures of patriarchal control that perpetuate rape culture and to exploit this knowledge in order to effect change."[50] Classes on Claudio Monteverdi's *L'Arianna* or Giovanni Battista Guarini's *L'Idropica*, says Gordon, enable students to engage the disturbing narration and aesthetic presentation of nonconsensual sexual acts. If instructors and students are willing to go there—there, meaning beyond the sanitized conventions of polite pedagogy—even musical artifacts from long ago can impart urgent strategies for listening and speaking up.

If the idea of art for art's sake is dead, our autopsy would show that it perished not simply from unrealistic ideals, ontological falsity, and hero worship, but also from its moral untenability.[51] To my ears, *aesthetic autonomy* brings echoes of *academic freedom*. It's not that they're synonymous, but that recommendations of *Let music be music* bear injunctive similarities to *Let scholars be scholars*, the belief that academics have a right to pursue their work free from political pressures and without fear of termination.[52] Such freedom can nurture creative thought. *But how can one ethically claim such extreme immunities without also attending to others' extreme vulnerabilities?* Scarry declares there's nothing about being a scholar that exempts her from matters of justice. If anything, being a scholar "actually increases [her] obligation," given her privileged capacity for research and her position to engage with and care for students.[53] Scarry admits various impediments to reparative work, including "the difficulty of seeing an injury, the sense of futility of one's own small efforts, the shame or embarrassment of acting, and the special difficulty of lifting complex ideas into the public space."[54] She concludes, however, that believing any issue to be a lost cause is never sufficient reason to waive duties as caregivers and social agents.

In the wake of aesthetic autonomy, a fashionable rebranding of agency has flourished. Proponents of actor-network theory (ANT), thing theory, and object-oriented ontology nominate alternatives to anthropocentric models of effectivity and action.[55] Everyday objects—computers, musical instruments, baseballs—are said to possess agency by virtue of having an impact on the world and its labors.[56] This might sound at once progressive and regressive: progressive, because it poses an exciting challenge to human exceptionalism and egotism; regressive, because a vision of things coming to life already abounds in childhood fantasies and kids' cartoons (think of the toys in *Toy Story*, the kitchenware in *Sleeping Beauty*, and the backpack in *Dora the Explorer*). ANT isn't infantile, but it is, on some level, epistemologically playful. For adults, one question is whether these games of imagination are ethical. Just because we're intellectually capable of theorizing the agencies of a yoga mat or a teddy bear, does this make it a morally expedient enterprise?

For ANT's subscribers, attending to a plethora of implements and agents may enable us to understand *better* the power relations in the world. ANT, argues Bruno Latour, compels us to be "scrupulous in checking whether power and domination are explained by the multiplicity of objects given a central role and transported by vehicles which should be empirically visible."[57] ANT anchors its conversations with materials, the gritty safety valves that preclude us from talking about authority and asymmetry in the abstract. For Richard Taruskin, however, a Latourian social world appears virtually anarchic. It is, he says, "a place I don't want to live in. If guns are actors then it is they who kill people and we can empty our jails. . . . I don't want anyone to have an alibi. I want actors to take responsibility, and I think it a waste of time to argue about whether a gun, a chanson, or a context is a responsible actor."[58] As with aesthetic autonomy, ANT (especially in the eyes of people who read only a summary of it, or cherry-pick quotes without sufficient context) can come across as a wishful thought experiment, one that does not hold up in real-world courts where matters of life and death hang in the balance.

Some fans of ANT thus claim it to be ethically sound, while other (mis)interpreters somehow see the exact opposite, complaining that notions of nonliving agents are too weightless, too ethereal to sit on the scales of justice. This debate can be recalibrated by stressing one point. Taruskin states that, by attributing agency to nonconscious beings, "the concept of *action* is emptied of real meaning . . . to no good purpose."[59] *Good* and *purpose* are key words. If, according to Latour, actors are entities that "make a difference," our attention should linger on questions about the differences worth making.[60] Rethinking human agency can do a lot of good. It can impugn social hierarchies, promote animal rights, and rectify the disempowering and dehumanizing representations of people who identify as disabled or queer. These are a few concrete examples of issues that stand to benefit from ANT's reflexive critiques of actors (who), networks (who *else*), and theories (inquiries therefrom).

In his 2015 Dewey lecture, philosopher Peter Railton spoke about the academic imperatives of pursuing theories and truths. Toward the end of his talk, he disclosed his personal battles with depression. Depression, he said, cannot be fended off with sheer logic or "steely-eyed, careful critique."[61] It can be crushing and its stigmatization equally so. "I know what has held me back all these years," remarked Railton. "Would people think less of me? Would I seem to be tainted, reduced in their eyes, someone with an inner failing whom no one would want to hire or whom no one would want to marry or have children [with]? Would even friends start tip-toeing around my psyche? Would colleagues trust me with responsibility?"[62] Railton acknowledged that his status as an established scholar came with the privilege of mitigating some, though not all, of these anxieties. Yet, he continued, "Think how these questions can resonate in the mind of a depressed undergraduate or graduate student, trying and failing to do his work, trying to earn the confidence and esteem of his teachers, worried what his friends and parents will think, afraid to show his face in the Department, struggling to find his first job. Will he feel free to come forward and ask for help?"[63] Speaking about one's depression—like speaking about chronic pain, or about queerness or disability—can involve difficult processes of coming out. Railton's words touch on a chief quandary of professionalism's meritocratic logic. Scholars of high standing have relative freedom to divulge personal ails without compromising job security, while junior scholars, whose careers remain contingent, are the ones who are urged to succeed by merit alone, to eschew first-person narratives, and to let their research do the talking (figure 2.1). In brief, those who may most desperately need to share private stories of self-doubt, vulnerability, and discrimination are the same people who are advised to leave identity politics behind and simply to work hard, keep their heads down, and try, try again.[64] I'm not sure what to call this. A bitter irony? A paradox? A necessary evil? In recent years, the *Chronicle of Higher Education* and similar outlets have increasingly featured articles about academics facing challenges of mental health. Given how, as one writer puts it, "academia promotes the blurring of lines between the personal and the professional," scholars "are seldom trained in how to firmly draw that line and value themselves beyond their work."[65]

How close do such issues need to hit home before we reach out to shelter others?

Celia Cain declares that disability, "visible or non-visible, is seen as ugly, malforming, queer."[66] The same could be said about depression and debility. "Our colleagues fear contagion," says Cain. "We fear they smell weakness, so we remain hidden, speaking in whispers, silenced when the visibly healthy walk by. When caught, we downplay, dismiss and deny the centrality of pain or impairment in our lives—betrayed by survival instinct and our bodies. When else is 'coming out' seen as weakness?"[67] (Not usually when it comes to mainstream showcases of LGBTQ pride, as the next chapter soon shows.) Truth and care pose a false yet stubborn dichotomy in intellectual pursuits and in ideas of moral personhood. Maladies of academia inhere in the very question of whether a scholar's physical and psychological well-being truly constitutes a matter of scholarship. Shouldn't there be ways to determine an individual's personhood beyond lines on a CV or apparent contributions to the field? Although *curriculum vitae* loosely translates to *the course of my life*, it can't be the only course of life and livelihood worth caring about. Publish-or-perish models of career advancement insist that we prioritize mind over matter and, as Chomsky might say, production over people.[68] Resisting this neoliberal mindset goes hand in hand with a radical commitment to reparative motions. It begins with finding truth in care, and with reevaluating what really matters across efforts to sound good and to be heard.

These days, the advent of job wikis has created new arenas of convenient yet sometimes combative exchange. Wikis allow academics to post job listings, share updates, and comment anonymously. Many users

Figure 2.1. Cards, sold on Etsy, intended for academics (notably graduate students). The card on the left reads, "I'm sorry you cried in front of your advisor," while the one on the right reads, "Guh—Ah, so . . . I don't know how to—Uh. Feelings, right?"

foster a tone of collegiality and even congratulate successful job recipients; on other occasions, the websites break into venting and gossip. Complaints pertain to unethical hiring practices, the monetary expenses of applications (when, say, Interfolio is required), the underappreciation of (and systemic overreliance on) contingent faculty, and the sheer dearth of employment opportunities.[69] Despondency, anger, and jealousy expectedly rear their heads and threaten to cast down the better angels of respect and generosity. Some users have even tried to discern and out others' identities by tracing IP addresses or via deduction. Phil Gentry, in a blog post, bleakly described the 2009 Musicology Wiki experience as follows: "False rumors are spread willy-nilly, useful discussions are summarily (and anonymously) deleted. Job postings were hidden until after the deadline date. The nadir was when one anonymous participant threatened to commit suicide if s/he didn't find employment by year's end. A few urged him or her to seek help, but really, what can you do?"[70] To take Gentry's important question seriously (and nonrhetorically) is first to acknowledge that the apparent hopelessness of the collective situation—*What can we do?*—does not, as Scarry would say, a priori exempt us from working toward solutions nonetheless. Emily Wilbourne was one of the people who reached out to the suicidal Wiki user. I've asked Emily if she could recall what she posted, since the 2009 Musicology Wiki has been taken down and its contents are no longer viewable online. She replied: "I imagine I just said [to this person] to talk to someone real (not a computer screen) and to remind themselves to differentiate between a system that is constructed to grind up the people, and the other people who were subject to similar situations; that they weren't alone, though it was easy to feel that way."[71] Emily's gesture of care resonates with her reflections on the lessons imparted by her own mentor, Suzanne Cusick, who "has lent her ear and her time to countless peers and junior scholars, bending her considerable intellect to their problems."[72] Receiving care—knowing what it feels like and sensing the difference it makes—can serve as a significant impetus for showing care in turn and paying things forward.

In the face of job market meltdowns, financial need, professional strife, and outright pain, declarations of support—especially when posted online by anonymous colleagues (many of whom are competing for the same pool of scarce resources)—may not sound helpful or sincere enough. Strangers who voice care are trying to do good, but no one can guarantee that it gets better. Indeed, paranoid conventions of criticism have given academics, as much as anyone, cause to be suspicious of optimism and optimistic endeavors, such as the famous It Gets Better Project aimed at queer youths. Hope, like care, can itself feel queer because it doesn't traffic normatively in reason or hard evidence. As far as reparative affects go, hope is simultaneously a misfit and a necessity in moments of gravest precarity. How does someone *stay* hopeful when facing a stark absence of justifications for *staying* at all (staying in a profession, staying in difficult relationships, staying alive)? As good as hope sounds, what are we left with when its tune starts to crack?

CHAPTER 3

How Hopeful the Queer

✦ ✦ ✦

Many trauma survivors who endured much worse than I did, and for much longer, found, often years later, that it was impossible to go on. It is not a moral failing to leave a world that has become morally unacceptable. I wonder how some can ask, of battered women, "Why didn't they leave?" while saying, of those driven to suicide by the brutal and inescapable aftermath of trauma, "Why didn't they stay?"

—Susan Brison[1]

Gay Bashes

Midway through my freshman year of college, a gay friend of mine (let's call him Jerry) decided to throw a series of coming-out parties. These weren't parties for gay-identified individuals; they were for dormmates he believed to be gay, but who had not confirmed this to be the case. Armed with noisemakers and snacks, Jerry rounded up peers decked out in bright costumes. The group would march into someone's room and yell, "Welcome!" The first party supposedly went well: the honoree enjoyed the attention and playfully asked if he was *so* obvious. The second party didn't happen: the person, it turned out, was gay-friendly but not gay, and casually waved off the undeserved festivity.

The third party was a disaster. I know this because I was there, eager to see what all the ruckus was about.

You can guess what went wrong. Although the guest of honor might have been gay, he definitely wasn't ready to come out. This fêted young man, eyes wide with horror, said nothing. Here's how one of my friends remembers it (I reached out to her for factual corroboration):

> [Jerry] had written a song for the occasion. I remember the refrain, "Hey, hey, hey, we're so glad you've got some gaaaaaaaaay in you." I recall him doing a dance that only he could do . . . arms waving slowly, eyes half closed, legs proceeding in a run-hop-run sort of pattern. I recall [another dormmate] was standing right behind him. She kept tapping him on the shoulder, saying, "Hey, maybe he doesn't want to celebrate right now?!" Then I recall how you pulled [Jerry] backwards out the door, pinching the back of his "shirt," a towel that he'd wrapped around himself along with streamers and Mardi Gras beads.[2]

Following the song and dance (which I've apparently blocked out of my memory), a painful awkwardness ensued. After what felt like minutes of frozen stares, I remember that Jerry bolted, beads jingling as he beelined for an exit at the end of the hall. The rest of us mumbled apologies, then shuffled away in silence.

A simple gloss of this encounter would report a collision between gay pride and gay shame. A bunch of out-and-proud, loud, musical freshmen ambushed a potentially closeted dormmate who, throughout the confrontation, stayed mute out of shame. Yet we, the queer posse, became ashamed in equal measure, disgraced and penitent for turning an exercise in good-humored recruitment into a crisis of forced conscription. Word got out that a group of hooting queens was going around East Florence Moore Hall kicking down people's doors—news that must have caused some people considerable paranoia.

But there was no need to sound the alarm, for the group disbanded immediately after the embarrassing incident. Beads and noisemakers and rainbow scarves were stuffed back into closets or tossed out altogether, forfeit reminders of pride turned pitiful.

Hoping against Hope

Even Adorno, the great belittler of popular pleasures, can be aghast at the ease with which intellectuals shit on people who hold on to a dream.
                                                                —Lauren Berlant[3]

In queer life, paranoid and reparative drives remain odd bedfellows. "Even aside from the prestige that now attaches to a hermeneutics of suspicion in critical theory as a whole," noted Eve Sedgwick, "queer studies in particular has had a distinctive history of intimacy with the paranoid imperative."[4] For good reason: closeted individuals live in anxiety of being found out, while those who are out still face pressures of fitting in. On the other side of the rainbow, homophobes stew in panic about the great gay agenda, whether it's same-sex marriage's assault on traditional family values or, as Nadine Hubbs points out, the bigoted rumors in the twentieth century about a "gay mafia" ruling American classical music.[5] Paranoid motives also summed up Don't Ask, Don't Tell. The defunct policy's semantic symmetry (two pithy words on each side of the comma) spun cruel poetry, a flimsy Band-Aid tendering a win-win solution under the fair swap of *I won't show you mine if you don't show me yours.*

In 1968, one year before the Stonewall Riots, the *Journal of Health and Social Behavior* published an article called "Paranoia, Homosexuality and Game Theory." The authors, sociologists Marvin Scott and Stanford Lyman, proposed that "[homosexuals] may come to see all or part of their world in terms of a conspiracy in which they must constantly be on guard against physical or financial harm, exploitation, or loss of status. . . . The paranoid explores, in game-theoretic fashion, the possibilities of all encounters."[6] As retrograde as this article sounds in its terminology and sensibilities, the authors' framework of game theory remains intriguing. Paranoid individuals indeed seek strategic defenses in the face of plausible precarity. By performing "emotional eavesdropping" on people around them—by seeking a hyperawareness of what others know—paranoiacs work to separate friend from foe.[7] Although Scott and Lyman did not cite Sigmund Freud, their views resonate with this psychoanalyst's sweeping hypothesis that paranoid delusions spring from repressed homosexual desires.[8] Game theory aside, think of the various games at play in queer dealings more generally: guessing games (*is he or isn't he*), reindeer games (activities predicated on exclusion and oppression), and language games (ciphers and circumlocutions that pussyfoot around the giant peacock in the room). These games aren't just for laughs. Depending on the playing field, grievous penalties await.

Amid queer tensions, reparative affects are a hard sell in academic perspectives. Negativity, cynicism, antinormativity, and antifuturity come more easily, with promises of deconstructionist vigor and political vigilance.[9] In a book on queerness and social class, Lisa Henderson points to queer studies' "near-ubiquitous" reliance on paranoid readings, which offer "negativity as truth and the exposure of textual or social violence as grail."[10] Cumulatively, there's far more theorization of gay shame than of gay pride, with the latter relegated to, as Alice Kuzniar describes, "something almost to be embarrassed about," or at least, something that doesn't have to be written about (figure 3.1).[11] One explanation for queer theory's allergy to pride may be that pride doesn't seem to need critical excavation to begin with. Unlike shame and its sexy covert essences, pride is already bombastically out there in the rainbow stripes, campy music, and parades where freak flags fly.

In 2007, the year I entered graduate school, an LGBTQ group called the Welcoming Committee launched an experiment by the name of Guerrilla Queer Bar (GQB) in the Greater Boston area. At the beginning of each month, organizers used social media to announce a planned takeover of an establishment. It began with bars and nightclubs: queers would show up en masse and turn the heterosexual majority on its head. If you got to the bar early in the evening, you could observe the regular crowd growing visibly confused about the steady trickle of gays onto the scene. The Welcoming Committee has since spread to ten U.S. cities and diversified its venues, hosting outings to sports games (Fengay Park), casinos, ski resorts, and Bette Midler concerts (where admittedly GQB's efforts are unnecessary). Although its events push for queer visibility, the Welcoming Committee doesn't frame its agenda in political terms.[12] "It's not a protest—it's a party," declares the GQB homepage. "Is it aggressive? No. Is it awesome? Yes."[13] GQB's message takes pride as a given, then proceeds to insist that gays just want to have fun.[14]

In recent years, authors have begun building up optimism and utopianism as rubrics of queer critique. It has been an uphill battle. "Optimism's very sanguinity," Michael Snediker says, "implies epistemological deficit."[15] Or, according to José Esteban Muñoz: "Shouting down utopia is an easy move. . . . The antiutopian critic of today has a well-worn war chest of poststructuralist pieties at her or his disposal to shut down lines of thought that delineate the concept of critical utopianism. Social theory that invokes the concept of utopia has always been vulnerable to charges of naiveté, impracticality, or lack of rigor."[16] Granted, positivity is by no means simple, nor is it the exclusive orientation of the allegedly simple-minded. As Snediker and Sara Ahmed point out, optimism is "interesting" in the way it gestures toward (yet necessarily fails to promise) happiness.[17] Optimism, explains Lauren Berlant, can also be "cruel" when "something you desire is actually an obstacle to your flourishing."[18] Berlant goes on to ask: "Why do people stay attached to conventional good-life fantasies—say, of enduring reciprocity in couples, families, political systems, institutions, markets, and at work—when the

HARVARD UNIVERSITY

From a fund established by

Douglass Roby
A.B. 1965

To portray a positive image
of homosexuality
and gay men and gay women

HARVARD COLLEGE LIBRARY

Figure 3.1. My friend Michaela Bronstein brought this to my attention: the
Harvard library bookplate for Heather Love's *Feeling Backward: Loss and
the Politics of Queer History* specifies a fund "to portray a positive image
of homosexuality and gay men and gay women"—which is by no means
what Love, in her rigorous book, straightforwardly portrays. In an email
exchange, Michaela remarked how she saw this as an example of a "clash
between academic paranoia and institutional optimism."

evidence of their instability, fragility, and dear cost abounds?"[19] Conversely, I have asked in *Just Vibrations* why people who have it pretty good might nevertheless anticipate, in paranoid and pessimistic fashion, the loss of present peace, obsessing over future adversity and the finitude of all good things. In the end, if reparative affects are elusive in queer theory and in criticism more generally, maybe it's because they hide in plain sight. Much of queer theory *is* queer pride insofar as it contributes to compassionate understandings of diversity, tolerance, and justice, albeit via gloomy and tortuous avenues of inquiry. Pride pops up between the lines. Put another way, positives already tend to reside in the photonegatives of critical production.

For an overt example of reparative work outside academia, consider the crowdsourced It Gets Better Project (IGBP), initiated by Dan Savage and Terry Miller in September 2010 as a response to the suicides of bullied youths who were gay (or were suspected as much by their peers). Aiming to deter self-harm, the project amassed thousands of video contributions from celebrities, public officials, and ordinary people testifying that life improves after high school. The project sounded unabashedly promissory in its reparative agenda. Personal testimonies that it *got* better (from people who had overcome adversity in their own lives) slipped into general assurances that it *gets* better. Although some contributors admitted that fortune can be fickle, most messages were unequivocal in their vows of greener pastures. IGBP's tone of certainty presumably aspired to maximize pride and uplift. According to this logic, what dejected youths needed was faith (things *will* get better), not reality or ambivalence (things *might* get better). By using the impersonal pronoun "it" as the subject, the slogan also painted bright futures as foregone conclusions rather than as points of personal or collective responsibility—"*It* gets better" in place of, say, "*Make* it better."

Academic responses to IGBP came fast and, in some cases, furious. Scholars homed in on the project's implicit inscriptions of white, male, and cis hegemony and the elisions of racial, ethnic, and class issues. Jumping off the insights of Tavia Nyong'o, Jasbir Puar described Savage's motto as a sanctimonious "mandate to fold oneself into urban, neoliberal gay enclaves: a call to upward mobility."[20] Such mobility remains more feasible for someone like Savage, who is "able-bodied, monied, confident, well-travelled, suitably partnered," than for "queer people of colour, trans, genderqueer and gender nonconforming youth, and lesbians."[21] The gist of these disclaimers is that, for some privileged people, it gets better *better*, while for others, it doesn't get better at all. But although it's painfully true that life can get worse, IGBP wasn't concerned with truth. Its purposes were foremost to offer selective care and to buy time. As with any politics of optimism, the project was epistemically treacherous yet pragmatically vital. And to the credit of the paperback anthology for IGBP, the editors include stories by diverse authors. Some stories even show flashes of skepticism about the viability of optimism, but, for better or for worse (that *is* the question), typically land on the sunnier side of hope. Here are a few excerpts from the anthology:

> JENNIFER FINNEY BOYLAN: It's hard to be gay, or lesbian. To be trans can be even harder. There have been plenty of times when I've lost hope. . . . Some of the people I most expected to lose, when I came out as trans, turned out to be loving, and compassionate, and kind.[22]
>
> ALEX R. ORUE (TRANSLATED FROM SPANISH): I'm a nineteen-year-old, Latino gay guy from Mexico City. . . . I'd always gotten the message that being gay was wrong. That it was evil. That it was an illness. . . . Eventually you'll find that person that will make you happy and whom you'll make happy, too. But for that to happen, you gotta hold on.[23]
>
> GABRIELLE RIVERA: As a gay woman of color, I just want to let the youth know that it kind of doesn't get better. All these straight, rich celebrities, I'm not even going to name them, they can tell you that it gets better because they've got money and people don't care what they do. . . . So, do I say it gets easier? No, but you get stronger. And you get more beautiful. And you believe in yourself harder.[24]
>
> MARK RAMIREZ (TRANSLATED FROM AMERICAN SIGN LANGUAGE): I lost my hearing when I was nine years old. We don't know exactly how it happened, maybe nerve damage, but it did. . . . I got suspended from school for participating in sexual activities with another male. . . . If you stand strong, be who you are, and know that even though people might not support you now, the days only get brighter if you believe in yourself.[25]

Reading these stories, I think back to my own angsty adolescence and wonder whether a viral sensation such as IGBP would have given me heart. No, I wouldn't have been able to relate to Dan Savage any more easily than I could to the Fab Five on *Queer Eye*. But I might have gone searching for videos featuring Asian immigrants, for example, in hopes that someone might lend advice on how to come out to traditional Taiwanese parents. At age eighteen, I told my parents I was gay and got a serving of full-on denial. For the next four years, my mother sporadically pleaded and bargained with me, asking what it would take for me to straighten up. I saw before me the arduous task of extinguishing her grim wish day by day. Her optimism felt cruel. So I asked my girl friends to stop calling the home phone, explaining to them that if my mother picked up and heard their voices, she would convince herself that lady suitors were on the line. I also asked these friends, after evenings out, to drop me off a few blocks from my house so that my parents wouldn't see us in the car together and get wrong ideas. Some of these games may sound childish and paranoid, but at the time, the battle felt heartbreaking and unwinnable. Seeing my sexuality as a repairable illness, my parents prayed for me to *get better*. So it was me versus them, hope against hope. From my perspective, I alone had the right to hope; they had to let theirs go. Eventually, they did, through blunt dialogue and raised voices and tears and work. Today, my parents are hoping tenfold for something different: for my chronic pain condition to resolve, for things to get better where it matters.

In an essay titled "It Gets Worse . . . ," Jack Halberstam calls out IGBP's toxic masculinities and whitewashed sermonizing. Not all gay youth suicides, Halberstam adds, result definitively from despair about gayness. Halberstam's criticisms build toward an all-out indictment of the project: "The touchy-feely notion embraced by this video campaign that teens can be pulled back from the brink of self-destruction by taped messages made by impossibly good looking and successful people smugly recounting the highlights of their fabulous lives is just PR for the status quo. . . . By all means make cute videos about you and your boyfriend, but don't justify the self-indulgence by imagining you are saving a life."[26] In a paranoid reading of IGBP, Halberstam slams its schmaltzy, gallant ventures at repair, presuming self-centered motives and ineffectual efforts. Of course, most people who recorded videos for IGBP were imagining precisely that they *could* save a life, and my guess is that several lives were indeed bettered as a result. For that matter, if Halberstam or Puar or Nyong'o had made their own It Gets Better videos, in which they tried to queer IGBP by speaking about the project's problematic normativities (and reflecting on their personal challenging paths toward becoming influential queer theorists and educators), their messages might have reached receptive ears as well—maybe the ears of despondent high school or college students eager to engage queerness radically, critically, and colorfully.

But scholars by and large did not record videos for IGBP. I, for one, didn't think to do so. Based on academics' quotes above, you might assume this owed primarily to elitism (*we know better*) and ivory tower insularity. But I believe the answer is more complex. I believe there's a worry that hope weakens critical inquiry—that when we cling to dreams, we slacken our grips on the darker realities of why hope is never enough. IGBP, for all its imperfections, helped some people. But perhaps it's always too soon to celebrate, because for so many left unsaved, it was too late. So first, we mourn: we remind ourselves that all lives are grievable.[27] Then, we dare to hope, recognizing that *not good enough* (critique's impulse) shouldn't have to mean *not good at all.* The bar isn't always blanket revolution. Sometimes, things have to begin with patchwork repair, little efforts sewn together to cover those most vulnerable, as many as we can.

A common problem with demanding strength is how it implicitly dumps the onus of survival and flourishing on the individual—whether it's enjoining queer kids to tough it out, or telling a chronic pain patient or underemployed instructor to hang in there, or mandating preemptive resiliency training in the U.S. Army so that returning veterans with posttraumatic stress disorder or physical injuries are less likely to ask for help and resources.[28] It gets better—as mere mantra, as just vibrations—can't always make good on its promises. Yet are the battle lines between camps like IGBP and academic skepticism necessary? Are they overdrawn? A do-it-yourself maker of an It Gets Better video and a scholar of postcolonial queer-of-color critique might not care much for (or even know much about) each other. These respective labors, however, depend on each other. They need to be held in tension and held mutually accountable, but one doesn't need, in neoliberal fashion, to co-opt or cannibalize its counterpart.

Academics have legitimate reasons to feel disempowered by the thought that someone's five-minute It Gets Better video could achieve more immediate results than a five-hundred-page monograph with a university press. As scholars lambast the pomp and pretentiousness of IGBP, they're led to grapple with their own feelings of helplessness in facing youth suicides and other crises. In the end, the operative affect behind scholars' heated reactions against IGBP is not, as I hear it, resentment or rage. It is anguish, a hope to hope, slipping all the while. No guarantees, no happily-ever-afters. Yet the overwhelming magnitude of any reparative task doesn't release us from trying. It simply means we try that much harder, in more ways than one, hoping against hope that some good can come to pass.

How to Sound Musicological

There's nothing like music to teach you that eventually if you work hard enough, it does get better. You see the results.

— Chuck Todd[29]

All musicians, we must remember, are faggots in the parlance of the male locker room.

— Philip Brett[30]

Since the 1990s, feelings of pride and duty have driven musicologists toward queer topics. But especially in cases of classical composers, researchers have not typically positioned pride itself as an explicit affective locus in their work. Musicologists have tended to focus instead on aesthetic traces of passing and sublimation, from Handel's psyche to Tchaikovsky's angst, from Ravel's repression to Elgar's secrets.[31] Although sorting out musical codes and closets served reparative agendas (remedying prior silences), pioneers of this work faced their own share of paranoia.[32] Early scholars of queer musicology had to brace themselves for resistance and ridicule, worrying about reputation, employment, tenure, and professional adversity. Yet even with all of these risks, musicologists went around pinning postmortem rainbow badges onto canonical composers, thanking them (with elaborate hermeneutic tributes) for their brave service in the trenches of the creative arts.

Both homosexuality and musicality, as Philip Brett memorably noted, can connote deviance. For gay youths who "often experience a shutdown of all feeling as the result of sensing their parents' and society's disapproval of a basic part of their sentient life, music appears as a veritable lifeline."[33] This rings true to my own experience. On the one hand, my musicianship made me vulnerable to accusations of homosexuality: in school, I was called a fag or fairy on some occasions, though my male flutist friends got it worse. On the other hand, being a musician offered perfect plausible deniability. I could sound out gaily on the ivories while insisting that this is *simply the way you play piano*—just sounds, just vibrations, none of it admissible evidence in the court of bullies.[34] If people further assumed I took lessons due to pressure from a tigerish Asian mom, then I had license to play as queerly as I wanted (arch my wrists, trill with pinkies up), leaving no one the wiser.

At a 2014 conference in Milwaukee (jointly for the American Musicological Society and the Society for Music Theory), a session titled "Queer Music Theory" ruffled feathers when multiple presenters began harping on a common theme: that maybe music theory, particularly music formalism, has been queer for some time, certainly far queerer than its own early snipes at gay and lesbian musicology would suggest. The panelist Roger Mathew Grant remarked that it is not just the "play with surface and depth, visibility and invisibility that formalist music analysis shares with gay identity," but that such "contemplation of art and pure form is also characteristic of the queer dandy, whose careful self-stylization and meticulous control over details allowed him to exist in a universe somehow distant from and untouched by the concerns of the surrounding quotidian world. Music theory's world was and still is somewhat like this: rarefied, out-of-touch, completely obsessed with nuance, style, and form."[35] Gay sensibilities resonate in formalism's doting demeanor and curatorial approaches to music.[36] Analyses show careful labor, proof of effort and devotion. In this sense, music analysis can appear precious, even sentimental, belying its reputation as a severe and domineering task, a form of strong theory with a high barrier of intellectual entry. At the same Milwaukee panel, Judith Peraino stressed how music theory articles almost ubiquitously depend on the device of the reduction— Schenkerian, neo-Riemannian, and set theory diagrams that distill musical pieces into daunting lines and figures.[37] Reductions jibe with paranoid readings in that both boast command over the text at hand, decrypting and reencrypting it via feats of interpretative and rhetorical prowess. A reduction can disorient certain readers not least by how it enfolds, distorts, and deconstructs the time frames and proportions of the original musical composition. Just as queer critics have lately rolled out sophisticated theories of futurity, asynchrony, and temporality, so music theory, Peraino observed, has relied on such time-bending devices for over a century.[38]

Given the troubled history between music theory and queer musicology, it's easy to find gratification and even glee in taking shots at the former's own queer tendencies. It's the same kind of satisfaction that some people derive from outing homophobic politicians who get caught tapping their feet under restroom stalls at airports, or from peeling back the veiled homoeroticism of slur-saturated rap lyrics.[39] Crying hypocrite is a national pastime. Go watch some reruns of the *Daily Show* or the *Colbert Report*, and you can see how most punch lines hinge on the faux pas and dry humor of hypocrisy in the news. But is the point really to fight fire with fire, to drum up paranoia through accusations of self-loathing? Or is it to recognize how insecurities drive us all to make mistakes from time to time, and then to find ways forward across bridges worth repairing?

From the AMS 2014 conference in Milwaukee, rewind one year to AMS 2013 in Pittsburgh, where an evening session for the LGBTQ Study Group welcomed the prominent scholar David Halperin. The session was called "How to Sound Gay," and the abstract read: "Halperin and [Ryan] Dohoney will discuss the broad range of musical influences and implications of Halperin's most recent book, *How to Be Gay*, including the role of music in the formation of LGBTQ cultures, sound's ability to produce queer affect, and the role music plays in both queer identity-formation and dissolution."[40] Although the session drew a large and enthusiastic crowd, the mood of the room began to waver as the evening wore on, partly for one odd reason: despite *How to Be Gay*'s frank discussions of gay countertenors, opera queens, and Broadway musicals' queer appeal, Halperin (who teaches in an English department) insisted to the audience over and over again that he was *not* a musicologist.[41] He said so virtually every time he was asked by Dohoney (who remained deferential and patient throughout) about the musical dimensions of performance, gesture, and song. These repeated disavowals of disciplinary affiliation came to sound both comical and confusing. On the one hand, Halperin was replicating the identity games of the closet, producing queer resonances between ashamed claims of *not gay!* and cautious pronouncements of *not a musicologist!* On the other hand, Halperin, though far outnumbered at the event by scholars of a certain musical persuasion, voiced abject disclaimers that queered musicology itself—presuming musicology to be an Other, a camp resistant to newcomers who don't fit the part. Halperin's hemming and hawing ultimately led Emily Wilbourne from the audience to stand up and declare that, on behalf of her colleagues, she dubs him a musicologist. The beknighting drew chuckles and applause. Heather Hadlock recalls the moment:

> Emily W made a final comment in which she granted Halperin the title and status of "musicologist" because he has written interesting things about music. . . . She recalled a conversation with a scholar in theater studies, where she referred to Wayne Koestenbaum as a musicologist and the theater scholar said, "Koestenbaum's not a musi-

cologist," and Emily said, "Sure he is, he's written about opera and I read him in musicology seminars," and the theater scholar said something to the effect that Koestenbaum's writing doesn't have musical examples, ergo Not Musicologist. This seemed like a self-evidently silly criterion, and got a big laugh.[42]

Is a lack of technical musical know-how enough to disqualify someone from claiming musicological identity? Perhaps not, yet Halperin's song and dance made him appear as if he feared speaking to a room of music-analytical wizards who would condemn him for the slightest slip in vocabulary or aesthetic judgment. Halperin, in short, evinced paranoia about sounding bad (musicologically) and being shamed by people (musicologists) he wouldn't call his own.[43] The original aims of this AMS session went off the rails through Halperin's discomfort with musicological affinity, but this queer failure broached valuable issues nonetheless. How does one *sound* musicological? And who's to judge?

Rewind again, this time two more decades, to a musicological controversy that pitted paranoia against repair: the inquisition of Franz Schubert's sexuality.[44] The question went unresolved. No one managed to forge a historicist or hermeneutic silver bullet to establish Schubert's orientation one way or the other—which was the takeaway lesson. The whole affair exposed the means, stakes, and risks of music exegesis. Alongside contemporaneous studies in critical musicology, the kerfuffle around Schubert alerted the community to the importance of rhetorical nuance. With expansive vocabularies and theoretical toolkits, judicious scholars have since learned to lead with abundant disclaimers about music's semantic promiscuity and the contingencies of interpretive frameworks, taking care not to overtax or overdetermine a musical work's evidentiary capacity.

Susan McClary penned some of the most high-profile contributions regarding Schubert's sexuality and subjectivity.[45] Apart from the battles that McClary's work stoked in academic circles, Marcia Citron has described its curious reception in her own undergraduate classroom. I quote Citron's illuminating anecdote at length:

Each year in the survey of [classical] and romantic music that I teach to sophomore-level music majors, we read Susan McClary's article on Schubert's "Unfinished" Symphony. . . . With considerable contextualization and explanation, McClary suggests that such a narrative [in the second movement] *might* reflect an alternative sexual identity on the part of the composer. She is careful to explain that this is not an essentialist relationship; she sets it up as a possibility. McClary also provides background by relating the fiasco of having presented this hypothesis at a [1992] Schubert symposium at the 92nd St. Y in New York, and of its disastrous reception at the time and in print: snide comments in the ladies' room and the question session after the presentation, and the mocking post-mortems in the *New York Times*. As for my music history class, this is our first foray into gendered analysis, and one reason I choose the essay is because of its care in framing contentious issues. So imagine my surprise when, at least twice in recent years, the reaction to the article is something like, "Just say it! If you mean that Schubert was gay, and that's what's coming across in his music, then don't apologize for it. Don't bring all these other issues into it." . . . Now, these are very smart students and excellent musicians, and they're not just blowing off steam or a historical mindset. No—they value it. But I think they're annoyed with the sensibility behind the arguments. They don't want what they see as fudging; they're ready to hear a direct call and seem to respect this approach more—or at least think they respect it more.[46]

What can be more disheartening and paranoia-inducing than overhearing "snide comments in the ladies' room" about one's research, like a scene straight out of *Mean Girls*?[47] What better demonstration of how schoolyard bullying and petty gossip snake their way into adulthood? McClary's project was caught in a double bind from the start. Some of Citron's students were frustrated by the caution that McClary displayed, preferring that she not dance around what they took to be the point of her article—namely, the outing of Schubert through musical analysis. They wanted her to "just say it" (do ask, do tell). From the opposite corner, McClary's professional detractors—those with rigid attachments to a heterosexual, masculine image of Schubert—wanted her to refrain from saying "it" (*gay*) at all, no matter how deft the euphemisms and rhetorical choreography. For some homophobes, even insinuation was too much. On the topic of Schubert and sexuality, the only acceptable stance was silence.[48] *Let music be music* (or *Let Schubert be Schubert*), they'd argue—it's just music, just vibrations; to which an activist might respond, *Not until you let gays be gays* (or, perhaps, *Not until you let Schubert be Schubert*).

Just say it, don't say it: a no-win, can't-please-everyone situation. Unfortunate, but also unsurprising given that there are no real winners when paranoia is in play. Suspicion begets more suspicion, more defensive formations, and more ping-ponging of negative affects. To sail into repara-tive horizons is to get out of this game for a moment and to explore what lies outside its vicious magic circle. Because within this circle, good is scarce. Media reports often emphasize how youth suicides result from shame, humiliation, and bullying. Comparable emotions and offenses come up in academic exchanges, albeit with less (or, one could say, few-er) tragic consequences. Following the terminologies of psychologist Sil-van Tomkins, Sedgwick used the label "humiliation theory" as another name for "strong theory."[49] Proceeding from paranoid motives, humili-ation theory is "monopolistic" in its aim to ward off contradictions, and can "snowball" in its aspirations to colonize larger and larger swaths of epistemic terrain.[50] Authors wield humiliation theories to avoid being humiliated by others' criticisms. In the process, this writing might humil-iate peers and predecessors so as to seize an intellectual high ground.[51] Conventional wisdom tells us that bullies might bully because they have themselves been bullied (either at school or at home), and that they join in bullying to escape being bullied.[52] Adversariality in scholarship isn't so different. Sometimes it can feel like the only option to avoid being prey is to play predator.

Hitting Close to Home (A Parable)

In this era of viral publicity, bullies morph into the bullied and back again with dizzying speed. We feel constantly pushed around and always on our last nerve.
—Tavia Nyong'o[53]

In an episode titled "Bully" from season 1 of the dramedy *Louie*, the pro-tagonist (played by comedian Louis C.K.) goes to a New York diner with a date. Rowdy teenagers nearby start making noise, and Louie, unable to carry on a conversation, yells, "Guys! Can you keep it down, please? *Thank you.*" Moments later, one of these teens, knuckles bruised and face scarred, comes over to Louie's table. He asks Louie when he last had his ass kicked, then asks if he's scared. Louie says no, because he's "a grown man" and "not afraid of some young kid, some high-school bully." But as the teen escalates his threats, Louie grows visibly nervous about whether it's just empty words. The teen says if Louie asks him nicely, maybe he won't get beaten up. Facing a choice between pride and physi-cal self-preservation, Louie mumbles: "Please don't kick my ass, okay?" The amused teens take off, leaving Louie to sort out the aftermath of emasculation with his date, who, throughout the ordeal, wore a mixed expression of disbelief and exasperation.

The story doesn't end here. After parting ways with his turned-off lady friend, Louie catches sight of the teen bully at a subway entrance and, for whatever reason, follows him all the way to his house in New Jersey. Louie goes into the house and confronts the parents, tattling on this teen's misdeeds. The father summons his son and, when he appears, begins to beat him. Louie immediately intervenes. "Stop hitting him! How do you think he turned out like this?" Louie exclaims to the dad. "You teach him to just hit people; what was he gonna be but a stupid bully? I mean, you never gave him a chance!" In a sardonic turn, the teen's mother takes offense and goes after Louie for telling her how to raise her child. She calls Louie an "Obama-loving faggot" and chases him out of the house while smacking his head.

But against all odds, the scene ends with a whiff of repair. The boy's father comes out of the house to see Louie, and the two smoke some cigarettes. They engage in calm, honest conversation. In response to Louie's exhortation against spanking children, the father says: "Well, that's what I know. My dad hit me, and his dad him." The two men sit on the front stoop, swap more stories, then fall silent. The only sound that lingers is the wail of a distant siren.

Moments from this *Louie* episode capture many of the dilemmas born of bullying: the troubled teen's use of brute intimidation; Louie's feminized passivity (cowering in the diner) and exceptionally proactive gesture thereafter (following the boy home); the mother's wholesale rejection of criticism and use of a politicized gay slur; and the father's revelation of systemic violence. These are the sorts of concerns that ripple through queer life, academic toils, and everyday precarities. Even more revealing is how the episode ends on the front steps of a house, on the physical and symbolic threshold of a residence. Moral and behavioral lessons, this closing scene conveys, may begin and end at home, and yet, according to the teen's abusive domestic life, not all homes feel safe. For scholars who consider musicology their disciplinary *home turf*, business might proceed as usual until a guest like David Halperin invites reconsiderations of what real and imagined boundaries circumscribe the field. For *homeless* queer youths whose voices and lives remain underaddressed by well-meaning projects such as It Gets Better, hope alone isn't enough. Trans people, people with disabilities, and others who face stigmatization might not always feel *at home* in societies or even in their own bodies. So I repeat verbatim a question posed in the previous chapter when I quoted Peter Railton's reflections on depression, interpersonal responsibility, and the life of the mind: How close do issues need to *hit home* before we reach out to shelter others?

A musicological ear, by way of a final note, can read more deeply into how the *Louie* episode ends with the sound of a siren in the distance. In television shows and movies, sirens are a common sound effect, typically used (alongside honks of cars and general buzz of traffic) to delineate an urban, maybe disorderly, setting. But when we hear a siren in the real world, we rarely process it as just background noise. Whether we're inside our house or at school or on the road, a siren compels us to wonder, *Is it getting farther or closer?* Loosely translated—is it someone else's problem, or could the problem hit close to home? Is there reason to care? Sure, once out of earshot, the siren is out of mind. If it starts getting louder, however, the noise begins to remind us that emergencies can land on any of our doorsteps.

Sirens, alarms, and calls to arms: no mere vibrations.

CHAPTER 4

Earsplitting

✦ ✦ ✦

In 1969, two Phantoms were sent to sow fear in the skies of Cairo. A year later, Phantoms from the Patishim ("Hammers") squadron did this in the skies of Damascus. This is how a bully demonstrates his strength. Over the years, we also used this method in the skies of Lebanon. But our enemies have never known the type of wholesale booms like those of recent weeks in Gaza. Anyone who has never awakened in a house full of children and infants at the sound of this thunder cannot understand how frightening it is. I once heard a boom like this over the Jenin refugee camp, and I was unable to breathe for a moment.
—Gideon Levy, describing the fear-mongering
tactics of Israeli jets' sonic booms over the Gaza Strip[1]

Unjust Vibrations

Musicologists or not, most of us don't have much control over music and sound in the grand scheme of things. We can elegantly theorize, analyze, and contextualize sonorous objects, but their unruly energies—their uses and abuses in daily life—take few cues from what we write or say. This doesn't usually occur to us until we find ourselves facing unwanted noise: a roommate's late-night racket, the thumping bass of a passing vehicle's radio, Muzak at the mall, or rowdy teenage bullies at a diner. With some cases of noise pollution (say, another person's car alarm), we have few means of addressing the offense. In other scenarios (raucous neighbors), we could be in a position to intervene, yet might choose not to act.

Noisy offenses breed suspicious minds. As we sit idly on the train, quietly fuming at the audacity of a commuter playing music through her iPhone's speakers, we are prone to wonder: *Is she aware of how loud her music sounds to other passengers? Does she know and not care? Is she doing this* on purpose, *just to be cool and rebellious, to give a middle finger to the world, or even to get a rise out of* me *specifically, since I'm sitting right across from her and maybe trying too hard to look like I don't notice?* This might not be the verbatim inner monologue of every disgruntled by-listener, but it gets to the heart of how acute annoyances can lead to chronic mistrust.[2] Paranoia means we assume the worst of noisemakers. Are television commercials and Internet ads disproportionately, gratingly loud relative to the main programming (or is it just our imaginations)? Is the on-hold music of a company's customer service line deliberately insipid, repetitive, and staticky in order to drive inquirers off the phone and to regulate call volumes? Are *vrooming* motorcyclists desperate for attention, measuring their badassery by the number of heads turned? Adopting paranoid relations to sound is to suspect and even to resent the acoustic output of service providers, marketers, motorists, and noisemakers at large—believing they are out to get us and make life less pleasant, vibe by vibe.

Such paranoia gets cranked up to eleven when the issue turns from everyday noise pollution to the deliberate weaponization of sound. An egregious example is music torture, which has received growing critical attention in recent years. In its war on terror, the American government has interrogated prisoners with systematic techniques of noise bombardment.[3] As with any form of torture, a core issue is control: the detainee has none, while the interrogator has more than any human should have over another. The torture victim has reason to be perpetually paranoid, dreading the administration of intolerable, unpredictable punishments, which leave any hope for repair—relief, release, rejuvenation—beyond reach.[4] With music torture, there's also the matter of whether we are dealing with *music* at all. Suzanne Cusick observes:

> Whether the sounds used in detention camps functioned as music or not, among the most horrifying aspects of these practices is the degradation of the thing we call "music." . . . The thing we have revered for an ineffability to which we attribute moral and ethical value is revealed as morally and ethically neutral—as just another tool in human beings' blood-stained hands. This feels like the stripping away of a soul from a body, and therefore like some kind of violent, violating death. It is, therefore, as horrifying *for us* as it is for its obvi-

ously intended victims (though not as painful), tearing away parts of the collective subjectivity—the culture—we have for so long taken for granted, and subsumed under the heading of "Western values."[5]

Have darker words about music ever been uttered? Cusick's wrenching statement pinpoints the difficulties of coming to terms with a world where grave abuses of music exist. No art, to be sure, is inviolate. In one sense, the idea of music torture sounds wildly unbelievable. But in another sense, the tactic seems coolly logical. Loudness hurts. So with advances in audio reproduction and amplification, wasn't it only a matter of time before music crept into the interrogator's arsenal?

In December 2014, media firestorms broke out following the U.S. Senate Intelligence Committee's damning report on the CIA's torture practices during the George W. Bush administration. The findings exposed the CIA's deceits, identified previously unknown victims, outlined heretofore unpublicized interrogation methods, and stressed torture's ineffectiveness at obtaining accurate and actionable information. The 525-page declassified portion of the report refers to over two dozen cases of interrogators using loud music and white noise (figures 4.1, 4.2, and 4.3).[6] In every instance, sound-based tactics receive mention in conjunction with additional torture methods: restraints, hoods, interrupted sleep, sensory deprivation, and sexual humiliation, to name only a few. At no point does the report isolate music or elaborate much on its specific abuses. Music torture gets lost in the mix, just one weapon in the battalion, fading into the background amid the buzz surrounding torture scandals writ large.

Casting music torture into a heinous miscellany of interrogation methods poses a problem—not because music torture is unequivocally more or less abhorrent than other forms of torture, but rather because of the exceptional ease with which perpetrators of music torture rationalize the practice as "no-touch torture" (or not "torture" at all), an enhanced interrogation technique within legal and ethical bounds.[7] It's just music and just vibrations, the argument goes—when, in actuality, it may be the most *unjust* deployment of music imaginable. For especially when music is extremely loud, repetitive, and imposed, it can do far more than touch. It pricks the skin, pummels the bone, penetrates the viscera, and unhinges the mind. It can discombobulate, traumatize, and humiliate.[8] It breaks down subjectivity, rendering prisoners unable to hear themselves think. The vibrations, while invisible, do leave visible marks on their victims: twitches and tremors, the aftershocks of injury

(T̶S̶/̶/̶██████████/̶/̶N̶F̶) On August 5, 2002, the day after Abu Zubaydah's interrogation using the CIA's enhanced interrogation techniques at DETENTION SITE GREEN began, CIA Headquarters authorized the proposed interrogation plan for al-Najjar, to include the use of loud music (at less than the level that would cause physical harm such as permanent hearing loss), worse food (as long as it was nutritionally adequate for sustenance), sleep deprivation, and hooding.[260]

(T̶S̶/̶/̶██████████/̶/̶N̶F̶) More than a month later, on September 21, 2002, CIA interrogators described al-Najjar as "clearly a broken man" and "on the verge of complete breakdown" as result of the isolation.[261] The cable added that al-Najjar was willing to do whatever the CIA officer asked.[262]

(T̶S̶/̶/̶██████████/̶/̶N̶F̶) In October 2002, officers from the U.S. military conducted a short debriefing of al-Najjar at DETENTION SITE COBALT and subsequently expressed an interest in a more thorough debriefing.[263] On November █, 2002, a U.S. military legal advisor visited DETENTION SITE COBALT and described it as a "CIA detention facility," noting that "while CIA is the only user of the facility they contend it is a [Country ██████████] facility."[264] The U.S. military officer also noted that the junior CIA officer designated as warden of the facility "has little to no experience with interrogating or handling prisoners." With respect to al-Najjar specifically, the legal advisor indicated that the CIA's interrogation plan included "isolation in total darkness; lowering the quality of his food; keeping him at an uncomfortable temperature (cold); [playing music] 24 hours a day; and keeping him shackled and hooded." In

Figure 4.1. Senate Committee on Intelligence report, 53 (my highlights)

(T̶S̶/̶/̶██████████/̶/̶N̶F̶) After being rendered to CIA custody on July █, 2004, Janat Gul was subjected to the CIA's enhanced interrogation techniques, including continuous sleep deprivation, facial holds, attention grasps, facial slaps, stress positions, and walling,[816] until he

---

[809] At the time of this CIA representation, the CIA had held at least 109 detainees and subjected at least 33 of them (30 percent) to the CIA's enhanced interrogation techniques.

[810] July 6, 2004, Memorandum from Condoleezza Rice, Assistant to the President for National Security Affairs, to the Honorable George Tenet, Director of Central Intelligence, re Janat Gul. CIA Request for Guidance Regarding Interrogation of Janat Gul, July 2, 2004.

[811] For additional details, see Volume III.

[812] July 6, 2004, Memorandum from Condoleezza Rice, Assistant to the President for National Security Affairs, to the Honorable George Tenet, Director of Central Intelligence, re Janat Gul.

[813] July 29, 2004, Memorandum for the Record from CIA General Counsel Scott Muller, "Principals Meeting relating to Janat Gul on 20 July 2004."

[814] The one-paragraph letter did not provide legal analysis or substantive discussion of the interrogation techniques. Letter from Attorney General Ashcroft to Acting DCI McLaughlin, July 22, 2004 (DTS #2009-1810, Tab 4).

[815] See Volume III for additional details.

[816]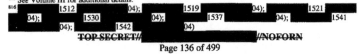

---

experienced auditory and visual hallucinations.[817] According to a cable, Janat Gul was "not oriented to time or place" and told CIA officers that he saw "his wife and children in the mirror and had heard their voices in the white noise."[818] The questioning of Janat Gul continued, although the CIA ceased using the CIA's enhanced interrogation techniques for several days.

Figure 4.2. Senate Committee on Intelligence report, 136–37 (my highlights)

confinement violated the Detainee Treatment Act. To support this analysis, the CIA asserted to the OLC that loud music and white noise, constant light, and 24-hour shackling were all for

[2399] Memorandum for John A. Rizzo, Senior Deputy General Counsel, Central Intelligence Agency, from Steven G. Bradbury, Principal Deputy Assistant Attorney General, Office of Legal Counsel, May 30, 2005, Re: Application of United States Obligations Under Article 16 of the Convention Against Torture to Certain Techniques that May be Used in the Interrogation of High Value Al Qaeda Detainees.
[2400] Memorandum for John A. Rizzo, Senior Deputy General Counsel, Central Intelligence Agency, from Steven G. Bradbury, Principal Deputy Assistant Attorney General, Office of Legal Counsel, May 30, 2005, Re: Application of United States Obligations Under Article 16 of the Convention Against Torture to Certain Techniques that May be Used in the Interrogation of High Value Al Qaeda Detainees, pp. 10-11, citing IG Special Review, pp. 85-91.
[2401] The Detainee Treatment Act passed on December 30, 2005. Letter from Senior Deputy General Counsel John Rizzo to Acting Assistant Attorney General Bradbury, December 19, 2005 (DTS #2009-1809).
[2402] April 19, 2006, Fax from ▮▮▮▮▮▮, ▮▮ Legal Group, CIA Counterterrorism Center to DOJ Command Center for Steve Bradbury (DTS #2009-1809).
[2403] Email from: ▮▮▮▮▮▮; to: [REDACTED]; cc: ▮▮▮▮▮▮, John Rizzo; subject: FW: Summary of *Hamdan* Decision; date: June 30, 2006, at 4:44 PM.
[2404] Department of Justice Office of Professional Responsibility; Report, Investigation into the Office of Legal Counsel's Memoranda Concerning Issues Relating to the Central Intelligence Agency's Use of 'Enhanced Interrogation Techniques' on Suspected Terrorists, July 29, 2009 (DTS #2010-1058).

TOP SECRET// ▮▮▮▮▮▮ //NOFORN

Page 428 of 499

UNCLASSIFIED

UNCLASSIFIED

TOP SECRET// ▮▮▮▮▮▮ //NOFORN

security purposes, that shaving was for security and hygiene purposes and was conducted only upon intake and not as a "punitive step," that detainees were not exposed to an "extended period" of white noise, and that CIA detainees had access to a wide array of amenities.[2405] This information is incongruent with CIA records. Detainees were routinely shaved, sometimes as an aid to interrogation; detainees who were "participating at an acceptable level" were permitted to grow their hair and beards.[2406] The CIA had used music at decibels exceeding the representations to the OLC. The CIA had also used specific music to signal to a detainee that another interrogation was about to begin.[2407] Numerous CIA detainees were subjected to the extended use of white noise.[2408] The CIA further inaccurately represented that "[m]edical

Figure 4.3. Senate Committee on Intelligence report, 428–29 (my highlights)

echoing in flesh.[9] It's all the more crucial, then, to ask what ideological, material, and ontological dimensions of music torture have enabled it (more so than, certainly, waterboarding and graphically shocking methods) to receive administrative sanction, elude media coverage, and fly under the public's sonar.

One explanation has to do with music's connotations of culturedness and leisure. Music, in the popular imagination, is a thing of pleasure. How bad can it be?

Failures of Imagination

[Torture] corrupts the whole social fabric because it prescribes a silencing of what has been happening between those two bodies, it forces people to make believe that nothing, in fact, has been happening, it necessitates that we lie to ourselves about what is being done not far from where we talk, while we munch a chocolate bar, smile at a lover, read a book, listen to a concerto, exercise in the morning. Torture obliges us to be deaf and blind and mute. Or we could not go on living. With that incessant awareness of the incessant horror, we could not go on living.

—Ariel Dorfman[10]

In a *Charmed* episode titled "Primrose Empath," a demon secretly curses the good witch Prue, granting her the capability to sense everyone else's feelings. The scenario begins comically, with Prue catching the laughing bug from a dentist patient who's under the effects of nitrous oxide. Then she begins empathizing willy-nilly with her sisters' and friends' emotions of love, shame, and denial. But soon, Prue finds herself shouldering the weight of the world. Murmurs of others' anguish thunder through her mind until she becomes, in her words, "one big raw nerve ending." She retreats to her basement and curls up into a ball, tortured and afraid. "There are these people and they're in my head, and they're in my heart, and it just hurts," she cries (figure 4.4). A priest arrives and tells Prue to embrace the (dis)ability as a gift rather than a scourge. "You have a once-in-a-lifetime opportunity to feel the world's emotions," he proclaims. "All it means to be human: the good *and* the bad." Prue listens, and then—in a display of resilience and overcoming—channels her motley feelings into sheer power, using a mix of magic and martial arts to vanquish the demon responsible for her affliction.

Ariel Dorfman, in his epigraph, declares that torture is a crime not just against the body, but also against the imagination. By this, he means that torture "craves the abrogation of our capacity to imagine others' suffering, dehumanizing them so much that their pain is not our pain."[11] To go on with our ordinary lives, Dorfman says, we must turn off (or at least turn down) our empathic impulses and block out these victims' presumed hollers of pain and pleas for relief. We, the nontortured, are impelled to compress these cries into white noise—random, indiscriminate frequencies emptied of meaning and human value. Although I find Dorfman's assertion persuasive, it rubs against the common ways in which people, when talking about torture, *try* to put themselves in the detainee's shoes. In a five-minute segment about "*Sesame Street* Music Torture" on the popular online news show *Young Turks*, the two hosts,

Figure 4.4. Prue in *Charmed* (*left*) retreats from the world and (*right*) returns to fight the good fight. Closed captions in original.

Cenk Uygur and Ana Kasparian, discuss the music torture used at Guantánamo Bay. Uygur and Kasparian play a few seconds of the *Sesame Street* theme song and note how the detainees were subjected to this music at extraordinarily loud volumes and long durations (matching the decibel level of a jackhammer for up to two hours). Here's an excerpt from the segment:

> ANA KASPARIAN: They used *Sesame Street* music to drive these detainees crazy during interrogation.
> CENK UYGUR: I could hardly stand it [the *Sesame Street* theme] for five seconds. . . . Now *imagine* listening to that at deafening volume for hours on end. . . .
> KASPARIAN: *Imagine* listening to a jackhammer for two hours. I could barely handle it when I'm walking by.
> UYGUR: Yeah, and *imagine*—I think that it's in some ways worse with music 'cause it's so repetitive, and, you know, bores down into your head.[12]

As Kasparian and Uygur verbally work through their thoughts and feelings about music torture, they repeatedly call on the imperatives of imagination. Yet even as they say *imagine, imagine, imagine,* the chant rhetorically pronounces its own failings in light of unimaginable injury.[13] Predictably, this *Young Turks* video also set its viewers' imaginations on fire. Aside from the usual trolls dangling incendiary bait about religion and terrorism, hundreds of YouTube users offered ideas for the types of music that could be most effective for music torture. People recommended dubstep, ABBA, Rebecca Black, and other genres and artists for interrogators' playlists.

Misguided presumptions about torture's imaginability may account in part for why debates persist at all about torture's legality, the grounds for permissibility, and ticking time-bomb scenarios.[14] In other words, moral opposition to torture is enabled largely by people's ability to draw on their own memories of pain and the consequent efforts to empathize; yet the reason such opposition is not absolute or unanimous owes to the imperfections of such empathy. In everyday speech, people use the word "torture" to color and amplify expressions of distress, such as "why waiting in line is torture"[15] (according to a *New York Times* op-ed) or the "little academic tortures"[16] experienced by young scholars. (And sure enough, among the prevalent metaphors containing *torture* is the term *tortured metaphor.*) One could argue that these are just idioms, just verbal vibrations, hyperbolic yet harmless. But might the very circulation of torture's metaphors signal a faulty imagination of torture's realities? For if thorough understanding prevailed, could people really stand to deploy its linguistic charge in banal contexts? Is it possible that trite references to torture dilute the perceived severity of actual torture and thus mask the urgency of antitorture measures?

Media's abundant representations of torture have long risked normalizing the practice and glorifying it as a way (and the only way) to obtain information from suspected criminals. We see torture in television (infamously, *24*), film (*Zero Dark Thirty*), and even books popular with youths (*Harry Potter* and its Cruciatus curse).[17] In the first season of the show *Homeland*, CIA agents capture a presumed al-Qaeda terrorist and detain him in a room. They subject him to cold temperatures, blinking lights, and a loud grindcore song (a cross between thrash, industrial, and punk). Every few seconds, the song cuts out before starting up again.[18] Agents observe the room on a monitor for several hours. The detainee eventually gives up an email address that proves useful. As viewers of the show, we necessarily fail to grasp the nature and magnitude of what the music-based interrogation entails: the scene itself lasts only fifty seconds total; it alternates between shots of the detainee and shots of an agent *watching* the detainee on a monitor, hence allowing us to be twice removed via embedded screens; and we retain the option of turning down the volume of the torturous music as it pipes through our television speakers or our headphones (figure 4.5). This effort to represent

Figure 4.5. Carrie in *Homeland* watches the interrogation of a suspected terrorist.

music torture remains hopelessly sanitized, glossed over by flat images and flattened (standardized-for-television) audio levels.

It's further worth noting that, prior to this interrogation scene, the show's protagonist (CIA agent Carrie Mathison) explicitly claims it to be *not* torture. During preparations, Carrie explains to onlooker Nicholas Brody that she needs to "unsettle [the detainee], to prove we have complete control, to demonstrate our omnipotence."

"One question," says Brody.

"Go ahead," replies Carrie.

"Will he be tortured?"

Carrie breaks into a gentle smile and shakes her head sagely, almost patronizingly: "We don't do that here."

Cue music.

Although some shows and movies problematize torture, they nonetheless tend to depict it as effective and utilitarian, as a means of drastically injuring one person so that many others may live. In a mission from Rockstar Games' acclaimed 2013 video game *Grand Theft Auto V* (GTA V), torture becomes a playable, interactive assignment. The player, controlling the protagonist Trevor Philips, is tasked with extracting information from an unarmed captive. Actions available to the player include electric shocks, blunt force, pulling teeth, and waterboarding (figures 4.6 and 4.7). If the captive isn't pushed far enough, he won't give up intelligence. But if the captive is pushed too far, he flatlines, and a shot of adrenaline is needed to revive him. The game asks the player to exercise cruel imagination and to think like a torturer: what is the right mix and sequence of injurious techniques needed to draw out actionable intelligence?[19] It must be stressed that while GTA V has dozens of optional missions, this one is mandatory. The mission has to be undertaken to advance the game's main story. The player thus faces a choice: either complete this torture simulation or forfeit the chance to play subsequent story missions. Even players who are turned off by the torture mission are likely to tough it out—regarding it as a necessary evil—so that they can get on with the rest of the game (a game they have presumably paid for and already sunk dozens of hours into). It almost doesn't sound like a choice at all . . . except it *is*. Among the few people I've found who reported permanently quitting GTA V upon reaching the torture mission, one gamer wrote: "Witnessing a man beg for his life passively in a film like *Reservoir Dogs* as he has his ear forcibly removed and gets doused in gasoline is disturbing enough. But having to slowly and deliberately select which weapons to use before entering the button prompts to rip a man's teeth out, break his kneecaps or almost drown him to death as he screams and begs for mercy is something else entirely."[20] Amnesty International, Freedom from Torture, and activist organizations protested this portion of GTA V. But fans defended the scene as satire.[21] Just a game, just a simulation, they claimed; why so serious?

With all this talk of imagination, let's conduct our own simulation. How might someone react upon hearing about music torture for the first time? For this hypothetical scenario, I extrapolate from several of my own experiences where I've mentioned the existence of music torture to people who had never before given the topic any thought. I encourage readers likewise to test out such conversations and see whether their outcomes align with or differ from mine. In any case, let's call our interlocutor Jon. When Jon hears about how the American government has subjected detainees to the songs of Britney Spears and Barney the Dinosaur, he appears at first confused, even amused. As if by instinct, he lets out a chuckle—not because he's a mean person, but because the case admittedly sounds absurd. It doesn't take long for Jon to recognize, however, that this is no laughing matter and that musical bombardment can be grievous indeed. Jon requires no hand-holding to arrive at this conclusion. He draws on his own memories of unpleasant noise, and tries to

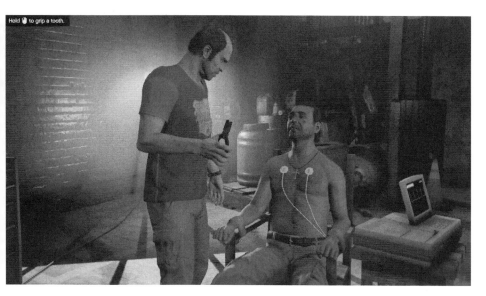

Figure 4.6. Torture sequence in *Grand Theft Auto V*—pulling teeth

Figure 4.7. Torture sequence in *Grand Theft Auto V*—waterboarding

imagine these feelings boosted hundredfold. He comes to feel a little ashamed of his initial response. All he really needed was a few extra seconds to think through, on his own, the terrible potential of music when it is flagrantly repeated, amplified, and wielded as a weapon. But these extra few seconds are *everything*. The lag—the time it takes for comprehension to dawn, for bemusement to turn to horror, for a chuckle to be stifled—harbors the alibis of music torture, the sneaky reasoning that enables interrogators to pass off the practice as torture-lite. For even though it doesn't take much thought to grasp the severity of music torture, it takes *some* thought nonetheless. And if people aren't prompted to give this transgression any thought at all, then it's already game over.

Jonathan Pieslak, who has studied music's usages in psychological warfare, recounts how, when he presented a paper at a conference on this subject and played Barney's "I Love You" on a loop for seventy-five seconds, "a chorus of groans and laughter erupted from the audience."[22] Given that torture is no laughing matter, the audience's laughter was riven with contradiction: on the one hand, audience members didn't immediately grasp the true horrors of music torture (for if they did, they probably wouldn't have been so quick to laugh); on the other hand, they may have perceived such an offense to be eminently graspable because, as Pieslak notes, they *think* they can "relate to the situation of having to listen to music they do not like," and whether it's "loud party or techno music blasting from a house at 3 am, the muzak of a doctor or dentist's office, or a heavy metal guitarist practicing for hours in an adjacent apartment, the shared response to being annoyed by music often involves laughter."[23] Many people, not least parents of young kids, know what it's like to be irked by repetitive children's songs. Such humdrum annoyance is a common irritant, as demonstrated by the existence of a YouTube video (linkable from the *Young Turks* torture feature) called "Can You Survive 10 Minutes of Barney Saying 'I Love You'?"[24] It's easy to shame people for laughing during a presentation on torture. But one reason for such laughter owes to the fact that a seventy-five-second clip of "I Love You" is a far cry from a real interrogation scenario. Pieslak did not play the music for two hours at 130 decibels. A conference room is a safe space where attendees aren't subjected to extreme temperatures, stress positions, starvation, humiliation, and other traumas that prisoners *always suffer alongside* music torture (as the Senate Committee on Intelligence report made brutally clear). Imagining music torture as involving *only* music—just vibrations—is to miss the broader regime of injury at the scene of criminal interrogation.

Given what I've said so far, a reader has reason to assume I would advocate against comparisons between music torture and quotidian sonic annoyances. Instead, I believe comparisons are necessary. I propose that, while we must not facilely conflate injuries big and small, we have to reflect on how our problematic mentalities toward acoustic offenses (big *or* small) intersect and interrelate. If people are antsy about the utterance of *music torture* and *freakin' car alarm* in the same breath, it's for fear of trivializing the former's exceptional status. The (paranoid) assumption is that the speaker must be connecting the two examples and insensitively asserting their equivalency. But in some ways, what I see is overcorrection—a denial of any connection whatsoever, a denial that lets us off the hook. We cannot understand or work against music torture unless we glean why such extraordinary torture goes largely unquestioned in public domains. And this we cannot do without taking stock of social attitudes toward ordinary sonic disturbances. My most pressing question, specifically, is this: are we, as members of society, in any way capable of mobilizing our littlest everyday behaviors to illuminate (or even to counteract) the government's grandest operations of music torture?

Quiescence: Microrepair?

First, let's consider the most obvious means of protesting music torture: speaking out. Musicians have taken varied stances on the issue. In 2008, Christopher Cerf (composer for *Sesame Street*), Pearl Jam, R.E.M., Tom Morello, Rosanne Cash, Trent Reznor, and other artists formed a coalition called Zero dB to decry the use of music in interrogations. Stevie Benton of Drowning Pool, however, voiced the opposite, saying: "I take it as an honor to think that perhaps our song could be used to quell another 9/11 attack or something like that."[25] And then there's the strange case of Canadian industrial band Skinny Puppy, who, upon learning that their music had been co-opted for purposes of torture, demanded a devilish $666,ooo in royalties from the U.S. Department of Defense.[26]

In academic circles, three leading music organizations—the American Musicological Society, the Society for Ethnomusicology, and the Society for American Music—proposed individual resolutions in 2007–8 condemning torture, with a focus on music torture. "Some critics," Suzanne Cusick points out, "have dismissed these resolutions as ineffectual vainglory, 'feel good' gestures that served only to substitute public sanctimony for real political action."[27] Such dismissals target the ivory tower stereotype, the notion that academics, through bids for social relevance, are all bark and no bite. Consider the resolution introduced at the 2007 Business Meeting of the Society for American Music:

> Whereas, We, the Society for American Music, join the chorus of protest and dissent against the use of torture in military interrogations; whereas, we, as scholars and musicians, who devote our lives to sustaining American music, protest the contamination of our culture by the heinous misappropriation of music as part of psychological torture; whereas, art has an ethical, in fact spiritual dimension, no matter what style or genre, and its corruption shames us all; Resolved, we, the Society for American Music, condemn the use of music as torture in military interrogations and in particular the debasement of American music in such a fashion.[28]

This resolution is admirable, yet raises several questions. For all its emphasis on music's ethical dimensions and musicians' shame toward sound-based interrogation techniques, the text omits overt references to the victims of torture. The particular mention of *American* music also comes across unnecessarily narrow. Is it that this Society's members feel qualified to speak out against torture only by citing their core expertise in American music? Does such wording reflect an excessive mind-set of compartmentalized protest—that musicologists should rally against music torture, queer theorists against sexual humiliation, and physicians against forced medication?[29] Does the specter of aesthetic autonomy and disciplinary division haunt this resolution's vocabularies?

Official petitions, public denunciations, and legal indictments can bring about change and awareness. But without discounting their efficacy, these interventions come off as socially conventional, as they seek, with paranoid motives, to expose the authorities and to out their sins. A more radical question—one that may yield reparative possibilities of a different stripe—pertains to how the everyday sonic habits of a general population resonate with its government's interrogation strategies.[30] Even if it sounds like a long stretch, how might we evaluate the responsibilities and complicities of a citizenry whose ruling bodies practice music torture?

A public's role in regimes of acoustic offense can be plotted through a number of behaviors. First, we, the people, compose a culture of sonic impropriety when we inflict undesirable noise on others, contributing actively to cacophony by violating explicit laws or implicit customs for the respective noise levels of neighborhoods, apartments, dormitories, hospitals, libraries, the Amtrak Quiet Car, and different times of day. Second, even if we're mindful of our own sonic footprints, we can, through inaction and apathy, enable the proliferation of noisy infractions. When we abstain from asking a stranger on the subway, *Please turn down the loud music from your iPod*, we show passive acceptance of acoustic disturbance, hence forfeiting any janitorial duties we might bear with respect to noise. And third, we endorse the social glorification of loudness when we enter into spaces and events that pump up the volume in the name of celebration (New Year's Eve in Times Square), competition (a football game), or basic pursuit of a good time (at a concert or a club).

In cultures that flaunt audio amplification, people reciprocally flaunt their tolerance of amplified sounds that verge on the intolerable— decibels that cause discomfort, even pain. At the risk of aural distress, we might bring earplugs to a rock concert but end up leaving them in our pockets because we decide that the volume isn't *totally* unbearable. Or picture the nightclub: even if the music is too loud for our taste, we head onto the thumping dance floor because most of our friends are there and that's where all the fun is, where actions speak louder than words. Once on the dance floor, there's collective recognition of thunderous noise as the cost of clubbing cool. Thus even noise-averse patrons play along as convincingly as they can, grinding and merging into all the other shiny happy people and becoming worthy of emulation in turn. Enduring loudness becomes a point of pride, a show of strength and resilience. It's a way of declaring that we can take it (yes, we can)!

A common urban occurrence involves fire trucks and ambulances screaming down the streets, bringing sounds that elicit despair as well as reassurance (signaling a nearby crisis while insisting that, have no fear, help is on its way). As a pedestrian, I sometimes cover my ears as the emergency vehicles zoom by—both ears if I can, or just one ear if I'm carrying something in my hand. Then there are times when I'm on the fence about whether covering my ears is necessary, and by the time I decide, the vehicles have passed, rendering the decision moot. Finally, there are instances when I feel the impulse to protect my ears, yet end up choosing not to, for fear of appearing weak, delicate, queer. As best as I can describe, I feel a twinge of embarrassment for instinctively wanting to cup my ears. Maybe it's because the sirens of emergency vehicles are among the few sounds of the city that have legitimate reason to be loud. Their loudness literally helps save lives, enabling rescuers to cut through mazes of moving metal. Furthermore, the sirens need to be loud only because the rest of the urban environment is so irrepressibly loud. They must drown out miscellaneous clamor to reach the ears of inhabitants who are keen on tuning out the city—iPod-carrying joggers, radio-piping drivers, and cyclists talking on headsets.[31] As odd as it sounds, then, my hesitation to cover my ears might stem from an anxiety about showing disrespect. Perhaps I'm worried that my act of self-concern would look uncouth, as if, by raising my hands, I'd be gesturally linking my fleeting aural discomfort with the far graver suffering of the people whom the emergency vehicles are rushing to save.

Ambivalent anecdotes aside, all of this is to say that our relationships and responses to music and everyday sounds aren't so simple. They can be riddled with uncertainty, irrationality, paranoia, and self-consciousness. We make a lot of noise, don't always redress others' noisy habits, and put up with noise at detrimental amplitudes out of peer pressure, habit, or vanity. Given sound's phenomenal pretext as somehow ephemeral and relatively innocuous, people might overlook or downplay how noises can put them in bad moods, deprive them of rest, and impair overall well-being. Quiescence toward noise ripples through society. It may not causally or straightforwardly trickle up to a political administration's practices of music torture, but civilian complacency does validate noise's free passes on smaller levels, codifying cultures where acoustic violations are too easily waved off with *Eh, not that bad*. With each display of passivity, sonic offenses inch toward the boundary of the normal, fortifying their status as typical and tolerable. And although it's scientifically evident that sustained exposure to loud sounds can lead to hearing loss, people continue to underestimate such consequences in part because this loss is so gradual.

Not all noise needs suppressing. We can opt to celebrate loud sounds knowing full well the risks; admire people who blast music as champions of social audacity, artistry, and free speech; and embrace emergency sirens as gratifying signals of medical aid. We can, in sum, try to absorb and absolve a rip-roaring world through a rose-tinted aural lens, listening to and through the noise for hints of playfulness, generosity, humor, pride, love, and invigorating affects. A reparative acoustemology would accommodate these possibilities while calling for simultaneous pursuits of alternative sonic regimes. To achieve more aurally tolerable and accessible environments, we have to play the long game. The goal? Not to dial down noise per se, but maybe to edge toward a world where something such as music torture would be *inconceivable as anything but unequivocal torture*—where the question of whether music torture can be torturous wouldn't be asked in the first place. The same could be said of torture in general: the goal isn't just to pass and follow laws that prohibit torture, but moreover to work toward a world where torture's absolute prohibition starts sounding axiomatic and feeling commonsensical.[32] These lofty objectives bubble with idealism, but their means are grounded in the real: palpable actions, rectifications, and results. "The ideal, then, is real," muses Martha Nussbaum. "At the same time, the real also contains the ideal. Real people aspire. They imagine possibilities better than the world they know, and they try to actualize them."[33] One has to start somewhere, sometime. So why not here, now? And if not us, then who?

In the spring of 2015, I taught an undergraduate course at Dartmouth College on music, media, and politics. For a unit called "Defense against the Dark Arts," during which we discussed music's weaponization, the students received the following assignment:

> *Step 1.* Find a situation involving what you perceive to be a noise violation.
> *Step 2.* Do something about the infraction, or don't. Do not put yourself in any danger (when in doubt, play it safe).
> *Step 3.* Attempt to articulate the social, psychological, and circumstantial factors that drove you to action or inaction.

Over the course of a few weeks, students found situations that included noisy dormmates, ruckus in the library, a disruptive passenger on a bus, and the music of Phi Delta Alpha, a Dartmouth frat house notorious for the way it blasts songs every evening using outward-facing loudspeakers. Two of the ten students chose action: one simply asked a dormmate to turn down his music (took all of three seconds), while the other met with a friend from Phi Delta Alpha for a half-hour debate over why the frat members insist on dominating the sonic airspace of Webster Avenue night after night. Other students shied away from direct confrontation and resorted to throwing dirty glances, sighing audibly, putting on headphones, and venting on social media.

One student wrote about a time when she was the *source* of noise. She and her marching band had gone around campus giving a late-night tour to prospective Dartmouth students. Although the band members didn't think they were bothering anyone, they decided to consult Yik Yak, an app that lets users post and view anonymous messages (sortable by up-votes) within a ten-mile radius.[34] "We checked Yik Yak," the student noted, "and saw such Yaks as 'not saying that I wanted to sleep, but if I did, it'd be great if the band would shut up' and 'The marching band needs to get the f**k off gold coast lawn.' We gained an insight to the true thoughts and feelings of our fellow students. . . . We laughed at the fact that people thought we were on the Gold Coast lawn, which is half way across campus, but also realized how far our sound traveled, and how many people we were disturbing."[35]

In the following class, all students read their papers out loud and together worked through their motives for action or inaction. Consensus formed around factors such as anxiety about confrontation, concerns of shaming or being shamed, and fear of developing a reputation as a whiner. In simple terms, complaining about noise isn't cool, least of all for college students. Doing so hurts their hip image and can make them come across as curmudgeons who gripe about *damn kids and their music.* For what it's worth, musicologists aren't supposed to rant about noise either. Scholars are presumably meant to exemplify open-mindedness, to recuperate noise as art, and to study soundscapes without moral judgment.[36]

Little inactions add up. But for all the paranoia that can inflect our relations to noise, reparative orientations are possible. A request or gesture to quell a disturbance, a brief reflection on sound's infractions and inevitabilities—little victories add up too. In the romantic chaos of consequence, the flutter of an insect's wings makes a sound, vibrations beget vibrations, and difference is made. Call it what you will: the butterfly effect, grassroots activism, bottom-up democracy, affective citizenship, or minority influence.[37] If these models sound like optimism for suckers, we could recall how, even as children, we were taught that change begins with a single person, that every recycled bottle matters, and that only we can prevent forest fires. For all the talk about microaggressions in daily life (concerning race, class, sexuality, disability), we can think constructively about microrepair—little acts that add up to something big.[38] A "micro-politics of justice," suggests Michael Shapiro, "references a process in which individuals and collectives, who are affected by legality/illegalities, participate in a culture of feelings or sensibilities and subsequently engage in discursive encounters about what is just."[39] Micropolitics can productively challenge and complement justice's macropolitics, namely how "states, through their decision-making bodies, promulgate, execute, and administer the law."[40] Individual optimism doesn't have to breed complacency. Believing things *could* get better is sometimes precisely what cheers us to fight harder for a world worth redeeming.

Insisting on greater attention to noise and its potential harms isn't antithetical to respecting articulations of Deaf Gain (countering notions of deafness as deficit), biodiversity, and alternate embodiments.[41] (Some Deaf people, for that matter, might pick up and prefer loud voices in conversations, or enjoy high-volume music and its sensational pressures on the dance floor.) Nor is this to say that normative hearing abilities are universally desirable and extra-deserving of preservation. The point is to recognize the injustices and calls for help that sometimes don't get heard—or seen, signed, felt, sensed, cared for—amid the competing clamor of modern life. We often don't speak up against public disturbances because, as my students pointed out, these awkward interventions are prone to mark us as peculiar and, in terms of societal expectations, veritably queer. To keep noise abatement from crossing into censorship and sanctimony, the focus can't be on the indiscriminate silencing or bullying of noisemakers, as this would introduce yet more shame into networks of paranoid exchange. The objective, where possible, is to find creative means of retuning the world. In certain cases, the relief can feel very real, not just for ourselves but also for people around us—even if they don't thank us out loud.

Overloaded / Understanding

If an agenda of quiescence still sounds too idealistic, it's worth keeping in mind the individuals for whom quiet can be an especially valuable commodity. Some people on the autism spectrum, for example, experience sensory overload in everyday settings (variably called sensory defensive disorder or sensory integration disorder).[42] Buzzing machinery, flickering lights, scents, tastes, fabrics, temperatures, and other stimuli can feel disturbing and even overwhelming. Cynthia Kim, an Autistic adult, describes her aural sensitivities born of Asperger's syndrome: "It's not like I want to hear the person sitting next to me in the library chewing gum and typing and breathing, but I can't *not* hear it. This barrage of sound often results in sensory overload in public places, especially crowded public places like stores, restaurants, or public transit. It can also make it difficult to follow conversations or make out speech in environments with a lot of background noise."[43] Educators invested in inclusivity have advocated for sensory-friendly environments and for students' freedom to customize the intake of their surroundings via noise-canceling headphones, sunglasses, and additional devices.[44] Students who begin to feel overloaded may also benefit from the option of temporarily leaving the classroom and accessing a sensory retreat (a quiet and peaceful room) elsewhere in the school.

Such accommodations are important because they make good on the understanding that not everyone hears or feels the world in the same way, and just as crucially, that it's vital yet difficult to empathize with the sensory experiences of others. Consider the free browser simulation *Auti-Sim*, designed by Taylan Kay for the 2013 Hacking Health Vancouver event, which brought together "health professionals and technologists to work together to prototype and problem-solve new ways to deliver healthcare."[45] Kay's interactive *Auti-Sim* sought to depict the following encounter:

> The player navigates through a playground as an autistic child with auditory hypersensitivity. Proximity to loud children causes sensory overload for the player, impacting cognitive functions. This impact is represented as visual noise and blur, as well as audio distortion. Participants described the experience as visceral, insightful and compelling.[46]

According to players' comments, reactions in fact varied widely. Some appreciated the simulation and thanked the creator for a revelatory experience. But others, including those who identified as Autistic, scorned the simulation for misrepresenting the sensory realities of their everyday lives and for portraying all Autistic subjects as hopelessly antisocial. Case in point: if the player's avatar spends too much time around raucous (and supposedly nondisabled) children, the visual and auditory output whips up a machine-like aesthetic of autism's sensorium. Static, shrieks, blips, and alarming signs of failure verge on dehumanizing the protagonist, conjuring a broken, glitched victim (figure 4.8). The simulation presents the child as someone tortured by noises that, to most ears, sound harmless, even good (laughter, conversation, and euphony of children at play).

The designer of *Auti-Sim* displayed good intentions and, in his responses to players' feedback, has expressed willingness to take criticism under advisement.[47] But despite the potential for *Auti-Sim* to raise awareness and to do good, the problem with the simulation—indeed, with any program or exercise in imagination—is that it may lead participants to feel overconfident about their understanding of the condition and lifestyle in question. Critics of *Auti-Sim* worry that "having taken part in a simulation exercise, non-disabled people will believe they fully

Figure 4.8. (*left*) Approaching crowds on the playground (loud and blurry stimuli) and (*right*) moving away from crowds in *Auti-Sim*

understand disability. [People with disabilities] say that unless you are disabled and live with the knock-on consequences like unemployment, pain and prejudice, it doesn't give a true picture."[48] Overconfidence can be the enemy of empathy if it fast-tracks to complacency and halts further inquiry. When we're too certain that we know what it's like to live in someone else's mind and body, we risk feeling entitled to cease listening to their stories. The apparent catch in empathy simulations is that, for people who actually endure challenging conditions, the game *is* reality and doesn't have easy solutions. (Besides disability simulations, controversial examples of recent empathy exercises have included Tyra Banks wearing a fat suit to incur judgmental stares and to understand obesity, Gwyneth Paltrow trying—and failing—to live on food stamps for a week, and rampant cases of slum and poverty tourism. Banks took off her fat suit after one day, Paltrow went back to eating like a millionaire, and tourists, by definition, always return home.)[49]

Recall the many pleas for imagination and the crises of empathy throughout this chapter's discussions of sound, injury, and quiescence: Prue in *Charmed* experiencing sensory overload and, against her will, empathically absorbing the world's chronic pain; the *imagine, imagine, imagine* rhetoric of the *Young Turks* hosts as they pondered music torture; the necessarily imperfect and even misleading simulations of torture in *Homeland* and *Grand Theft Auto V*; a conference audience groaning and laughing as Jonathan Pieslak played a few iterations of Barney's "I Love You"; and Gideon Levy, in his epigraph, insisting that if you've never experienced the roof-knocking sonic booms of fighter planes, you can't understand how it feels. Empathy, according to Martha Nussbaum, involves "a kind of 'twofold attention,' in which one both imagines what it is like to be in the sufferer's place and, at the same time, retains securely the awareness that one is not in that place."[50] Because empathy entails affective approximation rather than total equation, it remains, as Susan Brison argues, *a necessary but not sufficient* foundation for justice.[51] Hurdles in empathy, however, don't release us from attempting and hoping to empathize widely, creatively, and generously. Challenges of care and compassion serve as reminders that, beyond our verbal claims of resonating with one another (*I feel you*), the next step is action (. . . *and I'd like to help*).

Action might mean dialing down noise. But on some occasions, it could demand the opposite: cranking up the volume in the name of all-out protest.

Coda

If We Break . . .

♦ ♦ ♦

This book has been concerned with ideas and ideologies of music as I have apprehended them. . . . It would be silly to conclude it on a note of prediction. A coda is no place for presentiments. I draw attention to the above trends as hopes, not as predictions: as hopes for motion.

—Joseph Kerman, *Contemplating Music*, final lines[1]

Unvoiced

As I write this, America is burning. Protests sweep the country coast to coast, from Ferguson to Baltimore to Chicago; from Mizzou to Yale to Dartmouth College. Windows and hearts are breaking amid civilian demonstrations against police brutality, racism, hate crimes, and systemic injustice. Shouts of Black Lives Matter have reached fever pitch yet somehow, in various political and social domains, still seem to go unheard. In addition to using batons, tear gas, stun guns, smoke grenades, and rubber bullets, officers in several cities have been employing Long Range Acoustic Devices (LRADs), which can weigh over three hundred pounds and fire cones of noise up to almost 150 dB and 2.5 kHz. Development efforts for the LRAD originated in the wake of the 2000 terrorist attack on the USS *Cole* in Yemen. Since then, the LRAD Corporation, based in San Diego, has sold its line of products to military and security personnel worldwide. Thanks to strong international business, LRAD's revenues totaled $24.6 million in the fiscal year 2014, up 44 percent from $17.1 million the year before.[2] As of today, more than seventy countries have purchased LRAD systems.[3]

The LRAD Corporation markets its devices in benevolent, caring terms. Promotional materials stress LRADs' utility for wildlife protection, emergency mass notification, public safety, and rescue operations (such as talking a suicidal person off a bridge or communicating with stranded hikers on a mountain). The website states, complete with emphases: "LRAD is *not* a weapon; LRAD *is* a highly intelligible, long range communication system and a safer alternative to kinetic force."[4] Nonkinetic, *no-touch* maneuvers—we've heard this claim before. A blanket denial of LRADs as weapons runs counter to the maker's proud claims about the devices' potential to scare off sea pirates and overcome enemy combatants in wars abroad. "If [LRADs'] maker tempered its initial [weapon] metaphors," Juliette Volcler points out, "it's because this allows distributors to sidestep the U.S. and European prohibitions on weapons sales to China that have been in place since the Tiananmen Square massacre in 1989. It allows . . . the LRAD Corp. to publish glowing notices after its products are used to distribute information to survivors of natural disasters, such as in Haiti, or to counter anti-capitalist protesters in Canada."[5] LRADs use a technology called piezoelectric transducers to focus sound waves into a narrow field of impact (hence their moniker of *sound cannons*). In January 2010, the Disorder Control Unit of the NYPD released a seven-page briefing on the LRAD (figure 5.1). One section stated that "while the sound being emitted in front of the LRAD may be very loud, it is substantially quieter outside the 'cone' of sound produced by the device. In fact, someone could stand next to the device or just behind it and hear the noise being emitted at much lower levels than someone standing several hundred feet away, but within the 'cone' of sound being emitted."[6] Security forces and governing bodies to date have not subjected LRADs to extensive regulation, presumably because the devices fly under the radar as weapons in their own right.

Underestimations of LRADs' deleterious potential can contribute to their treatment by police as mere tools or even toys. LRADs' ability to focus sound into a narrow field doesn't eliminate the risk of collateral damage. In any case, the promise of exactitude doesn't make LRADs less problematic than drones (with purported capacity to carry out precision strikes) or sniper rifles (in the hands of a mass murderer). More generally, there's a lack of research on LRADs' injurious capabilities. Here's

Some examples of sound levels for comparison, in decibels (dB):	
Whisper	30 dB
Normal speech	60 dB
Telephone Dial Tone	80 dB
Vacuum Cleaner	85 dB
Sustained exposure may cause hearing loss	90-95 dB
Subway at 200 feet	95 dB
Motorcycle	105
Power Saw	110
Sandblasting	115
Pain may begin	120-125 dB
Shot gun	120
Short term exposure can cause permanent damage	140 dB
LRAD sustained at maximum power/audio	146 dB
Ear drum breaks	160 dB

Figure 5.1. Page 3 of the "Briefing on the LRAD by New York City Police Department: Special Operations Division/Disorder Control Unit" (January 2010)

Amnesty International's report on the use of LRADs in the Ferguson protests:

On the night of Aug. 18 [2014] at approximately 10:00 p.m., following the reported throwing of bottles at police and a group of protesters stopping in front of a police line in defiance of the five second rule, law enforcement activated a Long Range Acoustic Device (LRAD). The LRAD was pointed at [a] group of stationary protestors on the street approximately fifteen feet away. Members of the media and observers were likewise about the same distance from the device. No warning from law enforcement that an LRAD would be used was given to the protesters. After providing earplugs to a member of Amnesty International, a St. Louis County police officer says, "This noise will make you sick." Several members of the delegation reported feeling nauseous from the noise of the LRAD until it was turned off at approximately 10:15 p.m. LRADs emit high volume sounds at various frequencies, with some ability to target the sound to particular areas. Used at close range, loud volume and/or excessive lengths of time, LRADs can pose serious health risks which range from temporary pain, loss of balance and eardrum rupture, to permanent hearing damage. LRADs also target people relatively indiscriminately, and can have markedly different effects on different individuals and in different environments. Further research into the use of LRADs for law enforcement is urgently needed.[7]

A well-documented case of LRAD's power took place during the protests at the G-20 Summit in Pittsburgh on 24 September 2009. Karen Piper, a scholar of globalization and a visiting professor at Carnegie Mellon University, stopped to take photographs of protesters and their signs. Suddenly, she found herself caught in the blast zone of an LRAD, activated with no warning (figure 5.2). Later, Piper filed a lawsuit, describing how she "suffered immediate pain in her ears," became nauseated, and "was forced to sit down . . . unable to walk."[8] Her long-term injuries included "permanent nerve hearing loss; tinnitus; barotrauma; left ear pain and fluid drainage."[9] In an interview with the American Civil Liberties Union, Piper recalled how the LRAD's noise made her think she was dying of an aneurysm.[10] She won a (meager) settlement of $72,000 from the city of Pittsburgh.

Despite Piper's lawsuit, LRADs have only grown in popularity among security personnel. On 12 December 2014, attorney Gideon Orion Oliver sent the NYPD commissioner a memo on behalf of several people who claimed to have been injured by an LRAD while protesting the Staten Island grand jury's failure to indict the primary police officer involved in the death of Eric Garner.[11] Oliver requested that the NYPD refrain from using LRADs until thorough and independent testing has been conducted, until guidelines have been drafted and published, and until officers have received appropriate training to operate these devices. But a hurdle in such pleas lies in a lack of public awareness and empathy. Unless, like Karen Piper, you've been bombarded by an LRAD, it's difficult to imagine or even believe the degree and nature of pain that this sonic artillery can inflict. The fact that LRADs, like music torture, tend to leave *few* visible traces of injury on victims' bodies doesn't make the devices any less in need of regulation than, say, bullets and batons. LRADs are a sonorous smokescreen: because a relative absence of discernible wounds raises the victim's burden of proof in a court of law, these devices require stricter, not laxer, operational guidelines. It's too easy to write off an LRAD's deployment as mere warning shots that precede escalation of true force. In a video that shows a nighttime demonstration in Ferguson, we first hear the sounds of LRADs and police instructions; then we hear

Figure 5.2. Protest and LRAD at the 2009 Pittsburgh G-20 Summit. Note the striking diversity of people's protective actions against the LRAD: some cover their ears tightly, while others do not (choose to) cover their ears at all.

and see rubber bullets and tear gas lobbed into the crowd.[12] No matter how piercing the LRADs may have felt to this crowd, our attention (as YouTube viewers here and now, as protesters then and there) necessarily jerks toward the bullets once they start flying. Because look: *bullets.* During violent confrontations, nonlethal weaponry can serve practically as a euphemism for *pre*lethal. The announcement of a technology that's unlikely to kill nonetheless augurs the presence of external force and the weighted options of consequent lethality.[13] By the same mortal token, a tragic reality in the name Black Lives Matter is how it comes fueled by laments that black *deaths* matter—for it is black deaths that repeatedly and horrifically make the news, inciting outrage and after-the-fact damage control.[14]

LRADs leave protesters with little choice but to cover their ears with both hands. There's yet another brutal irony here given how one of the rallying cries of Black Lives Matter is precisely, "Hands up! Don't shoot!" Many protesters in the above-mentioned Ferguson video already had their hands raised above their heads to signal their weaponless status and to decry police killings of unarmed individuals. Police actions that force protesters to cup their ears effectively strip the hands-up-don't-shoot gesture of its symbolic charge. The raising of hands transforms from a deliberate sign of willful pacifism into a reflexive show of self-preservation.

So beyond the capacity of LRADs to inflict harm, the devices pervert the protesters' choreographies of resistance. They also drown out protesters' words and music, overriding free speech and rendering dialogue among assemblies inaudible. For the wielders of an LRAD, a major selling point is the clarity with which it amplifies the speech of those controlling it. The makers declare that "LRAD's optimized driver and waveguide technology ensure every voice and deterrent tone broadcast cuts through wind, engine, and background noise to be clearly heard and understood."[15] Voices transmitted through the devices boast exceptional intelligibility and range. But are such clarion vibrations just when protesters' voices are getting muted? In this case of asymmetrical conflict, should police have access to a technology that broadcasts crystalline instructions when the people's calls for reform are going unheard?

A Different Kind of Love Song

Concerning her pathbreaking research on music torture in the war on terror, Suzanne Cusick laments: "Nothing could be more paranoid (or less reparative) than my torture project. Accusatory in its taxonomies, brimming with conscious and unconscious projections of fear and rage toward practices motivated by exactly those affects, and *so* obviously premised on the paranoid's belief in the power of exposure and demystification, it is the ultimate in paranoid musicology."[16] If reparative possibilities hinge on the salvage of love, then a "reparative musicology," Cusick writes, "would restore love for music; would reconstruct musical experiences so that we could love them."[17] I agree with Cusick's call, and would just add that a reparative musicology would simultaneously restore love for people and reconstruct the opportunities for care among them. It means reflecting on our incentives to do good work; dissolving all objections over whether a graduate student's well-being is a scholarly concern; asking how we can make it better for people of all persuasions; and keeping the music—the conversations—going.

Because we all break from time to time. Our bodies, through torrents of pain. Our spirits, in times of depression and grief. Our group formations, when sirens make us scatter. Our selves, as shame takes over. A reparative stance has to urge collaboration and dialogue over pretention and coercion. For we see a surplus of humiliation as it is: childhood humiliation at the hands of schoolyard assailants, humiliation theory (the term used by Sedgwick and Tomkins) in academia, sexual humiliation in black-site interrogations, and humiliation tactics of *gotcha!* journalism. With modern media, opportunities for humiliation have indeed proliferated, from reality show pratfalls and political scandals to revenge porn and cyberbullying. Reparative endeavors involve holding accountable those who voice prejudice, sow injury, and do wrong. But just as important is learning to acknowledge people as more than the sum of their worst deeds and words. Mercy is an essential option, for others' sake as well as our own.

One challenge with reparative and caring work is that we don't always have a clear sense of what's real and what's fantasy. We roam a land of paper tigers: inflated targets of scholarly polemics; a music-blasting commuter who's oblivious rather than intentionally heinous; and other threats overblown by misperception or paranoid construction. Then there are the hidden dragons in the mist: youth bullying that gets written off as playful teasing; music torture passing as torture-lite; and additional dangers that elude intervention. So whereas paranoia entails constant and sometimes irrational suspicion of bad things—call it a doubt of benefit (that is, of beneficence, of people's trustworthiness and the world's goodness)—repair, in reverse, has to advocate benefit of the doubt. More than offering words of corroboration and flattery, a reparative agenda would insist on an active search for positivity and potential. In academia, this might manifest in magnanimous attempts to recognize others' expressions as worthwhile. With grading and peer reviews, we show this with compliment sandwiches, opening and closing with encouraging comments while tucking constructive criticism in between. We may, however, be so accustomed to such procedures that we follow them mostly out of courtesy and convention. A subtle but significant distinction exists between casually dispensing praise out of habit and actually cultivating the belief that there's value in all colleagues' and students' effortful contributions, no matter how unusual a piece of writing appears or how far a presentation strays from the institutional expectations of able-minded, good-sounding rhetoric. Epistemologically, suspicion and trust are two sides of the same coin, both grappling with things either not yet proven or outright unprovable. The former fears the bad. The latter hopes for better.

Hope is a funny thing because it's what we do when evidence remains incomplete. In ongoing situations, there's at once never and always reason to hold on to hope—because reason isn't omniscience. "The belief that things can, once and for all, be made right, makes no more sense than the belief (which takes hold of me, on average, once every few months) that everything is totally, irreparably, ruined," Susan Brison ponders. "But does it make any *less* sense?"[18]

Reader, it makes no less sense.

Calls for optimism don't discount a recurring need for suspicion, outrage, and protest.[19] As Barbara Ehrenreich warns, buying wholesale into cults of positive thinking can generate excessive pressure to be happy, counterproductively breeding discontent.[20] But the paranoid and the reparative are not locked in a zero-sum game. A rule of thumb would be to pursue repair where possible and to rely on paranoia when necessary. For as important as it may be to shoot for the reparative, it's even more vital to recognize that not everyone can afford to do so. Sociopolitically, foreswearing paranoia is a luxury reserved for those lucky enough to live under safe circumstances. It is not always a sound option for people oppressed by scarcity and states of emergency. And academically, the requirements for professional advancement still tend to favor scholarship that resembles paranoid criticism and its hermeneutics of suspicion (strong theories, virtuosic deconstruction, and spectacular demystification). Scholars who are seeking employment might therefore feel like they don't have enough job security or financial wherewithal to experiment with reparative readings and alternative writing styles. From the outset of *Just Vibrations*, I've stressed that because repair is a privilege, its exigencies should weigh that much more heavily on the shoulders of those who are in the most secure positions to undertake the task.

The theme of repair informs one of the first nursery rhymes that English-speaking children learn. Humpty Dumpty sat on a wall, then had a great fall. Despite the efforts of all the king's horses and men, he could not be put together again. Curiously, this is a story of failed repair, with pessimistic undertones belied by an uppity dactylic lilt. Although the ending isn't as traumatic as the grim conclusions of many fairy tales, it's a depressing narrative all the same, squeezed into just a few lines. We can imagine how youngsters, upon completing a concerted recitation of this bouncy rhyme, might feel rather melancholic about the cracked protagonist, letting the briefest moment of silence descend over the classroom before resuming their commitments to jovial noise. But maybe the rhyme's takeaway lesson is how a rescue mission was launched at all. If Humpty Dumpty couldn't be revived, it wasn't for lack of trying. The king took extraordinary measures, sending every man and horse at his disposal. He made repair and caregiving a public matter (figure 5.3).[21]

Frivolous though they may sound, childhood vignettes bookend and anchor *Just Vibrations* because they channel ageless wisdoms. The terror

Yes your Majesty, all of your horses and all of your men. It's a long shot, but it might just work.

Figure 5.3. Cartoon by Alex Matthews (2007)

of bullies, the poison of gossip, and the aching need to believe it gets better don't end with puberty or college or entry into esteemed jobs. Think about this game that children play shortly after learning the rudiments of language: you say something and they say, "Why?"; you respond thoughtfully, and then, "Why?"; you answer again, patience wearing thin, but still, "Why?"; and on it goes until you exclaim, "Okay, just stop!" ("Why?"—then finally, irritated silence). Children understandably find delight in this infinite deferral (they are keen little Derridas)—deferral not so much of meaning and context, but of bath times and bedtimes. Such a small word, so much power. As we age, these back-and-forth word games live on. They go by fancier names, whether it's dialectics or critique or legal adversariality. We uphold combative systems in the name of intellectual rigor, free speech, and fairness. In the process, we would do well to safeguard the reparative constellations of thriving in this world: love, care, empathy, respect, and other glints of good. Can we adopt these affects as foundations rather than as electives in everyday life, academic work, and relationships? Can we do so without fear of looking weak, feeling queer, or sounding like a clichéd cat poster or a self-help book or a Hallmark card?

Few of society's subjects are more vulnerable than children. Few make ruckus with more abandon. Fragile in physique and easy to deceive, they have the most reason to be paranoid, yet they can be among the most trusting (sometimes at their own great peril). Granted, children play *at* paranoia, conjuring foes and dangers for their games, dancing through the dark and bounding through the noise. But for the children who are relatively fortunate—the ones with homes, health, resources, social advantages—the make-believe threats in their lives are usually short-lived: tag's terrible *It* at recess becomes a friendly goofball once back in the classroom; the stuffed animals that look creepy at night revert to benign cuddle-things come daybreak; and the costumed scourge that overruns Halloween's carnivalesque streets is gone by the end of the evening, leaving only litters of candy wrappers as proof of prior antics. After flights of fancy, after raids of ninjas, order is magically restored.

Should children ever become genuinely afraid, they rarely think twice about voicing their concerns. As adults, however, we're no longer so quick to cop to anxieties and phobias. Paranoid about being judged, we obsess over showing strength, sounding good, racking up wins, and scrambling to the top of that wall. We're afraid to lose, to yield, to fail. Yet as Jack Halberstam puts it, failure may be what "preserves some of the wondrous anarchy of childhood and disturbs the supposedly clean boundaries between adults and children, winners and losers."[22] Boundaries stand to fall; most walls fall with time.

In the event we sound bad, who will care? As we slow down, who will keep pace? If we break, who will come put us back together again? Should our lives shatter, whose reflections show up in the shards? Rejection, loss, and heartache can sting so fiercely that they fire up promises never to aspire again. The cost of failing at repair is continued or added injury, from which recovery may be arduous as ever. The cost of shunning reparative efforts altogether is that there may eventually be nothing and no one worth recovering for anyway. Trust and suspicion, pride and shame, comfort and pain, love and indifference, hope and forfeit: a gamut of feelings rising early in life and shadowing us ever after. With each step, we face choices of how to face these shadows. Fear them, fight them, fold them into our innermost worlds—worlds for us to rue or repair, one vibe at a time.

Notes

✦ ✦ ✦

Introduction

1. See Brian Boyd, "Laughter and Literature: A Play Theory of Humor," *Philosophy & Literature* 28 (2004): 1–22; and Brian Sutton-Smith, John Gerstmyer, and Alice Meckley, "Playfighting as Folkplay amongst Preschool Children," *Western Folklore* 47 (1988): 161–76.

2. Paul de Man once called the advent of literary theory a "paper tiger" for its perceived threat to traditional critical methods. His description pokes at broader quirks in the metaphor: "If a cat is called a tiger it can easily be dismissed as a paper tiger; the question remains however why one was so scared of the cat in the first place. The same tactic works in reverse: calling the cat a mouse and then deriding it for its pretense to be mighty. Rather than being drawn into this polemical whirlpool, it might be better to try to call the cat a cat" (*The Resistance to Theory* [Minneapolis: University of Minnesota Press, 1986], 5). See also Molly Andrews, *Narrative Imagination and Everyday Life* (New York: Oxford University Press, 2014), 25–33.

3. See Jeremy Waldron, *The Harm in Hate Speech* (Cambridge, MA: Harvard University Press, 2012); Susan Brison, "Speech and Other Acts," *Legal Theory* 10 (2004): 261–72; and Frederick Schauer, "The Phenomenology of Speech and Harm," *Ethics* 103 (1993): 635–53.

4. Eve Kosofsky Sedgwick, "Paranoid Reading and Reparative Reading, or, You're So Paranoid, You Probably Think This Essay Is about You," in *Touching Feeling: Affect, Pedagogy, Performativity* (Durham, NC: Duke University Press, 2003), 123–51. Sedgwick first presented a paper on paranoid reading in 1995 (see Ellis Hanson, "The Future's Eve: Reparative Reading after Sedgwick," *South Atlantic Quarterly* 110 [2011]: 105).

5. For the Kleinian subject (versus the Freudian subject), Sedgwick notes that "omnipotence is a fear at least as much as it is a wish" ("Melanie Klein and the Difference Affect Makes," *South Atlantic Quarterly* 106 [2007]: 631). See also Meira Likierman, *Melanie Klein: Her Work in Context* (London: Continuum, 2002), 100–143.

6. Heather Love, "Truth and Consequences: On Paranoid Reading and Reparative Reading," *Criticism* 52 (2010): 236. On bids for authority, masculinity, and positions (tops versus bottoms) in music theory, see Fred Everett Maus, "Masculine Discourse in Music Theory," *Perspectives of New Music* 31 (1993): 264–93.

7. Paul Ricoeur, *Freud and Philosophy: An Essay on Interpretation*, trans. Denis Savage (New Haven: Yale University Press, 1970), 32. See also Ann Jurecic, "Empathy and the Critic," *College English* 74 (2011): 10–27; Rita Felski, "After Suspicion," *Profession* (2009): 28–35; Alison Scott-Baumann, *Ricoeur and the Hermeneutics of Suspicion* (London: Continuum, 2009); and Brian Leiter, "The Hermeneutics of Suspicion: Recovering Marx, Nietzsche, and Freud," in *The Future for Philosophy*, ed. Brian Leiter (New York: Oxford University Press, 2004), 74–105.

8. Sedgwick elaborated: "To call paranoia a strong theory is, then, at the same time to congratulate it as a big achievement (it's a strong theory rather as, for Harold Bloom, Milton is a strong poet) but also to classify it. It is one kind of affect theory among other possible kinds, and by [Silvan] Tomkins's account, a number of interrelated affect theories of different kinds and strengths are likely to constitute the mental life of any individual. Most pointedly, the contrast of strong theory in Tomkins is with weak theory, and the contrast is not in every respect to the advantage of the strong kind. The reach and reductiveness of strong theory—that is, its conceptual economy and elegance—involve both assets and deficits. What characterizes strong theory in Tomkins is not, after all, how well it avoids negative affect or finds positive affect, but the size and topology of the domain that it organizes" ("Paranoid Reading," 134).

9. Sedgwick, "Paranoid Reading," 138.

10. Sedgwick, "Paranoid Reading," 125–26. See also Steven Pinker, "Why Academics Stink at Writing," *Chronicle of Higher Education* (26 September 2014), http://chronicle.com/article/Why-Academics-Writing-Stinks/148989.

11. Rita Felski, "Suspicious Minds," *Poetics Today* 32 (2011): 229. See also Rita Felski, *The Limits of Critique* (Chicago: University of Chicago Press, 2015), 1–13; Peter Hitchcock, *Oscillate Wildly: Space, Body, and Spirit of Millennial Materialism* (Minneapolis: University of Minnesota Press, 1999), 1–8; and Richard Rorty, "The Pragmatist's Progress," in *Interpretation and Overinterpretation*, ed. Stefan Collini (Cambridge: Cambridge University Press, 1992), 89–108.

12. See Nina Sun Eidsheim, *Sensing Sound: Singing and Listening as Vibrational Practice* (Durham, NC: Duke University Press, 2015); Mary Simonson, *Body Knowledge: Performance, Intermediality, and American Entertainment at the Turn of the Twentieth Century* (New York: Oxford University Press, 2013); Tomie Hahn, *Sensational Knowledge: Embodying Culture through Japanese Dance* (Middletown, CT: Wesleyan University Press, 2007); and Carolyn Abbate, "Music—Drastic or Gnostic?" *Critical Inquiry* 30 (2004): 505–36; cf. Karol Berger, "Musicology According to Don Giovanni, or: Should We Get Drastic?" *Journal of Musicology* 22 (2005): 490–501.

13. Vladimir Jankélévitch, *Music and the Ineffable*, trans. Carolyn Abbate (Princeton, NJ: Princeton University Press, 2003), 11.

14. Lydia Hamessley, "How Did This All Start? Toward a History of the Feminist Theory and Music Phenomenon" (2009, revised 2015), http://www.femtheorymusic.org/ftm-history, quoted with permission. In an article about the underrepresentation of women composers in the music history curriculum, Rosemary Killam pointed out that "those who know both me and my writings know that when I write or speak in anger, I use a tone in which I am explicit about such anger" ("Response to Professor

Morse's Open Letter," *Music Theory Online* 3 [1997], http://www.mtosmt.org/issues/mto.97.3.4/mto.97.3.4.killam.html, par. 2); cf. Audre Lorde, "The Uses of Anger," in *Sister Outsider: Essays and Speeches* (Berkeley, CA: Crossing Press, 2007), 124–33 (first delivered as a keynote presentation at the National Women's Studies Association Conference in 1981).

15. On scholars' social responsibilities, Elaine Scarry writes: "The main work of the humanities is to ensure that books are placed in the hands of each incoming wave of students and carried back out to sea. Probably, though, teachers and readers need to do more. We should give more attention to making clear the lines of responsibility to real-world injuries and the call to that work that is embedded in the three key features of literature [its invitation to empathy, its reliance on deliberate thought, and its beauty]" ("Poetry, Injury, and the Ethics of Reading," in *The Humanities and Public Life*, ed. Peter Brooks with Hilary Jewett [New York: Fordham University Press, 2014], 47).

16. "AAU Campus Survey on Sexual Assault and Sexual Misconduct," *Association of American Universities* (2015), http://www.aau.edu/Climate-Survey.aspx?id=16525.

17. See Katherine Mangan, "1 in 4 Female Undergrads Experienced Sex Assault or Misconduct, AAU Survey Finds," *Chronicle of Higher Education* (21 September 2015), http://chronicle.com/article/1-in-4-Female-Undergrads/233281; and Emily Yoffe, "The Problem with Campus Sexual Assault Surveys," *Slate* (24 September 2015), http://www.slate.com/articles/double_x/doublex/2015/09/aau_campus_sexual_assault_survey_why_such_surveys_don_t_paint_an_accurate.html.

18. Granted, claims about *aboutness* can sound inherently political, circumscribing permissible versus impermissible (or relevant versus irrelevant) queries. Asking what something is (really) about might sometimes launch an evasive and (counterintuitively) counterproductive enterprise. See Stephen Yablo, *Aboutness* (Princeton, NJ: Princeton University Press, 2014), 7–9.

19. It is no coincidence that recent debates about "trigger warnings" have arisen concomitantly with expanding dialogues about sexual assault on campus. For different views, see Kate Manne, "Why I Use Trigger Warnings," *New York Times* (19 September 2015), http://www.nytimes.com/2015/09/20/opinion/sunday/why-i-use-trigger-warnings.html?_r=1&pagewanted=all; and Jack Halberstam, "You Are Triggering Me! The Neo-liberal Rhetoric of Harm, Danger and Trauma," *Bully Bloggers* (5 July 2014), http://bullybloggers.wordpress.com/2014/07/05/you-are-triggering-me-the-neo-liberal-rhetoric-of-harm-danger-and-trauma.

20. Phil Ford, "Disciplinarity (or, Musicology Is Anything You Can Get Away With)," *Dial M for Musicology* (28 June 2015), http://dialmformusicology.com/2015/06/28/disciplinarity.

21. Ford, "Disciplinarity." See also Robyn Wiegman, *Object Lessons* (Durham, NC: Duke University Press, 2012), 1–35.

22. I include here three excerpts from the American Musicological Society's "Guidelines for Ethical Conduct" as they appear in 2016 (last updated in October 1997 upon formal adoption by the board of directors). These excerpts are among the most relevant ones pertaining to AMS members' social and pedagogical duties. First, in the preamble: "Since the behavior of musicologists, in whatever professional capacities they serve, affects the well-being and reputation of the entire profession, members of the Society are expected to uphold these principles not only in their scholarly work but also in all their professional capacities" (*American Musicological Society 2015 Directory* [2015], http://www.ams-net.org/administration/ethics.php, xxx-

iv). Second, in a section on harassment: "Members of the AMS are therefore obliged not to abuse the power with which they are entrusted, but rather to create professional settings that foster respect for the rights of others. Furthermore, members of the AMS should neither condone harassment in any form nor disregard complaints of harassment or inequitable treatment from any person or group involved with the AMS and its activities" (xl). And third, in a section on teaching responsibilities: "In their roles as teachers, AMS members should maintain a strictly professional relationship with students while in a position of power over them, judging each student on merit alone. They should promote an atmosphere of respect for the personal difference and dignity of each student, and protect students' rights to confidentiality and privacy. The conditions for free exchange of ideas can be created only when such rights are observed" (xli).

23. Cynthia Wu, "Tenured and Happy," *Inside Higher Ed* (30 March 2015), http://www.insidehighered.com/advice/2015/03/30/essay-earning-tenure-and-considering-responsibilities-faculty-life. Wu continues: "My biggest concern as I face down another 25 years or so in this profession is not that I will become disaffected or stalled in my research. It's whether or not I can convince my fellow tenured colleagues to agree that we not pull the ladder up behind us and abandon the others in the interest of careerist gain. I don't find tenure depressing. I find it sobering. We need to use that sobriety to take collective responsibility for making the academy more livable for everyone."

24. Jennifer Ruth, "Slow Death and Painful Labors," in Michael Bérubé and Jennifer Ruth (coauthors), *The Humanities, Higher Education, and Academic Freedom: Three Necessary Arguments* (New York: Palgrave Macmillan, 2015), 72.

25. Ford, "Disciplinarity." See Susan McClary, *Feminine Endings: Music, Gender, and Sexuality* (Minneapolis: University of Minnesota Press, 1991); and Susan McClary, "The Making of a Feminist Musicologist," in *True Confessions: Feminist Professors Tell Stories out of School*, ed. Susan Gubar (New York: W. W. Norton, 2011), 301–10.

26. Some social scientists argue that rhetorical ability can even secure advantages in natural selection. See Hugo Mercier and Dan Sperber, "Why Do Humans Reason? Arguments for an Argumentative Theory," *Behavioral and Brain Sciences* 34 (2011): 57–111; and Dan Sperber et al., "Epistemic Vigilance," *Mind & Language* 25 (2010): 359–93.

27. See Elizabeth V. Spelman, *Repair: The Impulse to Restore in a Fragile World* (Boston: Beacon Press, 2002), 1–8.

28. See Roderick A. Ferguson, *Aberrations in Black: Toward a Queer of Color Critique* (Minneapolis: University of Minnesota Press, 2004), 1–29.

29. See Amy Sequenzia and Elizabeth J. Grace, eds., *Typed Words, Loud Voices* (Fort Worth, TX: Autonomous Press, 2015); and DMan Johnson, "The Role of Communication in Thought," *Disability Studies Quarterly* 31 (2011), http://dsq-sds.org/article/view/1717/1765.

30. See Luke Winslow, "The Undeserving Professor: Neoliberalism and the Reinvention of Higher Education," *Rhetoric & Public Affairs* 18 (2015): 201–46; Scott Yates, "Neoliberalism and Disability: The Possibilities and Limitations of a Foucauldian Critique," *Foucault Studies* 19 (2015): 84–107; and Robert Wilton and Stephanie Schuer, "Towards Socio-spatial Inclusion? Disabled People, Neoliberalism and the Contemporary Labour Market," *Area* 38 (2006): 186–95.

31. Akemi Nishida, "Neoliberal Academia and a Critique from Disability Studies," in *Occupying Disability: Critical Approaches to Community, Justice, and Decolonizing*

Disability, ed. Pamela Block, Devva Kasnitz, Akemi Nishida, and Nick Pollard (New York: Springer, 2015), 148. See also Lisa Duggan, *The Twilight of Equality? Neoliberalism, Cultural Politics, and the Attack on Democracy* (Boston: Beacon Press, 2003), ix–xx.

32. Eva Feder Kittay, "When Caring Is Just and Justice Is Caring: Justice and Mental Retardation," *Public Culture* 13 (2001): 559; cf. Martha Nussbaum, "The Future of Feminist Liberalism," in *The Subject of Care: Feminist Perspectives on Dependency*, ed. Eva Feder Kittay and Ellen K. Feder (Lanham, MD: Rowman & Littlefield, 2002), 186–214; and Michael Bérubé, "Value and Values," in Bérubé and Ruth, *Humanities*, 40–56.

33. Kittay, "When Caring Is Just," 560.

34. See Eva Feder Kittay, *Love's Labor: Essays on Women, Equality, and Dependency* (New York: Routledge, 1999). See also Nancy Fraser, *Fortunes of Feminism: From State-Managed Capitalism to Neoliberal Crisis* (New York: Verso, 2013), 83–110.

35. Eva Feder Kittay, "At the Margins of Moral Personhood," *Ethics* 116 (2005): 127. Portraying Sesha at age twenty-seven, Kittay elaborates: "No, Sesha's loveliness is not skin deep. How to speak of it? How to describe it? Joy. The capacity for joy. The babbling-brook laughter at a musical joke. The starry-eyed far away look as she listens to Elvis crooning 'Love Me Tender,' the excitement of her entire soul as the voices blare out 'Alle Menschen werden Brüder' in the choral ode of Beethoven's Ninth Symphony, and the pleasure of bestowing her kisses and receiving the caresses in turn" (*Love's Labor*, 151).

36. See Richard Leppert, "Music 'Pushed to the Edge of Existence' (Adorno, Listening, and the Question of Hope)," *Cultural Critique* 60 (2005): 92–133.

37. See John Rawls, *A Theory of Justice*, rev. ed. (Cambridge, MA: Belknap Press of Harvard University Press, 1999), 3–46.

38. See Amartya Sen, *The Idea of Justice* (Cambridge, MA: Belknap Press of Harvard University Press, 2009), xvii–xix, 75–77, and 109–11.

39. Bryan Stevenson, *Just Mercy: A Story of Justice and Redemption* (New York: Spiegel & Grau, 2014), 17–18.

40. See Elaine Scarry, "Beauty and the Scholar's Duty to Justice," *Profession* (2000): 21–31.

41. Kathleen Stewart, *Ordinary Affects* (Durham, NC: Duke University Press, 2007), 2.

42. See Virginia Held, *The Ethics of Care: Personal, Political, and Global* (New York: Oxford University Press, 2006); Fiona Robinson, *The Ethics of Care: A Feminist Approach to Human Security* (Philadelphia: Temple University Press, 2011), 9–17; and David Richards, *Resisting Injustice and the Feminist Ethics of Care in the Age of Obama* (New York: Routledge, 2013).

43. Seminal studies include Carol Gilligan, *In a Different Voice: Psychological Theory and Women's Development* (Cambridge, MA: Harvard University Press, 1982), 5–23; Nel Noddings, *Caring: A Feminine Approach to Ethics and Moral Education* (Berkeley: University of California Press, 1982); and Sara Ruddick, *Maternal Thinking: Toward a Politics of Peace* (Boston: Beacon Press, 1989), 127–40.

44. See Victoria Davion, "Autonomy, Integrity, and Care," *Social Theory and Practice* 19 (1993): 161–82; Claudia Card, "Caring and Evil," *Hypatia* 5 (1990): 101–8; and Marilyn Friedman, "Beyond Caring: The De-moralization of Gender," *Canadian Journal of Philosophy* 17 (1987): 87–110. See also Alison Reiheld, "Just Caring for Caregivers: What Society and the State Owe to Those Who Render Care," *Feminist Philosophy Quarterly* 1 (2015), http://ir.lib.uwo.ca/fpq/vol1/iss2/1; and Rose Hackman,

"'Women Are Just Better at This Stuff': Is Emotional Labor Feminism's Next Frontier?" *Guardian* (8 November 2015), http://www.theguardian.com/world/2015/nov/08/women-gender-roles-sexism-emotional-labor-feminism?CMP=share_btn_fb.

45. On the marginalization of care, see Joan Tronto, *Moral Boundaries: A Political Argument for an Ethic of Care* (New York: Routledge, 1994), 111–12.

46. A professor (writing under a pseudonym) describes the challenges of care-work in her encounters with students and colleagues who regularly come to her with dilemmas: "Just listening is the best you can do. With student mental-health issues on the rise and faculty stress running high, there is more and more care-work to do. While it would be nice if colleges and universities could find a way to recognize this as service work, the personal, confidential nature of these conversations makes that unlikely" (Myra Green, "Thanks for Listening," *Chronicle of Higher Education* [19 October, 2015], http://chronicle.com/article/Thanks-for-Listening/233825).

47. For a recent dialogue on the epistemic viability and vitalities of queerness, sex, and optimism, see Lauren Berlant and Lee Edelman, *Sex, or the Unbearable* (Durham, NC: Duke University Press, 2014). See also Michael Warner, "Queer and Then," *Chronicle of Higher Education* (1 January 2012), http://chronicle.com/article/QueerThen-/130161. More general debates about the politics and ethics of optimism have arisen from Steven Pinker's book, *The Better Angels of Our Nature: Why Violence Has Declined* (New York: Viking, 2011); see, for example, Nils Petter Gleditsch, ed. (with Steven Pinker, Bradley A. Thayer, Jack S. Levy, and William R. Thompson), "The Decline of War," *International Studies Review* 15 (2013): 396–419.

48. José Esteban Muñoz, *Cruising Utopia: The Then and There of Queer Futurity* (New York: New York University Press, 2009), 1.

49. Suzanne Cusick, "Let's Face the Music and Dance (or, Challenges to Contemporary Musicology)," in *AMS at 75*, ed. Jane Bernstein (Brunswick, ME: American Musicological Society, 2011), 29–30.

50. The scheduled panelists were Clara Latham, Elias Krell, Samantha Bassler, Margarita Restrepo, Nina Treadwell, Matilda Ann Butkas Ertz, and Cari E. McDonnell; Honey Meconi served as chair.

51. Carol Hess remarks: "How did musicology, so broadly defined in 1939, change to the point that we now feel compelled to distinguish 'public musicology' from . . . what? Some other kind of musicology? Program notes, pre-concert talks, writing articles and blogs for lay audiences may well be the forms of public musicology most familiar to us. But curating, government work, archival work, and oral history are other possibilities that greet those trained in our discipline. Do we need a theoretical underpinning to pursue these interests? Have our activities become constricted over the years—frozen in the academy, as it were—or have they expanded, even in these challenging economic times?" ("Public Musicology . . . 1939," *Musicology Now* [15 November 2013], http://musicologynow.ams-net.org/2013/11/public-musicology-1939.html). The blog post is excerpted in part from Carol Hess's "'De aspecto inglés pero de alma española': Gilbert Chase, Spain, and Musicology in the United States," *Revista de Musicología* 35 (2012): 263–96.

52. In 2014, the *Musicology Now* blog of the American Musicological Society released a four-part video series of musicologists explaining what they do; Andrew Dell'Antonio and Felicia Miyakawa began to edit a blog with W. W. Norton, *The Avid Listener*, which propounds that "music criticism can be literate *and* fun to read, . . . foster[ing] weekly discussions between scholars and novices alike" (see http://www.

theavidlistener.com/about.html, with Michael Fauver, managing editor); and W. Anthony Sheppard delivered a Tedx Talk titled "Pop Orientalism" as well as recorded a short video unraveling the musical magic of the hit song "Let It Go" from the Disney film *Frozen*. In early 2015, Westminster Choir College of Rider University hosted a three-day conference, "The Past, Present, and Future of Public Musicology," organized by Eric Hung.

53. Nicholas Cook, "We Are All (Ethno)musicologists Now," in *The New (Ethno)musicologies*, ed. Henry Stobart (Lanham, MD: Scarecrow Press, 2008), 48–70.

54. Mark Greif, "What's Wrong with Public Intellectuals?" *Chronicle Review* (13 February 2015), http://chronicle.com/article/Whats-Wrong-With-Public/189921.

55. The blog *Musicology Everywhere* features stories "on careers outside of, overlapping with, adjacent to, and beyond the academy" (http://musicologyeverywhere.wordpress.com).

56. The ethics and challenges of speaking to, for, and with others have long permeated postcolonial, feminist, queer, and ethnographic critique. As a sample, see Linda Alcoff, "The Problem of Speaking for Others," *Cultural Critique* 20 (1991–92): 5–32; Philip Bohlman, "Musicology as a Political Act," *Journal of Musicology* 11 (1993): 411–36; Kay Kaufman Shelemay, "The Impact and Ethics of Musical Scholarship," in *Rethinking Music*, ed. Nicholas Cook and Mark Everist (New York: Oxford University Press, 2001), 531–44; J. Maggio, "'Can the Subaltern Be Heard?': Political Theory, Translation, Representation, and Gayatri Chakravorty Spivak," *Alternatives: Global, Local, Political* 32 (2007): 419–43; and Michael B. Bakan, "Being Applied in the Ethnomusicology of Autism," in *The Oxford Handbook of Applied Ethnomusicology*, ed. Svanibor Pettan and Jeff Todd Titon (New York: Oxford University Press, 2015), 278–316.

57. See Eve Kosofsky Sedgwick, *Epistemology of the Closet* (Berkeley: University of California Press, 1990), 22, 27, 36, 40, 44, 48, and 59.

58. On the ethics of vitalism and vibration, see Jane Bennett, *Vibrant Matter: A Political Ecology of Things* (Durham, NC: Duke University Press, 2010), 12–16; cf. Veit Erlmann, *Reason and Resonance: A History of Modern Aurality* (New York: Zone Books, 2014), 9–27.

59. See Jeff R. Warren, *Music and Ethical Responsibility* (Cambridge: Cambridge University Press, 2014); Tia DeNora, *Music Asylums: Wellbeing through Music in Everyday Life* (Burlington, VT: Ashgate, 2013); and Garry L. Hagberg, "Jazz Improvisation and Ethical Interaction: A Sketch of the Connections," in *Art and Ethical Criticism*, ed. Garry L. Hagberg (Malden, MA: Blackwell, 2008), 259–85.

60. Joachim-Ernst Berendt, *The Third Ear*, trans. Tim Nevill (Perth, Australia: Element, 1985), 79.

61. My perspective draws from Atul Gawande's compassionate notes on end-of-life care in *Being Mortal: Illness, Medicine, and What Matters in the End* (London: Profile Books, 2014). On the critical and scholarly potential of memoirs, see Ann Cvetkovich, *Depression: A Public Feeling* (Durham, NC: Duke University Press, 2012), 11–15.

62. J. Jack Halberstam, *Gaga Feminism: Sex, Gender, and the End of Normal* (Boston: Beacon Press, 2012), xxiv. See also Steven D. Levitt and Stephen J. Dubner, *Think Like a Freak* (New York: HarperCollins, 2014), 87–104; and Patricia Shehan Campbell and Trevor Wiggins, eds., *The Oxford Handbook of Children's Musical Cultures* (New York: Oxford University Press, 2013).

63. On the queer precarities of childhood, see Kathryn Bond Stockton, *The Queer*

Child, or Growing Sideways in the Twentieth Century (Durham, NC: Duke University Press, 2009), 1–10. I'm grateful to Aimee Bahng for sharing this reference.

64. Amy Tan, "Mother Tongue," *Threepenny Review* 43 (1990): 7.

Chapter 1

1. Atul Gawande, *Complications: A Surgeon's Notes on an Imperfect Science* (New York: Picador, 2002), 126.

2. Elaine Scarry, *The Body in Pain: The Making and Unmaking of the World* (New York: Oxford University Press, 1985), 35–38; see also Ann Jurecic, *Illness as Narrative* (Pittsburgh: University of Pittsburgh Press, 2012), 43–66; David Biro, *Listening to Pain: Finding Words, Compassion, and Relief* (New York: W. W. Norton, 2010); Sarah Coakley and Kay Kaufman Shelemay, eds., *Pain and Its Transformations: The Interface of Biology and Culture* (Cambridge, MA: Harvard University Press, 2007); and Diane Ackerman, *A Natural History of the Senses* (New York: Random House, 1990), 101–10. In Jonathan Larson's *Rent*, the character Marc Cohen proclaims: "The opposite of war isn't peace; it's creation!"

3. See Rosemarie Garland-Thomson, *Extraordinary Bodies: Figuring Physical Disability in American Culture and Literature* (New York: Columbia University Press, 1996), 6–9; and Guy Dewsburg et al., "The Anti-social Model of Disability," *Disability & Society* 19 (2004): 145–58.

4. M. Celia Cain, "Of Pain, Passing and Longing for Music," *Disability & Society* 25 (2010): 748.

5. Sedgwick, "Paranoid Reading," 150; cf. Naomi Sunderland, Tara Catalano, and Elizabeth Kendall, "Missing Discourses: Concepts of Joy and Happiness in Disability," *Disability & Society* 24 (2009): 703–14.

6. For a reflection on scholarly identity and identification, see Rosemarie Garland-Thomson, "The Story of My Work: How I Became Disabled," *Disability Studies Quarterly* 34 (2014), http://dsq-sds.org/article/view/4254/3594.

7. See Carole-Ann Tyler, "Passing: Narcissism, Identity and Difference," in *Feminism Meets Queer Theory*, ed. Elizabeth Weed and Naomi Schor (Bloomington: Indiana University Press, 1997), 227–65; Steven Bruhm, *Reflecting Narcissus: A Queer Aesthetic* (Minneapolis: University of Minnesota Press, 2000); and Olu Jenzen, "Revolting Doubles: Radical Narcissism and the Trope of Lesbian Doppelgangers," *Journal of Lesbian Studies* 17 (2013): 344–64.

8. Tobin Siebers, *Disability Theory* (Ann Arbor: University of Michigan Press, 2008), 35–36. Philosophers in general are, as Susan Brison says, "trained to write in an abstract, universal voice and to shun first-person narratives as biased and inappropriate for academic discourse" (*Aftermath: Violence and the Remaking of a Self* [Princeton, NJ: Princeton University Press, 2002], 6). See also Thomas Nagel, *The View from Nowhere* (New York: Oxford University Press, 1986), 37–43.

9. A recent example of experimental academic rhetoric appeared in Patrick Stewart's Ph.D. architecture dissertation, which eschewed punctuation as a political display of deconstructionist grammatical resistance. See Brian Hutchinson, "UBC Student Writes 52,438-Word Architecture Dissertation with No Punctuation—Not Everyone Loved It," *National Post* (8 May 2015), http://news.nationalpost.com/news/canada/ubc-student-writes-52438-word-architecture-dissertation-with-no-punctuation-not-everyone-loved-it. A well-known example of formal innovation appears in Gilles Deleuze and Félix Guattari's rhizomatic *A Thousand Plateaus: Capitalism and*

Schizophrenia, trans. Brian Massumi (Minneapolis: University of Minnesota Press, 1987). A book modeled stylistically on *A Thousand Plateaus* is Steve Goodman's *Sonic Warfare: Sound, Affect, and the Ecology of Fear* (Cambridge, MA: MIT Press, 2010). See also Stewart, *Ordinary Affects,* 1–7; and David Wills, *Prosthesis* (Stanford, CA: Stanford University Press, 1995).

10. An example of a creatively organized and rhetorically diverse volume is Phil Smith, ed., *Both Sides of the Table: Autoethnographies of Educators Learning and Teaching with/in [Dis]ability* (New York: Peter Lang, 2013). I thank Andrew Dell'Antonio for recommending this book.

11. Rita Felski, "Digging Down and Standing Back," *English Language Notes* 51 (2013): 7.

12. See William Cheng, "My Students Never Use the First Person Voice. I Wish They Would," *Slate* (11 June 2015), http://www.slate.com/blogs/lexicon_valley/2015/06/11/my_students_never_use_the_first_person_voice_i_wish_they_would.html. The title I originally wanted to use (before it was changed by editors) was "For Students, What Letter Trumps an A?"

13. See Blake Howe, Stephanie Jensen-Moulton, Neil Lerner, and Joseph Straus, eds., *The Oxford Handbook of Music and Disability Studies* (New York: Oxford University Press, 2015).

14. Joseph Straus, email correspondence with author (17 November 2013), quoted with permission.

15. On the closet politics of disability, see N. Ann Davis, "Invisible Disability," *Ethics* 116 (2005): 153–213; Ellen Samuels, "My Body, My Closet: Invisible Disability and the Limits of Coming-Out Discourse," *GLQ: A Journal of Lesbian and Gay Studies* 9 (2003): 233–55; and Tanya Titchkosky, "Coming Out Disabled: The Politics of Understanding," *Disability Studies Quarterly* 21 (2001): 131–39.

16. Jonathan Sterne uses this phrase to describe auscultation in "Mediate Auscultation, the Stethoscope, and the 'Autopsy of the Living': Medicine's Acoustic Culture," *Journal of Medical Humanities* 22 (2001): 126. See also Tom Rice, "Sounding Bodies: Medical Students and the Acquisition of Stethoscopic Perspectives," in *The Oxford Handbook of Sound Studies,* ed. Trevor Pinch and Karin Bijsterveld (New York: Oxford University Press, 2011), 298–319; and Eric Topol, *The Patient Will See You Now: The Future of Medicine Is in Your Hands* (New York: Basic Books, 2015).

17. On supercrip and savant stereotypes, see Joseph Straus, "Idiots Savants, Retarded Savants, Talented Aments, Mono-Savants, Autistic Savants, Just Plain Savants, People with Savant Syndrome, and Autistic People Who Are Good at Things: A View from Disability Studies," *Disability Studies Quarterly* 34 (2014), http://dsq-sds.org/article/view/3407/3640; Wendy L. Chrisman, "A Reflection on Inspiration: A Recuperative Call for Emotion in Disability Studies," *Journal of Literary & Cultural Disability Studies* 5 (2011): 173–84; and Sharon L. Snyder and David T. Mitchell, "Introduction: Ablenationalism and the Geo-politics of Disability," *Journal of Literary and Cultural Disability Studies* 4 (2010): 113–25.

18. Norman Cousins, *Anatomy of an Illness as Perceived by the Patient* (New York: W. W. Norton, 1979), 80. I'm grateful to Maureen Ragan for this reference.

19. Cousins, *Anatomy of an Illness,* 80–81.

20. Concerning queer love for music, see Suzanne Cusick, "On a Lesbian Relationship with Music: A Serious Effort Not to Think Straight," in *Queering the Pitch: The New Gay and Lesbian Musicology,* 2nd ed., ed. Philip Brett, Elizabeth Wood, and Gary C. Thomas (New York: Routledge, 2006), 67–84.

21. The memoirs I read that summer included Frank Spinelli, *Pee-Shy* (New York: Kensington, 2014); Charles M. Blow, *Fire Shut Up in My Bones* (New York: Houghton Mifflin Harcourt, 2014); and Tim Anderson, *Sweet Tooth* (Seattle: Lake Union, 2014).

22. Jean-Luc Nancy, *Listening*, trans. Charlotte Mandell (New York: Fordham University Press, 2007), 12. The excerpt in French: "Être à l'écoute, c'est donc entrer dans la tension et dans le guet d'un rapport à soi: *non pas*, il faut le souligner, un rapport à 'moi' (sujet supposé donné) et pas non plus au 'soi' de l'autre (le parleur, le musicien, lui aussi supposé donné avec sa subjectivité), mais le *rapport en soi*, si je peux dire, tel qu'il forme un 'soi' ou un 'à soi' en général et si quelque chose de tel arrive jamais au terme de sa formation" (Jean-Luc Nancy, *À l'écoute* [Paris: Galilée, 2002], 30).

23. Nancy, *Listening*, 17. The original French: "Il faudrait ici s'arrêter longuement sur le rythme: il n'est pas autre chose que le temps du temps, l'ébranlement du temps lui-même dans la frappe d'un présent qui le présente en le disjoignant de lui-même. . . . Ainsi, le rythme disjoint la succession de la linéarité de la séquence ou de la durée: il plie le temps pour le donner au temps lui-même, et c'est de cette façon qu'il plie et déplie un 'soi'" (Nancy, *À l'écoute*, 37–38). See also Aden Evens, *Sound Ideas: Music, Machines, and Experience* (Minneapolis: University of Minnesota Press, 2005), 16–25; and Erlmann, *Reason and Resonance*, 185–216. Several months after reading *Listening* by Nancy, I came across Roger Mathew Grant's review of this book in the *Journal of the American Musicological Society* 62 (2009): 748–52. The review, which effectively parses the original French text and its English translation, illuminates many of Nancy's complex claims. See also Ryan Dohoney, "Echo's Echo: Subjectivity in Vibrational Ontology," *Women & Music* 19 (2015): 142–50; and Brian Kane, "Jean-Luc Nancy and the Listening Subject," *Contemporary Music Review* 31 (2012): 439–47.

24. In an iconic essay, Susan Sontag advised that people who study art "must learn to *see* more, to *hear* more, to *feel* more" (*Against Interpretation and Other Essays* [New York: Farrar, Straus & Giroux, 1966], 14).

25. See Mike Springer, "Noam Chomsky Slams Žižek and Lacan: Empty Posturing," *Open Culture* (28 June 2013), http://www.openculture.com/2013/06/noam_chomsky_slams_zizek_and_lacan_empty_posturing.html; see also Alan D. Sokal, *Intellectual Impostures: Postmodern Philosophers' Abuse of Science* (London: Profile Books, 1998). Postcolonial scholar Homi Bhabha has pushed back against criticisms of humanists' difficult language: "There is a damaging and self-defeating assumption that theory is necessarily the elite language of the socially and culturally privileged" (*The Location of Culture* [New York: Routledge, 1994], 28). Disciplinary envy, moreover, can cut both ways, seeing as how mathematicians and scientists often seek beauty and aesthetic value in their fields of inquiry. See, for example, Mario Livio's *The Golden Ratio: The Story of Phi, the World's Most Astonishing Number* (New York: Broadway Books, 2002) and *Is God a Mathematician?* (New York: Simon & Schuster, 2009).

26. For an analysis of this Hans Christian Andersen tale, see Hollis Robbins, "The Emperor's New Critique," *New Literary History* 34 (2003): 659–75.

27. Nancy, *Listening*, 63.

28. See Rolv-Ole Lindsetmo and Jonah Stulberg, "Chronic Abdominal Wall Pain—a Diagnostic Challenge for the Surgeon," *American Journal of Surgery* 198 (2009): 129–34; Radhika Srinivasan et al., "Chronic Abdominal Wall Pain: A Frequently Overlooked Problem," *American Journal of Gastroenterology* 97 (2002): 824–30; and William V. Applegate, "Abdominal Cutaneous Nerve Entrapment Syndrome

(ACNES): A Commonly Overlooked Cause of Abdominal Pain," *Permanente Journal* 6 (2002): 20–27.

29. Historical discourses about people's varying pain thresholds have often sprung out of racist, sexist, or otherwise discriminatory and dehumanizing perspectives. Claims about the higher pain thresholds of people of African origins, for example, fed apologias for chattel slavery. See Joanna Bourke, "Pain Sensitivity: An Unnatural History from 1800 to 1965," *Journal of Medical Humanities* 35 (2014): 301–19; Rachel Dudley, "Toward an Understanding of the 'Medical Plantation' as a Cultural Location of Disability," *Disability Studies Quarterly* 32 (2012), http://dsq-sds.org/article/view/3248/3184; and Marie Jenkins Schwartz, *Birthing a Slave: Motherhood and Medicine in the Antebellum South* (Cambridge, MA: Harvard University Press, 2006), 167–68. I thank Rosemarie Garland-Thomson for bringing these ideas to my attention.

30. Sir Winston Churchill quoted in Kingsley Martin, "Winston Churchill Interviewed in 1939," *New Statesman* (6 January 2014), http://www.newstatesman.com/archive/2013/12/british-people-would-rather-go-down-fighting; cf. Scarry, *The Body in Pain*, 52.

31. Cousins, *Anatomy of an Illness*, 41.

32. See Elizabeth Heideman, "'Inspiration Porn Is Not Okay': Disability Activists Are Not Impressed with Feel-Good Super Bowl Ads," *Salon* (2 February 2015), http://www.salon.com/writer/elizabeth_heideman; and Harilyn Rousso, *Don't Call Me Inspirational: A Disabled Feminist Talks Back* (Philadelphia: Temple University Press, 2013).

Chapter 2

1. Henry David Thoreau, *The Journal, 1837–1861*, ed. Damion Searls (New York: New York Review Books, 2009), 26.

2. Bruno Latour, "Why Has Critique Run out of Steam? From Matters of Fact to Matters of Concern," *Critical Inquiry* 30 (2004): 238–39.

3. See Elaine Scarry, *Thermonuclear Monarchy: Choosing between Democracy and Doom* (New York: W. W. Norton, 2014).

4. Latour, "Critique," 228.

5. Latour, "Critique," 228.

6. Deborah Tannen, *The Argument Culture: Stopping America's War on Words* (New York: Random House, 1998), 3.

7. For accounts of academics' fighting spirit, see Deborah Tannen, "Agonism in Academic Discourse," *Journal of Pragmatics* 34 (2002): 1651–69; and Jonathan Gottschall, *The Professor in the Cage: Why Men Fight and Why We Like to Watch* (New York: Penguin, 2015).

8. On debates about anti-intellectualism from the last half-century, see Catherine Liu, *American Idyll: Academic Antielitism as Cultural Critique* (Iowa City: University of Iowa Press, 2011); Martha Nussbaum, *Not for Profit: Why Democracy Needs the Humanities* (Princeton, NJ: Princeton University Press, 2010); Andrew Ross, *No Respect: Intellectuals and Popular Culture* (New York: Routledge, 1989); and seminally, Richard Hofstadter, *Anti-intellectualism in American Life* (New York: Knopf, 1963).

9. See William Cheng, "Pleasure's Discontents," *Journal of the American Musicological Society* 66 (2013): 840–44.

10. Allegations against ocularcentrism pop up frequently in sound studies and in musicology. See the respective introductions to Sumanth Gopinath and Jason Stan-

yek, eds., *The Oxford Handbook of Mobile Music Studies*, vol. 1 (New York: Oxford University Press, 2014); Pinch and Bijsterveld, *Handbook of Sound Studies*; and Jonathan Sterne, ed., *The Sound Studies Reader* (New York: Routledge, 2012).

11. The origin of this saying is contested: it has been variously attributed to Wallace Sayre, Henry Kissinger, and Richard Neustadt. See Ralph Keyes, *The Quote Verifier: Who Said What, Where, and When* (New York: St. Martin's Press, 2006), 1.

12. On how gamers and academics face comparable accusations of losing touch with reality, see William Cheng, *Sound Play: Video Games and the Musical Imagination* (New York: Oxford University Press, 2014), 15–16. Gamers are often asked why they spend so much time in virtual worlds, roaming fantastical lands and seeking castles in the sky. And at times, scholars—especially those in the arts and humanities—likewise get called out for holing up in ivory towers, debating and discoursing about a subject rather than *really* doing something about it (say, via social intervention, political activism, or obvious material contribution). In short, both groups are routinely charged with playing at something almost real, but not quite.

13. Margaret Price, *Mad at School: Rhetorics of Mental Disability and Academic Life* (Ann Arbor: University of Michigan Press, 2011), 8.

14. Suzanne Cusick, "Musicology, Torture, Repair," *Radical Musicology* 3 (2008), http://www.radical-musicology.org.uk/2008/Cusick.htm, par. 19.

15. Hanson, "The Future's Eve," 105. See also Jurecic, *Illness as Narrative*, 113–31.

16. See Elizabeth J. Donaldson and Catherine Prendergast, "Disability and Emotion: 'There's No Crying in Disability Studies!'" *Journal of Literary & Cultural Disability Studies* 5 (2011): 129–35.

17. Lauren Berlant, *Cruel Optimism* (Durham, NC: Duke University Press, 2011), 139.

18. Judith Halberstam, *The Queer Art of Failure* (Durham, NC: Duke University Press, 2011), 15.

19. Abbate, "Music: Drastic or Gnostic?," 516.

20. Abbate, "Music: Drastic or Gnostic?," 516.

21. Clifford Geertz, "Thick Description: Toward an Interpretive Theory of Culture," in *The Interpretation of Cultures: Selected Essays* (New York: Basic Books, 1973), 3–30.

22. John L. Jackson Jr., *Thin Description: Ethnography and the African Hebrew Israelites of Jerusalem* (Cambridge, MA: Harvard University Press, 2013), 153. See also Heather Love, "Close Reading and Thin Description," *Public Culture* 25 (2013): 401–34; and Wayne H. Brekhus, John F. Galliher, and Jaber F. Gubrium, "The Need for Thin Description," *Qualitative Inquiry* 11 (2005): 861–79. Yet another dichotomy in critical reading pertains to values of depth versus surface; see, for example, Robert Fink, "Going Flat: Towards a Post-hierarchical Music Theory," in Cook and Everist, *Rethinking Music*, 102–37.

23. Love, "Truth and Consequences," 239. Love continues: "A reading of [Sedgwick's] work as all about love suggests that we are not listening to her, nor watching how she moves" (239). See also Eve Kosofsky Sedgwick, *A Dialogue on Love* (Boston: Beacon Press, 1999); and Cindy Patton, "Love without the Obligation to Love," *Criticism* 52 (2010): 215–24.

24. On problematic expectations of rhetorical aptitude (in relation to disability and neurodiversity), see Shannon Walters, "Unruly Rhetorics: Disability, Animality, and New Kinship Compositions," *PMLA* 129 (2014): 471–77; Price, *Mad at School*,

37–46; and Brenda Jo Brueggemann and James A. Fredal, "Studying Disability Rhetorically," in *Disability Discourse*, ed. Mairian Corker and Sally French (Philadelphia: Open University Press, 1999), 129–30.

25. On control, trust, and vulnerability, see Martha Nussbaum, *The Fragility of Goodness: Luck and Ethics in Greek Tragedy and Philosophy*, rev. ed. (Cambridge: Cambridge University Press, 2001); and George W. Harris, *Dignity and Vulnerability: Strength and Quality of Character* (Berkeley: University of California Press, 1997).

26. See James Currie, "Music after All," *Journal of the American Musicological Society* 62 (2009): 189; cf. James Currie, *Music and the Politics of Negation* (Bloomington: Indiana University Press, 2012), xiv–xviii.

27. Kevin Korsyn, *Decentering Music: A Critique of Contemporary Musical Research* (New York: Oxford University Press, 2003), 16.

28. Diverse responses to *Decentering Music* pointed up Korsyn's claims about music scholarship's radical tensions. See reviews by Patrick McCreless in *Theory and Practice* 29 (2004): 252–66; by Martin Scherzinger in the *Journal of the American Musicological Society* 59 (2006): 777–85; and by Ruth Solie in *Music and Letters* 85 (2004): 418–23. Jonathan Pieslak describes these wildly different takes on Korsyn's book: "Korsyn speaks of the 'crisis' of discourse in musical scholarship, and, indeed, the disagreements about the 'crisis' and the contrasting ways scholars have read the book seem to affirm its existence. . . . If these varied reactions do not, themselves, indicate the 'crisis' Korsyn is talking about, it is at least, for me, confusing" ("Review of *Decentering Music*," *Music Theory Online* 14 [2008]: par. 10).

29. See Rosemarie Garland-Thomson, "Human Biodiversity Conservation: A Consensual Ethical Principle," *American Journal of Bioethics* 15 (2015): 13–15. See also Michael Sandel, *The Case against Perfection: Ethics in the Age of Genetic Engineering* (Cambridge, MA: Belknap Press of Harvard University Press, 2007), 85–100.

30. Amartya Sen, *Identity and Violence: The Illusion of Destiny* (New York: W. W. Norton, 2006), xiv; cf. Walter Benn Michaels, *The Trouble with Diversity: How We Learned to Love Identity and Ignore Inequality* (New York: Metropolitan Books, 2006). See also Olivia Bloechl, with Melanie Lowe, "Introduction: Rethinking Difference," in *Rethinking Difference in Music Scholarship*, ed. Olivia Bloechl, Melanie Lowe, and Jeffrey Kallberg (Cambridge: Cambridge University Press, 2015), 1–52 (esp. 47–49); Judith Peraino, "The Same, but Different: Sexuality and Musicology, Then and Now," *Journal of the American Musicological Society* 66 (2013): 825–31; and Ruth A. Solie, "Introduction: On 'Difference,'" in *Musicology and Difference: Gender and Sexuality in Music Scholarship*, ed. Ruth A. Solie (Berkeley: University of California Press, 1993), 1–20.

31. See Zosha Stuckey, *A Rhetoric of Remnants: Idiots, Half-Wits, and Other State-Sponsored Inventions* (Albany: SUNY Press, 2014); and Eva Feder Kittay and Licia Carlson, eds., *Cognitive Disability and Its Challenge to Moral Philosophy* (Malden, MA: Wiley-Blackwell, 2010).

32. One of the founding treatises for the Slow Movement was Carl Honoré's *In Praise of Slowness: Challenging the Cult of Speed* (San Francisco: HarperSanFrancisco, 2004).

33. Alison Mountz et al., "For Slow Scholarship: A Feminist Politics of Resistance through Collective Action in the Neoliberal University," *ACME: An International E-Journal for Critical Geographies* 14 (2015): 1253.

34. See Yvonne Hartman and Sandy Darab, "A Call for Slow Scholarship: A Case Study on the Intensification of Academic Life and Its Implications for Pedagogy,"

Review of Education, Pedagogy, and Cultural Studies 34 (2012): 49–60. See also Claire Barber-Stetson, "Slow Processing: A New Minor Literature by Autists and Modernists," *Journal of Modern Literature* 38 (2014): 147–65.

35. Nishida, "Neoliberal Academia," 148.

36. Price, *Mad at School*, 62. See also Julie Cosenza, "SLOW: Crip Theory, Dyslexia and the Borderlands of Disability and Ablebodiedness," *Liminalities* 6 (October 2010): 10 pages; and Irving Kenneth Zola, "Self, Identity and the Naming Question: Reflections on the Language of Disability," *Social Science and Medicine* 36 (1993): 167–73. In both terminology and subversive potential, "crip time" resonates with "queer time" (Judith Halberstam, *In a Queer Time and Place: Transgender Bodies, Subcultural Lives* [New York: New York University Press, 2005], 1–21) as well as "women's time" (Julia Kristeva, "Women's Time," trans. Alice Jardine and Harry Blake, *Signs* 7 [1981]: 13–35).

37. Luke Martell, "The Slow University: Inequality, Power and Alternatives," *Forum: Qualitative Social Research* 15 (2014): par. 36.

38. Debra Erickson, "Why It's So Hard to Leave Academe," *Chronicle of Higher Education* (7 October 2015), http://chronicle.com/article/Why-It-s-So-Hard-to-Leave/233670. The decisions of leaving versus staying in academia were powerfully articulated by Cari E. McDonnell in "Parenting a Special-Needs Child in Academe: Should I Stay or Should I Go?," paper presented at AMS 2015 in Louisville, KY (13 November 2015).

39. Felicia Miyakawa has described her decision to leave a tenured position in musicology as follows: "On the first day of the conference [on public musicology], I spoke about how/why I left academia. For the rest of the day and into the next, numerous people cornered me to tell me how brave I am. This is a comment I've been getting all too frequently since I quit my job. And it invariably comes from current academics who cop to sharing many of my experiences. I'll admit I feel just a little worse each time I am called 'brave,' because this comment drives home to me just how many people are unhappy or frustrated in their academic positions but have little power to change their situation. I am 'brave' because I escaped, because I found a way out, because I was willing to take a big risk and walk away from a broken system. It saddens me to know that so many of my peers are so frustrated. Or maybe there's a different way to interpret being brave. Let's talk about it" ("Going Rogue: On Leaving the Academy and Taking Risks" [1 February 2015], http://fmmiyakawa.com/2015/02/01/on-being-brave-publicmusicology).

40. Richard Taruskin, "Is There a Baby in the Bathwater? (Part II)," *Archiv für Musikwissenschaft* 63 (2006): 318 and 327; cf. Robert Fink, "Resurrection Symphony: El Sistema as Ideology in Venezuela and Los Angeles," *Action, Criticism, and Theory for Music Education* 15 (2016): 33–57.

41. For an early feminist critique of objectivity (with references to ocularcentrism), see Donna Haraway, "Situated Knowledges: The Science Question in Feminism and the Privilege of Partial Perspective," *Feminist Studies* 14 (1988): 575–99.

42. Brison, *Aftermath*, 109. See also Amy Allen, *The Politics of Our Selves: Power, Autonomy, and Gender in Contemporary Critical Theory* (New York: Columbia University Press, 2008), 10–13.

43. See Elaine Scarry, *On Beauty and Being Just* (Princeton, NJ: Princeton University Press, 1999), 3.

44. Scarry, *On Beauty*, 39. Scarry also writes: "It is the argument of this chapter that beauty, far from contributing to social injustice . . . actually assists us in the work

of addressing injustice, not only by requiring of us constant perceptual acuity—high dives of seeing, hearing, touching—but by the more direct forms of instruction" (42).

45. Scarry, *On Beauty*, 39. See also Ernest R. House, "Origins of the Ideas in *Evaluating with Validity*," *New Directions for Evaluation* 142 (2014): 9–15.

46. Pieter van den Toorn, "Politics, Feminism, and Contemporary Music Theory," *Journal of Musicology* 9 (1991): 292 and 293.

47. Van den Toorn, "Politics," 297.

48. Ruth A. Solie, "What Do Feminists Want? A Reply to Pieter van den Toorn," *Journal of Musicology* 9 (1991): 409–10. See also Susan Brison, "Everyday Atrocities and Ordinary Miracles, or Why I (Still) Bear Witness to Sexual Violence (but Not Too Often)," *Women's Studies Quarterly* 36 (2008): 188–98.

49. Bonnie Gordon, "Why We Matter," *Women & Music* 19 (2015): 117.

50. Gordon, "Why We Matter," 117. This article expands on Bonnie Gordon's earlier piece, "The UVA Gang Rape Allegations Are Awful, Horrifying, and Not Shocking at All," *Slate* (25 November 2014), http://www.slate.com/blogs/xx_factor/2014/11/25/uva_gang_rape_allegations_in_rolling_stone_not_surprising_to_one_associate.html.

51. See Stephen Downes, introduction, in *Aesthetics of Music: Musicological Perspectives*, ed. Stephen Downes (New York: Routledge, 2014), 1–11; Roger Savage, *Hermeneutics and Music Criticism* (New York: Routledge, 2010), 25–31; Richard Taruskin, "Is There a Baby in the Bathwater? (Part I)," *Archiv für Musikwissenschaft* 63 (2006): 163–85; Andrew Dell'Antonio, introduction, in *Beyond Structural Listening? Postmodern Modes of Hearing*, ed. Andrew Dell'Antonio (Berkeley: University of California Press, 2004), 1–12; and Max Paddison, "Music as Ideal: The Aesthetics of Autonomy," in *The Cambridge History of Nineteenth-Century Music*, ed. Jim Samson (Cambridge: Cambridge University Press, 2001), 318–42.

52. See Vijay Prashad, "Teaching by Candlelight," in *The Imperial University: Academic Repression and Scholarly Dissent*, ed. Piya Chatterjee and Sunaina Maira (Minneapolis: University of Minnesota Press, 2014), 281–97. See also Ward Churchill, "The Myth of Academic Freedom: Personal Experiences of a Liberal Principle in the Neoconservative Era (Fragments of a Work in Progress)," *Social Text* 25 (2007): 17–39.

53. Scarry, "Beauty," 24–25.

54. Scarry, "Beauty," 26.

55. See Ian Bogost, *Alien Phenomenology: or, What It's Like to Be a Thing* (Minneapolis: University of Minnesota Press, 2012); Bennett, *Vibrant Matter*, 1–13; and Bill Brown, ed., *Things* (Chicago: University of Chicago Press, 2004). Related streams of thought include vitalism, posthumanism, speculative realism, and flat ontology. See Andrew Cole, "The Call of Things: A Critique of Object-Oriented Ontologies," *Minnesota Review* 80 (2013): 106–18.

56. See Benjamin Piekut, "Actor-Networks in Music History: Clarifications and Critiques," *Twentieth-Century Music* 11 (2014): 191–215; Cheng, *Sound Play*, 8–9; and Nicholas Mathew and Mary Ann Smart, "Elephants in the Music Room: The Future of Quirk Historicism," *Representations* 132 (2015): 61–78.

57. Bruno Latour, *Reassembling the Social: An Introduction to Actor-Network Theory* (New York: Oxford University Press, 2005), 83; cf. Scarry, *The Body in Pain*, 278–323; and Geoffrey Galt Harpham, "Elaine Scarry and the Dream of Pain," *Salmagundi* 130–31 (2001): 202–34. See also Bruno Latour, *We Have Never Been Modern*, trans. Catherine Porter (Cambridge, MA: Harvard University Press, 1993), 82–94. I'm grateful to Ryan Dohoney for expanding my Latourian literacy.

58. Richard Taruskin, "Agents and Causes and Ends, Oh My," *Journal of Musicology* 31 (2014): 292.

59. Taruskin, "Agents and Causes," 291.

60. Latour, *Reassembling the Social*, 71.

61. Peter Railton, "Innocent Abroad: Rupture, Liberation, and Solidarity," Dewey Lecture, APA-Central (February 2015), http://www.lsa.umich.edu/UMICH/philosophy/Home/News/Railton%20Dewey%20Lecture%20Central%20APA%202015%20revised.pdf, 14.

62. Railton, "Innocent Abroad," 14.

63. Railton, "Innocent Abroad," 15. See also Jake Jackson, "On Critical Abyss-Gazing: Depression & Academic Philosophy," *PhDisabled* (19 August 2014), http://phdisabled.wordpress.com/2014/08/19/on-critical-abyss-gazing-depression-academic-philosophy; and Phil Ford, "What Good News Do You Bring?" *Dial M for Musicology* (11 March 2015), http://dialmformusicology.com/2015/03/11/what-good-news-do-you-bring.

64. See William Cheng, "Meritocracy's Darker Notes," *Huffington Post* (22 May 2015), http://www.huffingtonpost.com/william-cheng/meritocracys-darker-notes_b_7423774.html.

65. Nadine Muller quoted in Claire Shaw and Lucy Ward, "Dark Thoughts: Why Mental Illness Is on the Rise in Academia," *Guardian* (6 March 2014), http://www.theguardian.com/higher-education-network/2014/mar/06/mental-health-academics-growing-problem-pressure-university?CMP=share_btn_fb. See also Cvetkovich, *Depression*, 17–42; Melonie Fullick, "'My Grief Lies All Within': PhD Students, Depression & Attrition," *University Affairs* (14 December 2011), http://www.universityaffairs.ca/opinion/speculative-diction/my-grief-lies-all-within-phd-students-depression-attrition; Jennifer Ruark, "In Academic Culture, Mental-Health Problems Are Hard to Recognize and Hard to Treat," *Chronicle of Higher Education* (16 February 2010), http://chronicle.com/article/In-Academe-Mental-Health/64246; and Rachel Vorona Cote, "There's No Crying in Graduate School," *Chronicle of Higher Education* (5 June 2015), http://chroniclevitae.com/news/1026-there-s-no-crying-in-graduate-school.

66. Cain, "Of Pain," 748.

67. Cain, "Of Pain," 748–49. See also Stephanie L. Kerschbaum, "On Rhetorical Agency and Disclosing Disability in Academic Writing," *Rhetoric Review* 33 (2014): 55–71; and S. Naomi Finkelstein, "The Only Thing You Have to Do Is Live," *GLQ: A Journal of Lesbian and Gay Studies* 9 (2003): 307–19.

68. See Noam Chomsky, *Profit over People: Neoliberalism and Global Order* (New York: Seven Stories Press, 1999).

69. On battles for contingent faculty rights, see Bérubé and Ruth, *Humanities*, 121–41.

70. Phil Gentry, "The Polite Musicologist," 2′23″ (4 April 2009), http://blog.pmgentry.net/2009/04/polite-musicologist.html.

71. Emily Wilbourne, email correspondence with author (21 October 2015), quoted with permission.

72. Emily Wilbourne, "On a Lesbian Relationship with Musicology: Suzanne G. Cusick, Sound Effects," *Women & Music* 19 (2015): 6. See also Charles Hiroshi Garrett, "Enterprising Students and the Future of the American Musicological Society," in Bernstein, *AMS at 75*, 33–37.

Chapter 3

1. Brison, *Aftermath*, 65.

2. Avery Brown, email correspondence with author (28 May 2015), quoted with permission.

3. Berlant, *Cruel Optimism*, 123.

4. Sedgwick, "Paranoid Reading," 125–26. In a later essay, Sedgwick elaborated on the relationship between paranoia and queer theory: "I overlooked the crudest, most contingent, and probably also most important reason why paranoia seems so built into queer theory as such. To quite get that, I think one has to have experienced gay life in the 1980s and early '90s, when queer theory was still a tentative, emergent itinerary. That was also the moment when AIDS was a new and nearly untreatable disease—bringing a sudden, worse than Euripidean horror into the lives of urban gay men and their friends. It was not an uncommon experience then to be in a room of vibrant young people, conscious that within a year or two, all but a few of them would have sickened and died" ("Melanie Klein," 638).

5. Nadine Hubbs, "Homophobia in Twentieth-Century Music: The Crucible of America's Sound," *Daedalus* 142 (2013): 46.

6. Marvin B. Scott and Stanford M. Lyman, "Paranoia, Homosexuality and Game Theory," *Journal of Health and Social Behavior* 9 (1968): 184, 185.

7. Frieda Fromm-Reichmann quoted in Scott and Lyman, "Paranoia," 185.

8. See David Lester, "The Relationship between Paranoid Delusions and Homosexuality," *Archives of Sexual Behavior* 4 (1975): 285–94; and Morton Schatzman, "Paranoia or Persecution: The Case of Schreber," *Salmagundi* 19 (1972): 38–65.

9. See Robyn Wiegman and Elizabeth A. Wilson, "Introduction: Antinormativity's Queer Conventions," *differences* 26 (2015): 1–25; Kim Q. Hall, "No Failure: Climate Change, Radical Hope, and Queer Crip Feminist Eco-futures," *Radical Philosophy Review* 17 (2014): 203–25; Elahe Haschemi Yekami, Eveline Kilian, and Beatrice Michaelis, "Introducing Queer Futures," in *Queer Futures: Reconsidering Ethics, Activism, and the Political* (Burlington, VT: Ashgate, 2012), 1–15; and Lee Edelman, *No Future: Queer Theory and the Death Drive* (Durham, NC: Duke University Press, 2004).

10. Lisa Henderson, *Love and Money: Queers, Class, and Cultural Production* (New York: New York University Press, 2013), 11.

11. Alice A. Kuzniar, "Sublime Shame (review)," *GLQ: A Journal of Lesbian and Gay Studies* 15 (2009): 499. See also David Halperin and Valerie Traub, eds., *Gay Shame* (Chicago: University of Chicago Press, 2009); Heather Love, *Feeling Backward: Loss and the Politics of Queer History* (Cambridge, MA: Harvard University Press, 2007), 147; Jasbir Puar, *Terrorist Assemblages: Homonationalism in Queer Times* (Durham, NC: Duke University Press, 2007), 1–36; Kathryn Bond Stockton, *Beautiful Bottom, Beautiful Shame: Where "Black" Meets "Queer"* (Durham, NC: Duke University Press, 2006), 1–38; and Jack Katz, *How Emotions Work* (Chicago: University of Chicago Press, 1999), 142–74.

12. In his Dewey lecture, Railton noted that radical upticks in polls on gay marriage came about through "experience-based moral learning" whereby "enough gay individuals courageously took things into their own hands and came out publicly" ("Innocent Abroad," 13).

13. Home page of the Welcoming Committee; see http://thewelcomingcommittee.com/gqb.

14. At GQB events, pride effectively turns mundane as participants make attempts at (to riff on Harvey Sacks) queering being ordinary, or being queerly ordinary. See Harvey Sacks, "On Doing 'Being Ordinary,'" in *Structures of Social Action: Studies in Conversation Analysis*, ed. J. Maxwell Atkinson and John Heritage (Cambridge: Cambridge University Press, 1985), 413–29; cf. Heather Love, "Doing Being Deviant: Deviance Studies, Description, and the Queer Ordinary," *differences* 26 (2015): 74–95.

15. Michael Snediker, *Queer Optimism: Lyric Personhood and Other Felicitous Persuasions* (Minneapolis: University of Minnesota Press, 2009), 1. Snediker offers the concept of "queer optimism," which "doesn't aspire toward happiness, but instead finds happiness *interesting*. Queer optimism, in this sense, can be considered a form of meta-optimism: it wants to *think* about feeling good, to make disparate aspects of feeling good thinkable" (3).

16. Muñoz, *Cruising Utopia*, 10.

17. Snediker, *Queer Optimism*, 2; and Sara Ahmed, *The Promise of Happiness* (Durham, NC: Duke University Press, 2010), 161; cf. Sianne Ngai, *Our Aesthetic Categories: Zany, Cute, Interesting* (Cambridge, MA: Harvard University Press, 2012).

18. Berlant, *Cruel Optimism*, 1.

19. Berlant, *Cruel Optimism*, 2.

20. Jasbir K. Puar, "The Cost of Getting Better: Suicide, Sensation, Switchpoints," *GLQ: A Journal of Lesbian and Gay Studies* 18 (2012): 152. See also Patrick R. Grzanka and Emily S. Mann, "Queer Youth Suicide and the Psychopolitics of 'It Gets Better,'" *Sexualities* 17 (2014): 369–93; Michael Johnson Jr., "The It Gets Better Project: A Study in (and of) Whiteness in LGBT Youth and Media Cultures," in *Queer Youth and Media Cultures*, ed. Christopher Pullen (New York: Palgrave Macmillan, 2014), 278–91; Rob Cover, *Queer Youth Suicide, Culture and Identity: Unliveable Lives?* (Burlington, VT: Ashgate, 2012), 57–75; and Tavia Nyong'o, "School Daze," *Bully Bloggers* (30 September 2010), http://bullybloggers.wordpress.com/2010/09/30/school-daze.

21. Jasbir K. Puar, "In the Wake of It Gets Better," *Guardian* (16 November 2010), http://www.theguardian.com/commentisfree/cifamerica/2010/nov/16/wake-it-gets-better-campaign.

22. Jennifer Finney Boylan, "In the Early Morning Rain," in *It Gets Better: Coming Out, Overcoming Bullying, and Creating a Life Worth Living*, ed. Dan Savage and Terry Miller (New York: Dutton, 2011), 20.

23. Alex R. Orue, "The Person Worth Fighting For Is You," in Savage and Miller, *It Gets Better*, 35–37.

24. Gabrielle Rivera, "Getting Stronger and Staying Alive," in Savage and Miller, *It Gets Better*, 45–46.

25. Mark Ramirez, "An Identity Unfolded," in Savage and Miller, *It Gets Better*, 99–101.

26. Jack Halberstam, "It Gets Worse . . . ," *Social Text* (20 November 2010), http://socialtextjournal.org/periscope_article/it_gets_worse.

27. See Judith Butler, *Frames of War: When Is Life Grievable?* (New York: Verso, 2009); see also Ayo Coly, "Healing Is Not Grieving: We Must Not 'Move Forward' in the Wake of Massacre," *Truth-out* (3 July 2015), http://www.truth-out.org/opinion/item/31693-healing-is-not-grieving-we-must-not-move-forward-in-the-wake-of-massacre.

28. See Emily Hutcheon and Bonnie Lashewicz, "Theorizing Resilience: Critiquing and Unbounding a Marginalizing Concept," *Disability & Society* 29 (2014): 1383–97; Brad Evans and Julian Reid, *Resilient Life: The Art of Living Dangerously* (Cambridge:

Polity, 2014), 68–90; Jeannie Suk, "Laws of Trauma," in *Knowing the Suffering of Others: Legal Perspectives on Pain and Its Meanings*, ed. Austin Sarat (Tuscaloosa: University of Alabama Press, 2014), 220–21; Jonathan Joseph, "Resilience as Embedded Neoliberalism: A Governmentality Approach," *Resilience* 1 (2013): 38–52; and Alison Howell, "The Demise of PTSD: From Governing through Trauma to Governing Resilience," *Alternatives: Global, Local, Political* 37 (2012): 214–26. I'm grateful to Brianne Gallagher for pointing me to these sources.

29. Chuck Todd quoted in Joanne Lipman, "Is Music the Key to Success?" *New York Times* (12 October 2013), http://www.nytimes.com/2013/10/13/opinion/sunday/is-music-the-key-to-success.html?_r=0.

30. Philip Brett, "Musicality, Essentialism, and the Closet," in Brett, Wood, and Thomas, *Queering the Pitch*, 17–18.

31. See Gary C. Thomas, "'Was George Frideric Handel Gay?': On Closet Questions and Cultural Politics," in Brett, Wood, and Thomas, *Queering the Pitch*, 155–203; Timothy Jackson, *Tchaikovsky: Symphony No. 6 (Pathétique)* (Cambridge: Cambridge University Press, 1999); Michael J. Puri, "Dandy, Interrupted: Sublimation, Repression, and Self-Portraiture in Maurice Ravel's *Daphnis et Chloé* (1909–1912)," *Journal of the American Musicological Society* 60 (2007): 317–72; and Byron Adams, "Elgar's Later Oratorios: Roman Catholicism, Decadence and the Wagnerian Dialectic of Shame and Grace," in *The Cambridge Companion to Elgar*, ed. Daniel M. Grimley and Julian Rushton (Cambridge: Cambridge University Press, 2004), 81–105. See also Paul Attinello, "Performance and/or Shame: A Mosaic of Gay (and Other) Perceptions," *repercussions* 4 (1995): 97–130; and David Caron, "Shame on Me, or the Naked Truth about Marlene Dietrich," in Halperin and Traub, *Gay Shame*, 117–31.

32. See Brett, "Musicality," 14–18; J. Peter Burkholder, "From Radical Fairy to Tenured Faculty: Personal Reflections on Gayness, Music, and Musicology," *GLSG Newsletter of the American Musicological Society* 12 (2002): 3–8; Mitchell Morris, "Musical Virtues," in Dell'Antonio, *Beyond Structural Listening?*, 44–69; and Nadine Hubbs, *The Queer Composition of America's Sound: Gay Modernists, American Music, and National Identity* (Berkeley: University of California Press, 2004), 7–10.

33. Brett, "Musicality," 17. On the "deviant" connotations of musicality, Brett has also remarked that "it is surely no coincidence that among the many code words and phrases for a homosexual man before Stonewall (and even since), 'musical' (as in, 'Is he "musical" do you think?') ranked with others such as 'friend of Dorothy' as safe insider euphemisms" (11).

34. In addition to musical indicators, there are (mundane) sonic signifiers of queerness, whether it's the "gay lisp" or other stereotyped variables of tone, pitch, range, lexicon, and phraseology. See Erik C. Tracy et al., "Judgments of Self-Identified Gay and Heterosexual Male Speakers: Which Phonemes Are Most Salient in Determining Sexual Orientation?" *Journal of Phonetics* 52 (2015): 13–25; Benjamin Munson et al., "The Acoustic and Perceptual Bases of Judgments of Women and Men's Sexual Orientation from Read Speech," *Journal of Phonetics* 34 (2006): 202–40; and Rudolf P. Gaudio, "Sounding Gay: Pitch Properties in the Speech of Gay and Straight Men," *American Speech* 69 (1994): 30–57. See also David Thorpe's 2014 documentary, *Do I Sound Gay?* (distributed by Sundance Selects).

35. Roger Mathew Grant, "The Queen of Music Theory Goes to Milwaukee City, or, Yes I Am a Music Theory Queen," paper presented at AMS/SMT joint meeting in Milwaukee, WI (7 November 2014), quoted with permission.

36. I've ventured elsewhere that formal analyses, as much as any type of music

scholarship, "sometimes read and sound as if they're talking *around* pleasure, circumventing the snares of emotional candor and its possible implications of irrationality, emasculation, and deficit of control" (Cheng, "Pleasure's Discontents," 842).

37. See Judith Peraino, "On Phone Theory," paper presented at AMS/SMT joint meeting in Milwaukee, WI (7 November 2014).

38. See Carolyn Dinshaw, *How Soon Is Now? Medieval Texts, Amateur Readers, and the Queerness of Time* (Durham, NC: Duke University Press, 2012); Elizabeth Freeman, *Time Binds: Queer Temporalities, Queer Histories* (Durham, NC: Duke University Press, 2010); and Halberstam, *In a Queer Time*, 46–61.

39. See William Cheng, "Theory, Born This Way," response to Queer Music Theory panel at AMS/SMT joint meeting in Milwaukee, WI (7 November 2014).

40. "How to Sound Gay: David M. Halperin in Conversation with Ryan Dohoney," *AMS Pittsburgh 2013 (7–10 November) Program & Abstracts* (2013), http://www.amsnet.org/pittsburgh/abstracts.pdf, 138.

41. See David M. Halperin, *How to Be Gay* (Cambridge, MA: Belknap Press of Harvard University Press, 2012), 82–125.

42. Heather Hadlock, "How to Sound Gay—Discipline (and Punish)?" *Still a Musicologist* (20 November 2013), http://amsfellowtraveler.wordpress.com/2013/11. See also Wayne Koestenbaum, *The Queen's Throat: Opera, Homosexuality, and the Mystery of Desire* (New York: Poseidon Press, 1993).

43. One area where I feel *How to Be Gay* falters, irrespective of music, is its strategic yet impolitic neglect of queer categories and genres outside a predominantly privileged rubric of white, male, cis, middle-class, able-bodied, domiciled, youthful gays. As Halperin, at the AMS session, doubled down on the desirable aspects of embracing legible gayness, Stephan Pennington rose from the audience to voice the indispensable caveat that for many people—especially those who are, for example, trans, homeless, of color—markers of queerness can drastically heighten one's susceptibility to violence and injustice. Not everyone, in other words, has the security or wherewithal to benefit from knowing what it means (or takes) to be *straightforwardly gay* in the first place. See Heather Hadlock, "'How to Sound Gay' at the AMS 2013 Meeting in Pittsburgh," *Still a Musicologist* (12 November 2013), http://amsfellowtraveler.wordpress.com/2013/11/12/how-to-sound-gay-at-the-ams-2013-meeting-in-pittsburgh.

44. See Maynard Solomon, "Franz Schubert and the Peacocks of Benvenuto Cellini," *19th-Century Music* 12 (1989): 193–206; and Rita Steblin, "The Peacock's Tale: Schubert's Sexuality Reconsidered," *19th-Century Music* 17 (1993): 5–33.

45. See Susan McClary, "Constructions of Subjectivity in Schubert's Music," in Brett, Wood, and Thomas, *Queering the Pitch*, 205–33.

46. Marcia J. Citron, "Feminist Waves and Classical Music: Pedagogy, Performance, Research," *Women & Music* 8 (2004): 50.

47. McClary recounts: "I had several occasions to stand in a long line in the women's room, where I was privy to unrelieved carping about this woman who was 'determined to drag our Schubert through the mud.' [Maynard] Solomon's article had been circulated in advance, and some of those who spoke during the course of the day deemed it appropriate to take gratuitous swipes at him ('a pornographer'), with the obvious approval of the crowd" ("Constructions of Subjectivity," 206). See also Elaine Barkin, "either/or," *Perspectives of New Music* 30 (1992): 206–33.

48. Much ink has been spilled over how McClary's studies of music and sexuality have been mischaracterized, misunderstood, and misappropriated. Suzanne Cusick calls McClary "one of the most misquoted musicologists in history" ("Gender, Musi-

cology, and Feminism," in Cook and Everist, *Rethinking Music,* 488 n. 30); see also Robert Fink, "Beethoven Antihero: Sex, Violence, and the Aesthetics of Failure, or Listening to the Ninth Symphony as Postmodern Sublime," in Dell'Antonio, *Beyond Structural Listening?,* 109–53. McClary has reflected on the wild reception of *Feminine Endings,* noting that "no one (least of all this author) could have anticipated that a drab-looking little book from the University of Minnesota Press would be cause for a twenty-year reflection" ("Feminine Endings at Twenty," *TRANS: Revista Transcultural de Música* 15 [2011], http://www.sibetrans.com/trans/public/docs/trans_15_02_ McClary.pdf).

49. Sedgwick, "Paranoid Reading," 134.

50. Silvan S. Tomkins, *Affect, Imagery, Consciousness,* vol. 2, *The Negative Affects* (New York: Springer, 1963), 404–5. Bruno Latour puts it this way: "As soon as naïve believers are thus inflated by some belief in their own importance, in their own projective capacity, you strike them by a second uppercut and humiliate them again, this time by showing that, whatever they think, their behavior is entirely determined by the action of powerful causalities coming from objective reality they don't see, but that you, yes you, the never sleeping critic, alone can see. Isn't this fabulous? Isn't it really worth going to graduate school to study critique?" ("Critique," 239).

51. In seminal sociological projects, Erving Goffman proposed that people's everyday behaviors are structured by performative efforts to avoid the embarrassment of selves and others (see "Embarrassment and Social Organization," *American Journal of Sociology* 62 [1956]: 264–71; and *The Presentation of Self in Everyday Life* [Garden City, NY: Doubleday, 1959]). For concise reflections on the shame (and, in a way, sheepishness) that can attend the privileges of performing research in an age of Google and Wikipedia, see Benjamin Walton, "Quirk Shame," *Representations* 132 (2015): 121–29.

52. See Rev. Romal J. Tune, "Bullying Starts at Home," *Huffington Post* (21 May 2012), http://www.huffingtonpost.com/rev-romal-j-tune/bullying-starts-at-home_1_b_1528898.html.

53. Tavia Nyong'o, "The Student Demand," *Bully Bloggers* (17 November 2015), http://bullybloggers.wordpress.com/2015/11/17/the-student-demand. Nyong'o is writing here about Yale University's 2015 Halloween/housemaster controversy. See also Kate Manne and Jason Stanley, "When Free Speech Becomes a Political Weapon," *Chronicle Review* (13 November 2015), http://chronicle.com/article/When-Free-Speech-Becomes-a/234207.

Chapter 4

1. Gideon Levy, "Demons in the Skies of the Gaza Strip," *Haaretz,* available at *Lebanon Wire* (6 November 2005), http://www.lebanonwire.com/1105/05110601HZ. asp. See also María Edurne Zuazu, "Loud but Non-lethal: Acoustic Stagings and State-Sponsored Violence," *Women & Music* 19 (2015): 151–59.

2. See Steve Swayne, "Music Is Power: Michael Dunn, Jordan Davis, and How We Respond When People Turn up the Volume," *Pacific Standard* (5 March 2014), http://www.psmag.com/navigation/books-and-culture/music-power-volume-sound-michael-dunn-jordan-davis-75929; George Prochnik, *In Pursuit of Silence: Listening for Meaning in a World of Noise* (New York: Doubleday, 2010); Lisa Goines, "Noise Pollution: A Modern Plague," *Southern Medical Journal* 100 (2007): 287–94; and Stephen A. Stansfeld and Mark P. Matheson, "Noise Pollution: Non-auditory Effects on Health," *British Medical Bulletin* 68 (2003): 243–57. See also Michael C. Heller, "Between

Silence and Pain: Loudness and the Affective Encounter," *Sound Studies: An Interdisciplinary Journal* 1 (2015): 40–58.

3. See Suzanne Cusick, "'You Are in a Place That Is out of the World . . .': Music in the Detention Camps of the 'Global War on Terror,'" *Journal of the Society for American Music* 2 (2008): 1–26. Cusick urges readers to remember the "important, irrefutable fact that Americans have theorized and deployed music and sound as weapons of interrogation for at least fifty years. It is not a phenomenon of the current administration or the current wars; it is not news. The only news is that in the last few years we have become increasingly aware of it; that, and perhaps the unnerving fact that our awareness of this practice has provoked no public outcry" (3–4). On sound, war, torture, and ecologies of acoustic violence, see also J. Martin Daughtry, *Listening to War: Sound, Music, Trauma, and Survival in Wartime Iraq* (New York: Oxford University Press, 2015); James Kennaway, *Bad Vibrations: The History of the Idea of Music as Cause of Disease* (Burlington, VT: Ashgate, 2012), 147–53; Goodman, *Sonic Warfare*, 8–12; Bruce Johnson and Martin Cloonan, *Dark Side of the Tune: Popular Music and Violence* (Burlington, VT: Ashgate, 2009); and Jonathan Pieslak, *Sound Targets: American Soldiers and Music in the Iraq War* (Bloomington: Indiana University Press, 2009).

4. See Elaine Scarry, *Rule of Law, Misrule of Men* (Cambridge, MA: MIT Press, 2010), 132–33.

5. Cusick, "Musicology, Torture, Repair," par. 4.

6. Senate Committee on Intelligence, "Unclassified: Committee Study of the Central Intelligence Agency's Detention and Interrogation Program," released to the public on 9 December 2014. Document available at (among other sites) *New York Times*, http://www.nytimes.com/interactive/2014/12/09/world/cia-torture-report-document.html?_r=0.

7. See Suzanne Cusick, "Music as Torture / Music as Weapon," *TRANS: Revista Transcultural de Música* 10 (2006), http://www.sibetrans.com/trans/articulo/152/music-as-torture-music-as-weapon.

8. On music torture and sexual humiliation, Cusick explains: "The belief that music *could* torture emerges, in the blogosphere, among people who feel themselves to be 'tortured' by certain musics—rap music, disco, sentimental ballads, the music of Yoko Ono. Additionally, the idea that music could torture seems linked both to homophobia and to heterosexual fantasy; in fact, the most lively repertoire discussions propose as torturous popular musics easily associated with either homosexuality or the effeminacy perceived to come from being too emotionally engaged with women. These folk seem readily to imagine themselves moving from tortured to torturer, and imagine music torturing by either a racial/cultural affront or, more often, by feminizing and/or queerifying Muslim men: either way, detainees would be emasculated (and the bloggers' masculinity, presumably, strengthened)" ("Music as Torture").

9. The effects of musical bombardment go beyond mere facts of physical and psychic assault. Cusick describes how one particular detainee's attempts to "resist pain with thought" were acoustically "jammed" by continuous, subjectivity-invading music ("Towards an Acoustemology of Detention in the 'Global War on Terror,'" in *Music, Sound and Space: Transformations of Public and Private Experience*, ed. Georgina Born [Cambridge: Cambridge University Press, 2013], 284). See also Lily E. Hirsch, *Music in American Crime Prevention and Punishment* (Ann Arbor: University of Michigan Press, 2012), 119–20.

10. Ariel Dorfman, "The Tyranny of Torture," in *Torture: A Collection*, rev. ed., ed. Sanford Levinson (New York: Oxford University Press, 2006), 9.

11. Dorfman, "The Tyranny of Torture," 8.

12. "*Sesame Street* Music Torture," *Young Turks* (3 June 2012), http://www.youtube.com/watch?v=IJOc0bOycf8, emphasis added.

13. Elaine Scarry remarks that "the human capacity to injure other people is very great precisely because our capacity to imagine other people is very small" ("The Difficulty of Imagining Other Persons," in *Human Rights in Political Transitions: Gettysburg to Bosnia*, ed. Carla Hesse and Robert Post [New York: Zone Books, 1999], 285).

14. Exercises in selective imagination underscore the polemics of the infamous ticking time-bomb scenario (the hypothetical question of whether one would or should torture a terrorist who is believed to know the location of a presumed bomb about to go off in a city). Concerning moral and legal responsibility, Elaine Scarry notes: "It is a peculiar characteristic of such hypothetical arguments on behalf of torture that the arguer can always 'imagine' someone large-spirited enough to overcome (on behalf of a city's population) his aversion to torture, but not so large-spirited that he or she can also accept his or her own legal culpability and punishment" ("Five Errors in the Reasoning of Alan Dershowitz," in Levinson, *Torture*, 282); cf. Alan Dershowitz, *Why Terrorism Works: Understanding the Threat, Responding to the Challenge* (New Haven, CT: Yale University Press, 2004), 131–63.

15. Alex Stone, "Why Waiting Is Torture," *New York Times* (18 August 2012), http://www.nytimes.com/2012/08/19/opinion/sunday/why-waiting-in-line-is-torture.html?_r=0.

16. Ilias Chrissochoidis, "Composed in Hypocrisy," *Chronicle Review* (8 May 2009), http://chronicle.com/article/Composed-in-Hypocrisy/44313.

17. See David Danzig, "Countering the Jack Bauer Effect: An Examination of How to Limit the Influence of TV's Most Popular, and Most Brutal, Hero," in *Screening Torture: Media Representations of State Terror and Political Domination*, ed. Michael Flynn and Fabiola F. Salek (New York: Columbia University Press, 2012), 21–34.

18. The song in this *Homeland* scene is "Orphan" by the band Gridlink.

19. In an odd admission, this is what the player-character Trevor says to the detainee following the torture sequence: "The media and the government would have us believe that torture is some necessary thing. We need it to get information, to assert ourselves. Did we get any information out of you? Exactly. Torture's for the torturer . . . or for the guy giving orders to the torturer. You torture for the good times—we should all admit that. It's useless as a means of getting information" (Rockstar Games, *Grand Theft Auto V*).

20. Pigeonhammer, "Why the Torture Scene in GTA V Made Me Quit Playing," *IGN* (24 September 2013), http://www.ign.com/blogs/pigeonhammer/2013/09/24/why-the-torture-scene-in-gta-v-made-me-quit-playing.

21. See Erik Kain, "*Grand Theft Auto V* Torture Scene Is Satire," *Forbes* (21 September 2013), http://www.forbes.com/sites/erikkain/2013/09/21/grand-theft-auto-v-torture-scene-is-satire; and Alex Hern, "*Grand Theft Auto V* under Fire for Graphic Torture Scene," *Guardian* (18 September 2013), http://www.theguardian.com/technology/2013/sep/18/grand-theft-auto-5-under-fire-for-graphic-torture-scene.

22. Pieslak, *Sound Targets*, 172.

23. Pieslak, *Sound Targets*, 172. "If 'I Love You' were played repeatedly for an hour," suggests Pieslak, "the complete melody would be heard 120 times and the

main melodic motive would be heard 360 times. Adding to the repetition, the singing style of the children, presumably Barney's target audience of preschoolers or young children, seems unnaturally uniform and calm. It is hard to imagine a group of four- to six-year-olds singing with such precision, clarity, and restraint, and for me, the vocal performance is unnervingly artificial. The repetitive timbres of music intended for children make for a powerful source of antagonism" (171). Assuming a basic comprehension of English, moreover, a detainee's idea of what love is might break down from being forced to listen to sing-songy reiterations of "I love you" at high volumes and for hours on end. Semantics and affects crash together, twisting one's feelings and understandings of love even after the torture stops.

24. Ltlmason, "Can You Survive 10 Minutes of Barney Saying 'I Love You'?" *YouTube* (7 February 2012), http://www.youtube.com/watch?v=KOmVMWMyTBE.

25. Quoted in Andy Worthington, "Hit Me Baby One More Time," *Counterpunch* (15 December 2008), http://www.counterpunch.org/2008/12/15/hit-me-baby-one-more-time.

26. Sean Michaels, "Industrial Band Skinny Puppy Demand $666,000 after Music Is Used in Guantánamo Torture," *Guardian* (7 February 2014), http://www.theguardian.com/music/2014/feb/07/skinny-puppy-payment-guantanamo.

27. Cusick, "Musicology, Torture, Repair," par. 13; cf. Chrissochoidis, "Composed in Hypocrisy"; Jonathan Bellman, "Music as Torture: A Dissonant Counterpoint," *Dial M for Musicology* (21 August 2007), http://dialmformusicology.com/2007/08/21/music-as-tortur; and Lara Pellegrinelli, "Scholarly Discord," *Chronicle of Higher Education* (8 May 2009), http://www.chroniclecareers.com/article/Scholarly-Discord/44312.

28. Society for American Music, "Resolutions Introduced at the SAM Business Meeting" (3 March 2007), http://www.american-music.org/organization/tick_resolution.php.

29. On the restrictions—or lack thereof—imposed by the American Psychiatric Association, the American Medical Association, and the American Psychological Association concerning their members' direct participation in U.S. intelligence interrogations, see Jan de Vos, "Depsychologizing Torture," *Critical Inquiry* 37 (2011): 286–314; and Tom Bartlett, "What a Bombshell Report Tells Us about the APA's Abetting of Torture," *Chronicle of Higher Education* (13 July 2015), http://chronicle.com/article/What-a-Bombshell-Report-Tells/231543/?key=T2l2IgI7aScXZitiamwQaGsEOHd kYx1xayAYbC0iblBWEg.

30. As Cusick writes: "Every amplified sound in these camps, and therefore every bit of music, *is* the United States' transformation of the energy in Middle Eastern oil into violent, violating sonic energy aimed directly at the people whose land yielded that oil—people who are as powerless to resist our thirst for their lands' resources as they are to resist the use of those transformed resources against them" ("You Are in a Place," 18). See also Sally Macarthur, "Music and Violence," *Musicology Australia* 34 (2012): 101–10.

31. On the cultural and technological genesis of modern sirens (along with their sonorous powers and dangers), see Alexander Rehding, "Of Sirens Old and New," in *The Oxford Handbook of Mobile Music Studies*, vol. 2, ed. Sumanth Gopinath and Jason Stanyek (New York: Oxford University Press, 2014), 77–106.

32. Morag Josephine Grant states: "For the historical evidence suggests that as long as there is torture, there will be music used in the service of torture. The answer, then, is easy to say, but less simple to achieve: Show me a world without music torture,

and I will show you a world without torture" ("Pathways to Music Torture," *Transposition* 4 [2014]: par. 37).

33. Martha Nussbaum, *Political Emotions: Why Love Matters for Justice* (Cambridge, MA: Harvard University Press, 2013), 384.

34. Yik Yak's mottos include "Share your thoughts and keep your privacy," and "Get a live feed of what everyone's saying around you" (http://www.yikyakapp.com).

35. Scheridan Vorwaller, "The Marching Band Agreed to Yield," student paper (12 May 2015), quoted with permission.

36. See Marie Suzanne Thompson, "Beyond Unwanted Sound: Noise, Affect and Aesthetic Moralism," Ph.D. dissertation, Newcastle University (2014); Anahid Kassabian, *Ubiquitous Listening: Affect, Attention, and Distributed Subjectivity* (Berkeley: University of California Press, 2013); Khadija White, "Considering Sound: Reflecting on the Language, Meaning and Entailments of Noise," in *Reverberations: The Philosophy, Aesthetics and Politics of Noise*, ed. Michael Goddard, Benjamin Halligan, and Paul Hegarty (New York: Continuum, 2012), 233–43; Hans-Joachim Braun, "Turning a Deaf Ear? Industrial Noise and Noise Control in Germany since the 1920s," in Pinch and Bijsterveld, *Handbook of Sound Studies*, 58–78; Paul Hegarty, *Noise/Music: A History* (New York: Continuum, 2007), 153–66; and Jonathan Sterne, *The Audible Past: Cultural Origins of Sound Reproduction* (Durham, NC: Duke University Press, 2003), 117–22.

37. See Elaine Scarry, *Who Defended the Country?* (Boston: Beacon Press, 2003); Carol Johnson, "The Politics of Affective Citizenship: From Blair to Obama," *Citizenship Studies* 14 (2010): 495–509; and Serge Moscovici, Gabriel Mugny, and Eddy Van Avermaet, eds., *Perspectives on Minority Influence* (Cambridge: Cambridge University Press, 1985). With thanks to Graziella Parati for suggesting this literature on citizenship.

38. See Derald Wing Sue, *Microaggressions in Everyday Life: Race, Gender, and Sexual Orientation* (Hoboken, NJ: Wiley, 2010).

39. Michael J. Shapiro, *Studies in Trans-disciplinary Method: After the Aesthetic Turn* (New York: Routledge, 2013), 100.

40. Shapiro, *Studies in Trans-disciplinary Method*, 100.

41. See Irene W. Leigh, Donna A. Morere, and Caroline Kobek Pezzarossi, "Deaf Gain: Beyond Deaf Culture," in *Deaf Gain: Raising the Stakes for Human Diversity*, ed. H-Dirksen L. Bauman and Joseph J. Murray (Minneapolis: University of Minnesota Press, 2014), 356–71; H-Dirksen L. Bauman and Joseph J. Murray, "Deaf Studies in the 21st Century: 'Deaf-gain' and the Future of Human Diversity," in *The Oxford Handbook of Deaf Studies, Language, and Education*, vol. 2, ed. Marc Marschark and Patricia Elizabeth Spencer (New York: Oxford University Press, 2010), 210–25; and Michael Bérubé, "Disability, Democracy, and the New Genetics," in *Genetics, Disability, and Deafness*, ed. John Vickrey Cleve (Washington, DC: Gallaudet University Press, 2004), 202–20.

42. For a neuroscientific versus social-model discussion of autism and sensory overload, see respectively Catherine Manning et al., "Enhanced Integration of Motion Information in Children with Autism," *Journal of Neuroscience* 35 (2015): 6979–86; and Anne M. Donnellan, David A. Hill, and Martha R. Leary, "Rethinking Autism: Implications of Sensory and Movement Differences," *Disability Studies Quarterly* 30 (2010), http://dsq-sds.org/article/view/1060/1225. See also Michael B. Bakan, "'Don't Go Changing to Try and Please Me': Combating Essentialism through Ethnography in the Ethnomusicology of Autism," *Ethnomusicology* 59 (2015): 116–44; Richard Brom-

field, *Embracing Asperger's: A Primer for Parents and Professionals* (Philadelphia: Jessica Kingsley, 2011), 68–76; and Sharon Heller, *Too Loud, Too Bright, Too Fast, Too Tight: What to Do If You Are Sensory Defensive in an Overstimulating World* (New York: Harper Perennial, 2003).

43. Cynthia Kim, *Nerdy, Shy, and Socially Inappropriate: A User Guide to an Asperger Life* (Philadelphia: Jessica Kingsley, 2015), 111. See also Julia Bascom, ed., *Loud Hands: Autistic People, Speaking* (Washington, DC: Autistic Press, 2012); and Carol Stock Kranowitz, *The Out-of-Sync Child: Recognizing and Coping with Sensory Processing Disorder* (New York: Berkley Publishing Group, 2005). I'm grateful to Andrew Dell'Antonio and Michael Bakan for recommending these sources.

44. See Steve Silberman, *NeuroTribes: The Legacy of Autism and the Future of Neurodiversity* (New York: Avery, 2015), 471–72; and Alice M. Hammel and Ryan M. Hourigan, *Teaching Music to Students with Autism* (New York: Oxford University Press, 2013), 113.

45. "About Us," *Hacking Health* (2 October 2015), http://www.hackinghealth.ca/about/about.

46. Taylan Kay, "Description: Auti-Sim," *Game Jolt* (26 February 2013), http://gamejolt.com/games/auti-sim/12761.

47. One person (username andrewkilroy5) on the simulation's website wrote: "Should I laugh at this or should I be horrified by it? I am Autistic and I think this is terrible stereotyping." To which creator Taylan Kay responded: "Hi Andrew. I'm very sorry that you found this horrifying. I understand where you are coming from and wish that we could have done a better job at describing your experience with autism. The reality of the situation though is that it is not possible to make this a 100% accurate simulation for everyone with autism, as there is a wide variation in how each person experiences hypersensitivity. Chances are someone else on the ASD would find your description of it incomplete as well. I will concede that the 'Sim' in Auti-Sim might have caused a different expectation, and it is a valid criticism. Going forward, we should consider doing a better job of communicating the goal of our project, which is to raise awareness of and empathy for hypersensitivity" (andrewkilroy5 and Taylan Kay, "Comments: Page 9," *Game Jolt* [2 March 2013], http://gamejolt.com/games/auti-sim/12761?comment_page=9).

48. Emma Tracey, "Not Just a Game: Is It Right to 'Recreate' Disability?" *BBC* (11 June 2014), http://www.bbc.com/news/blogs-ouch-27763085.

49. See Kiri Blakeley, "Stop with the Stupid Fat Suit Experiments, Please," *Forbes* (26 October 2011), http://www.forbes.com/sites/kiriblakeley/2011/10/26/stop-with-the-stupid-fat-suit-experiments-please; Darlena Cunha, "Sorry, Gwyneth Paltrow, Poverty Tourism Is Gross," *TIME* (13 April 2015), http://time.com/3819349/gwyneth-paltrow-poverty-tourism; and Bob Ma, "A Trip into the Controversy: A Study of Slum Tourism Travel Motivations," *Penn Humanities Forum on Connections* (2010), http://repository.upenn.edu/cgi/viewcontent.cgi?article=1011&context=uhf_2010.

50. Martha Nussbaum, *Upheavals of Thought: The Intelligence of Emotions* (Cambridge: Cambridge University Press, 2003), 328. Nussbaum's description of empathy's "twofold" nature resonates with writers' depictions of games as imaginative exercises in double consciousness, wherein a player may identify with an avatar or a role yet retain an awareness of its artificiality (see Katie Salen and Eric Zimmerman, *Rules of Play: Game Design Fundamentals* [Cambridge, MA: MIT Press, 2004], 453).

51. Susan Brison, "On Empathy as a Necessary, but Not Sufficient, Foundation for

Justice (A Response to Slote)," in *Law, Virtue, and Justice*, ed. Amalia Amaya and Ho Hock Lai (Oxford: Hart, 2013), 303–9; see also Michael Slote, *The Ethics of Care and Empathy* (New York: Routledge, 2007); and Susan Sontag, *Regarding the Pain of Others* (New York: Farrar, Straus & Giroux, 2003).

Coda

1. Joseph Kerman, *Contemplating Music: Challenges to Musicology* (Cambridge, MA: Harvard University Press, 1985), 230.

2. LRAD Corporation, "LRAD Corporation Reports Fiscal Year 2014 Financial Results," *LRAD* (2014), http://www.lradx.com/press_release/lrad-corporation-reports-fiscal-third-quarter-2014-financial-results.

3. LRAD Corporation, "Winter 2015 Newsletter," *LRAD* (2015), http://www.lradx.com/investors/newsroom/press-releases/lrad-newsletter.

4. LRAD Corporation, "Safeguarding the Public & Protecting the Officers," *LRAD* (n.d.), http://www.lradx.com/application/law-enforcement. In a promotional video, Robert Putnam, senior marketing manager for the LRAD Corporation, says that "we really don't look at this as any kind of a weapon, non-lethal or otherwise" ("LRAD—Long Range Acoustic Hailing Devices," *AOL/YouTube* [14 September 2012], http://www.youtube.com/watch?v=1P3FsLMKwJE).

5. Juliette Volcler, *Extremely Loud: Sound as a Weapon*, trans. Carol Volk (New York: New Press, 2013), 112.

6. Quoted in Nick Pinto, "NYC Cops Are Blithely Firing a Potentially Deafening Sound Cannon at Peaceful Protesters," *Gothamist* (13 December 2014), http://gothamist.com/2014/12/13/lrad_nypd_protests_sound.php.

7. Amnesty International USA, "On the Streets of America: Human Rights Abuses in Ferguson" (24 October 2014), http://www.amnestyusa.org/research/reports/on-the-streets-of-america-human-rights-abuses-in-ferguson?page=show.

8. Witold J. Walczak et al., "Karen L. Piper vs. City of Pittsburgh et al.," full claim available at http://www.aclupa.org/download_file/view_inline/791/486, 5.

9. Walczak et al., "Karen L. Piper," 8.

10. American Civil Liberties Union, "ACLU-PA Client Karen Piper" (21 September 2011), http://www.youtube.com/watch?v=kNsaSyruods.

11. Gideon Orion Oliver, "The NYPD's Use of Long Range Acoustic Devices for Crowd Control," *Scribd* (12 December 2014), http://www.scribd.com/doc/250122281/The-NYPD-s-Use-of-Long-Range-Acoustic-Devices-for-Crowd-Control.

12. See Lily Hay Newman, "This Is the Sound Cannon Used against Protesters in Ferguson," *Slate* (14 August 2014), http://www.slate.com/blogs/future_tense/2014/08/14/lrad_long_range_acoustic_device_sound_cannons_were_used_for_crowd_control.html.

13. See Neil Davison, *"Non-lethal" Weapons* (New York: Palgrave Macmillan, 2009), 1–3. Even when an LRAD has been set to suppress mode, points out María Edurne Zuazu regarding Ferguson's protests, the "tone not only marked out and showed the site-specific impunity of police abuse but, because of their much-publicized ruthlessness and of the mobile repeatability of the LRAD tone, also predicted more extraordinary episodes" ("Loud but Non-lethal," 157).

14. See Marty Favor, "How Do They Matter?" *Huffington Post* (20 May 2015),

http://www.huffingtonpost.com/marty-favor/how-do-they-matter_b_7312320.html.

15. LRAD Corporation, "Extended Range & EOF Communication," http://www.lradx.com/application/defense.

16. Cusick, "Musicology, Torture, Repair," pars. 22–23.

17. Cusick, "Musicology, Torture, Repair," par. 20.

18. Brison, *Aftermath*, 116.

19. See Harris, *Dignity and Vulnerability*, 115; and Sen, *Idea of Justice*, 390–92.

20. See Barbara Ehrenreich, *Bright-Sided: How the Relentless Promotion of Positive Thinking Has Undermined America* (New York: Metropolitan Books, 2009), 1–13; cf. Walter Laqueur, *Optimism in Politics: Reflections on Contemporary History* (New Brunswick, NJ: Transaction Publishers, 2014).

21. See Martha Albertson Fineman, *The Autonomy Myth: A Theory of Dependency* (New York: New Press, 2004); and Mona Harrington, *Care and Equality: Inventing a New Family Politics* (New York: Knopf, 1999).

22. Halberstam, *Queer Art of Failure*, 3.

Works Cited

✦ ✦ ✦

"AAU Campus Survey on Sexual Assault and Sexual Misconduct." *Association of American Universities* (2015), http://www.aau.edu/Climate-Survey.aspx?id=16525.

Abbate, Carolyn. "Music—Drastic or Gnostic?" *Critical Inquiry* 30 (2004): 505–36.

"About Us." *Hacking Health* (2015), http://www.hackinghealth.ca/about/about.

Ackerman, Diane. *A Natural History of the Senses*. New York: Random House, 1990.

Adams, Byron. "Elgar's Later Oratorios: Roman Catholicism, Decadence and the Wagnerian Dialectic of Shame and Grace." In *The Cambridge Companion to Elgar*, edited by Daniel M. Grimley and Julian Rushton, 81–105. Cambridge: Cambridge University Press, 2004.

Ahmed, Sara. *The Promise of Happiness*. Durham, NC: Duke University Press, 2010.

Alcoff, Linda. "The Problem of Speaking for Others." *Cultural Critique* 20 (1991–92): 5–32.

Allen, Amy. *The Politics of Our Selves: Power, Autonomy, and Gender in Contemporary Critical Theory*. New York: Columbia University Press, 2008.

American Civil Liberties Union. "ACLU-PA Client Karen Piper" (21 September 2011), http://www.youtube.com/watch?v=kNsaSyruods.

Amnesty International USA. "On the Streets of America: Human Rights Abuses in Ferguson" (24 October 2014), http://www.amnestyusa.org/research/reports/on-the-streets-of-america-human-rights-abuses-in-ferguson?page=show.

Anderson, Tim. *Sweet Tooth*. Seattle: Lake Union, 2014.

Andrews, Molly. *Narrative Imagination and Everyday Life*. New York: Oxford University Press, 2014.

Applegate, William V. "Abdominal Cutaneous Nerve Entrapment Syndrome (ACNES): A Commonly Overlooked Cause of Abdominal Pain." *Permanente Journal* 6 (2002): 20–27.

Attinello, Paul. "Performance and/or Shame: A Mosaic of Gay (and Other) Perceptions." *repercussions* 4 (1995): 97–130.

Bakan, Michael B. "Being Applied in the Ethnomusicology of Autism." In *The Oxford*

Handbook of Applied Ethnomusicology, edited by Svanibor Pettan and Jeff Todd Titon, 278–316. New York: Oxford University Press, 2015.

Bakan, Michael B. "'Don't Go Changing to Try and Please Me': Combating Essentialism through Ethnography in the Ethnomusicology of Autism." *Ethnomusicology* 59 (2015): 116–44.

Barber-Stetson, Claire. "Slow Processing: A New Minor Literature by Autists and Modernists." *Journal of Modern Literature* 38 (2014): 147–65.

Barkin, Elaine. "either/or." *Perspectives of New Music* 30 (1992): 206–33.

Bartlett, Tom. "What a Bombshell Report Tells Us about the APA's Abetting of Torture." *Chronicle of Higher Education* (13 July 2015), http://chronicle.com/article/What-a-Bombshell-Report-Tells/231543/?key=T2l2IgI7aScXZitiamwQaGsEOHd kYx1xayAYbC0iblBWEg.

Bascom, Julia, ed. *Loud Hands: Autistic People, Speaking*. Washington, DC: Autistic Press, 2012.

Bauman, H-Dirksen L., and Joseph J. Murray. "Deaf Studies in the 21st Century: 'Deaf-gain' and the Future of Human Diversity." In *The Oxford Handbook of Deaf Studies, Language, and Education*, vol. 2, edited by Marc Marschark and Patricia Elizabeth Spencer, 210–25. New York: Oxford University Press, 2010.

Bellman, Jonathan. "Music as Torture: A Dissonant Counterpoint." *Dial M for Musicology* (21 August 2007), http://dialmformusicology.com/2007/08/21/music-as-tortur.

Bennett, Jane. *Vibrant Matter: A Political Ecology of Things*. Durham, NC: Duke University Press, 2010.

Berendt, Joachim-Ernst. *The Third Ear*. Translated by Tim Nevill. Perth, Australia: Element, 1985.

Berger, Karol. "Musicology According to Don Giovanni, or: Should We Get Drastic?" *Journal of Musicology* 22 (2005): 490–501.

Berlant, Lauren. *Cruel Optimism*. Durham, NC: Duke University Press, 2011.

Berlant, Lauren, and Lee Edelman. *Sex, or the Unbearable*. Durham, NC: Duke University Press, 2014.

Bérubé, Michael. "Disability, Democracy, and the New Genetics." In *Genetics, Disability, and Deafness*, edited by John Vickrey Cleve, 202–20. Washington, DC: Gallaudet University Press, 2004.

Bérubé, Michael, and Jennifer Ruth. *The Humanities, Higher Education, and Academic Freedom: Three Necessary Arguments*. New York: Palgrave Macmillan, 2015.

Bhabha, Homi. *The Location of Culture*. New York: Routledge, 1994.

Biro, David. *Listening to Pain: Finding Words, Compassion, and Relief*. New York: W. W. Norton, 2010.

Blakeley, Kiri. "Stop with the Stupid Fat Suit Experiments, Please." *Forbes* (26 October 2011), http://www.forbes.com/sites/kiriblakeley/2011/10/26/stop-with-the-stupid-fat-suit-experiments-please.

Bloechl, Olivia, with Melanie Lowe. "Introduction: Rethinking Difference." In *Rethinking Difference in Music Scholarship*, edited by Olivia Bloechl, Melanie Lowe, and Jeffrey Kallberg, 1–52. Cambridge: Cambridge University Press, 2015.

Blow, Charles M. *Fire Shut Up in My Bones*. New York: Houghton Mifflin Harcourt, 2014.

Bogost, Ian. *Alien Phenomenology: or, What It's Like to Be a Thing*. Minneapolis: University of Minnesota Press, 2012.

Bohlman, Philip. "Musicology as a Political Act." *Journal of Musicology* 11 (1993): 411–36.

Bourke, Joanna. "Pain Sensitivity: An Unnatural History from 1800 to 1965." *Journal of Medical Humanities* 35 (2014): 301–19.

Boyd, Brian. "Laughter and Literature: A Play Theory of Humor." *Philosophy & Literature* 28 (2004): 1–22.

Boylan, Jennifer Finney. "In the Early Morning Rain." In *It Gets Better: Coming Out, Overcoming Bullying, and Creating a Life Worth Living*, edited by Dan Savage and Terry Miller, 18–21. New York: Dutton, 2011.

Braun, Hans-Joachim. "Turning a Deaf Ear? Industrial Noise and Noise Control in Germany since the 1920s." In *The Oxford Handbook of Sound Studies*, edited by Trevor Pinch and Karin Bijsterveld, 58–78. New York: Oxford University Press, 2012.

Brekhus, Wayne H., John F. Galliher, and Jaber F. Gubrium. "The Need for Thin Description." *Qualitative Inquiry* 11 (2005): 861–79.

Brett, Philip. "Musicality, Essentialism, and the Closet." In *Queering the Pitch: The New Gay and Lesbian Musicology*, 2nd ed., edited by Philip Brett, Elizabeth Wood, and Gary C. Thomas, 9–26. New York: Routledge, 2006.

Brison, Susan. *Aftermath: Violence and the Remaking of a Self*. Princeton, NJ: Princeton University Press, 2002.

Brison, Susan. "Everyday Atrocities and Ordinary Miracles, or Why I (Still) Bear Witness to Sexual Violence (but Not Too Often)." *Women's Studies Quarterly* 36 (2008): 188–98.

Brison, Susan. "On Empathy as a Necessary, but Not Sufficient, Foundation for Justice (A Response to Slote)." In *Law, Virtue, and Justice*, edited by Amalia Amaya and Ho Hock Lai, 303–9. Oxford: Hart, 2013.

Brison, Susan. "Speech and Other Acts." *Legal Theory* 10 (2004): 261–72.

Bromfield, Richard. *Embracing Asperger's: A Primer for Parents and Professionals*. Philadelphia: Jessica Kingsley, 2011.

Brown, Bill, ed. *Things*. Chicago: University of Chicago Press, 2004.

Brueggemann, Brenda Jo, and James A. Fredal. "Studying Disability Rhetorically." In *Disability Discourse*, edited by Mairian Corker and Sally French, 129–35. Philadelphia: Open University Press, 1999.

Bruhm, Steven. *Reflecting Narcissus: A Queer Aesthetic*. Minneapolis: University of Minnesota Press, 2000.

Burkholder, J. Peter. "From Radical Fairy to Tenured Faculty: Personal Reflections on Gayness, Music, and Musicology." *GLSG Newsletter of the American Musicological Society* 12 (2002): 3–8.

Butler, Judith. *Frames of War: When Is Life Grievable?* New York: Verso, 2009.

Cain, M. Celia. "Of Pain, Passing and Longing for Music." *Disability & Society* 25 (2010): 747–51.

Campbell, Patricia Shehan, and Trevor Wiggins, eds. *The Oxford Handbook of Children's Musical Cultures*. New York: Oxford University Press, 2013.

Card, Claudia. "Caring and Evil." *Hypatia* 5 (1990): 101–8.

Caron, David. "Shame on Me, or the Naked Truth about Marlene Dietrich." In *Gay Shame*, edited by David M. Halperin and Valerie Traub, 117–31. Chicago: University of Chicago Press, 2009.

Cheng, William. "Meritocracy's Darker Notes." *Huffington Post* (22 May 2015), http://www.huffingtonpost.com/william-cheng/meritocracys-darker-notes_b_7423774.html.

Cheng, William. "My Students Never Use the First Person Voice. I Wish They Would." *Slate* (11 June 2015), http://www.slate.com/blogs/lexicon_valley/2015/06/11/my_students_never_use_the_first_person_voice_i_wish_they_would.html.

Cheng, William. "Pleasure's Discontents." *Journal of the American Musicological Society* 66 (2013): 840–44.

Cheng, William. *Sound Play: Video Games and the Musical Imagination.* New York: Oxford University Press, 2014.

Cheng, William. "Theory, Born This Way." Response to Queer Music Theory panel at AMS/SMT joint meeting in Milwaukee, WI (7 November 2014).

Chomsky, Noam. *Profit over People: Neoliberalism and Global Order.* New York: Seven Stories Press, 1999.

Chrisman, Wendy L. "A Reflection on Inspiration: A Recuperative Call for Emotion in Disability Studies." *Journal of Literary & Cultural Disability Studies* 5 (2011): 173–84.

Chrissochoidis, Ilias. "Composed in Hypocrisy." *Chronicle Review* (8 May 2009), http://chronicle.com/article/Composed-in-Hypocrisy/44313.

Churchill, Ward. "The Myth of Academic Freedom: Personal Experiences of a Liberal Principle in the Neoconservative Era (Fragments of a Work in Progress)." *Social Text* 25 (2007): 17–39.

Citron, Marcia J. "Feminist Waves and Classical Music: Pedagogy, Performance, Research." *Women & Music* 8 (2004): 47–60.

Coakley, Sarah, and Kay Kaufman Shelemay, eds. *Pain and Its Transformations: The Interface of Biology and Culture.* Cambridge, MA: Harvard University Press, 2007.

Cole, Andrew. "The Call of Things: A Critique of Object-Oriented Ontologies." *Minnesota Review* 80 (2013): 106–18.

Coly, Ayo. "Healing Is Not Grieving: We Must Not 'Move Forward' in the Wake of Massacre." *Truth-out* (3 July 2015), http://www.truth-out.org/opinion/item/31693-healing-is-not-grieving-we-must-not-move-forward-in-the-wake-of-massacre.

Cook, Nicholas. "We Are All (Ethno)musicologists Now." In *The New (Ethno)musicologies,* edited by Henry Stobart, 48–70. Lanham, MD: Scarecrow Press, 2008.

Cosenza, Julie. "SLOW: Crip Theory, Dyslexia and the Borderlands of Disability and Ablebodiedness." *Liminalities* 6 (October 2010): 10 pages.

Cote, Rachel Vorona. "There's No Crying in Graduate School." *Chronicle of Higher Education* (5 June 2015), http://chroniclevitae.com/news/1026-there-s-no-crying-in-graduate-school.

Cousins, Norman. *Anatomy of an Illness as Perceived by the Patient.* New York: W. W. Norton, 1979.

Cover, Rob. *Queer Youth Suicide, Culture and Identity: Unliveable Lives?* Burlington, VT: Ashgate, 2012.

Cunha, Darlena. "Sorry, Gwyneth Paltrow, Poverty Tourism Is Gross." *TIME* (13 April 2015), http://time.com/3819349/gwyneth-paltrow-poverty-tourism.

Currie, James. "Music after All." *Journal of the American Musicological Society* 62 (2009): 145–203.

Currie, James. *Music and the Politics of Negation.* Bloomington: Indiana University Press, 2012.

Cusick, Suzanne. "Gender, Musicology, and Feminism." In *Rethinking Music,* edited by Nicholas Cook and Mark Everist, 471–98. New York: Oxford University Press, 2001.

Cusick, Suzanne. "Let's Face the Music and Dance (or, Challenges to Contemporary

Musicology)." In *AMS at 75*, edited by Jane Bernstein, 25–32. Brunswick, ME: American Musicological Society, 2011.

Cusick, Suzanne. "Music as Torture / Music as Weapon." *TRANS: Revista Transcultural de Música* 10 (2006), http://www.sibetrans.com/trans/articulo/152/music-as-torture-music-as-weapon.

Cusick, Suzanne. "Musicology, Torture, Repair." *Radical Musicology* 3 (2008), http://www.radical-musicology.org.uk/2008/Cusick.htm, 24 paragraphs.

Cusick, Suzanne. "On a Lesbian Relationship with Music: A Serious Effort Not to Think Straight." In *Queering the Pitch: The New Gay and Lesbian Musicology*, 2nd ed., edited by Philip Brett, Elizabeth Wood, and Gary C. Thomas, 67–84. New York: Routledge, 2006.

Cusick, Suzanne. "Towards an Acoustemology of Detention in the 'Global War on Terror.'" In *Music, Sound and Space: Transformations of Public and Private Experience*, edited by Georgina Born, 275–91. Cambridge: Cambridge University Press, 2013.

Cusick, Suzanne. "'You Are in a Place That Is out of the World . . .': Music in the Detention Camps of the 'Global War on Terror.'" *Journal of the Society for American Music* 2 (2008): 1–26.

Cvetkovich, Ann. *Depression: A Public Feeling.* Durham, NC: Duke University Press, 2012.

Danzig, David. "Countering the Jack Bauer Effect: An Examination of How to Limit the Influence of TV's Most Popular, and Most Brutal, Hero." In *Screening Torture: Media Representations of State Terror and Political Domination*, edited by Michael Flynn and Fabiola F. Salek, 21–34. New York: Columbia University Press, 2012.

Daughtry, J. Martin. *Listening to War: Sound, Music, Trauma, and Survival in Wartime Iraq.* New York: Oxford University Press, 2015.

Davion, Victoria. "Autonomy, Integrity, and Care." *Social Theory and Practice* 19 (1993): 161–82.

Davis, N. Ann. "Invisible Disability." *Ethics* 116 (2005): 153–213.

Davison, Neil. *"Non-Lethal" Weapons.* New York: Palgrave Macmillan, 2009.

Deleuze, Gilles, and Félix Guattari. *A Thousand Plateaus: Capitalism and Schizophrenia.* Translated by Brian Massumi. Minneapolis: University of Minnesota Press, 1987.

Dell'Antonio, Andrew. Introduction. In *Beyond Structural Listening? Postmodern Modes of Hearing*, edited by Andrew Dell'Antonio, 1–12. Berkeley: University of California Press, 2004.

De Man, Paul. *The Resistance to Theory.* Minneapolis: University of Minnesota Press, 1986.

DeNora, Tia. *Music Asylums: Wellbeing through Music in Everyday Life.* Burlington, VT: Ashgate, 2013.

Dershowitz, Alan. *Why Terrorism Works: Understanding the Threat, Responding to the Challenge.* New Haven, CT: Yale University Press, 2004.

De Vos, Jan. "Depsychologizing Torture." *Critical Inquiry* 37 (2011): 286–314.

Dewsbury, Guy, et al. "The Anti-social Model of Disability." *Disability & Society* 19 (2004): 145–58.

Dinshaw, Carolyn. *How Soon Is Now? Medieval Texts, Amateur Readers, and the Queerness of Time.* Durham, NC: Duke University Press, 2012.

Dohoney, Ryan. "Echo's Echo: Subjectivity in Vibrational Ontology." *Women & Music* 19 (2015): 142–50.

Donaldson, Elizabeth J., and Catherine Prendergast. "Disability and Emotion: 'There's No Crying in Disability Studies!'" *Journal of Literary & Cultural Disability Studies* 5 (2011): 129–35.

Donnellan, Anne M., David A. Hill, and Martha R. Leary. "Rethinking Autism: Implications of Sensory and Movement Differences." *Disability Studies Quarterly* 30 (2010), http://dsq-sds.org/article/view/1060/1225.

Dorfman, Ariel. "The Tyranny of Torture." In *Torture: A Collection*, rev. ed., edited by Sanford Levinson, 3–18. New York: Oxford University Press, 2006.

Downes, Stephen. Introduction. In *Aesthetics of Music: Musicological Perspectives*, edited by Stephen Downes, 1–11. New York: Routledge, 2014.

Dudley, Rachel. "Toward an Understanding of the 'Medical Plantation' as a Cultural Location of Disability." *Disability Studies Quarterly* 32 (2012), http://dsq-sds.org/article/view/3248/3184.

Duggan, Lisa. *The Twilight of Equality? Neoliberalism, Cultural Politics, and the Attack on Democracy*. Boston: Beacon Press, 2003.

Edelman, Lee. *No Future: Queer Theory and the Death Drive*. Durham, NC: Duke University Press, 2004.

Ehrenreich, Barbara. *Bright-Sided: How the Relentless Promotion of Positive Thinking Has Undermined America*. New York: Metropolitan Books, 2009.

Eidsheim, Nina Sun. *Sensing Sound: Singing and Listening as Vibrational Practice*. Durham, NC: Duke University Press, 2015.

Erickson, Debra. "Why It's So Hard to Leave Academe." *Chronicle of Higher Education* (7 October 2015), http://chronicle.com/article/Why-It-s-So-Hard-to-Leave/233670.

Erlmann, Veit. *Reason and Resonance: A History of Modern Aurality*. New York: Zone Books, 2014.

Evans, Brad, and Julian Reid. *Resilient Life: The Art of Living Dangerously*. Cambridge: Polity, 2014.

Evens, Aden. *Sound Ideas: Music, Machines, and Experience*. Minneapolis: University of Minnesota Press, 2005.

Favor, Marty. "How Do They Matter?" *Huffington Post* (20 May 2015), http://www.huffingtonpost.com/marty-favor/how-do-they-matter_b_7312320.html.

Felski, Rita. "After Suspicion." *Profession* (2009): 28–35.

Felski, Rita. "Digging Down and Standing Back." *English Language Notes* 51 (2013): 7–23.

Felski, Rita. *The Limits of Critique*. Chicago: University of Chicago Press, 2015.

Felski, Rita. "Suspicious Minds." *Poetics Today* 32 (2011): 215–34.

Ferguson, Roderick A. *Aberrations in Black: Toward a Queer of Color Critique*. Minneapolis: University of Minnesota Press, 2004.

Fineman, Martha Albertson. *The Autonomy Myth: A Theory of Dependency*. New York: New Press, 2004.

Fink, Robert. "Beethoven Antihero: Sex, Violence, and the Aesthetics of Failure, or Listening to the Ninth Symphony as Postmodern Sublime." In *Beyond Structural Listening? Postmodern Modes of Hearing*, edited by Andrew Dell'Antonio, 109–53. Berkeley: University of California Press, 2004.

Fink, Robert. "Going Flat: Towards a Post-hierarchical Music Theory." In *Rethinking Music*, edited by Nicholas Cook and Mark Everist, 102–37. New York: Oxford University Press, 2001.

Fink, Robert. "Resurrection Symphony: El Sistema as Ideology in Venezuela and Los Angeles." *Action, Criticism, and Theory for Music Education* 15 (2016): 33–57.

Finkelstein, Naomi. "The Only Thing You Have to Do Is Live." *GLQ: A Journal of Lesbian and Gay Studies* 9 (2003): 307–19.

Ford, Phil. "Disciplinarity (or, Musicology Is Anything You Can Get Away With)." *Dial M for Musicology* (28 June 2015), http://dialmformusicology.com/2015/06/28/disciplinarity.

Ford, Phil. "What Good News Do You Bring?" *Dial M for Musicology* (11 March 2015), http://dialmformusicology.com/2015/03/11/what-good-news-do-you-bring.

Fraser, Nancy. *Fortunes of Feminism: From State-Managed Capitalism to Neoliberal Crisis.* New York: Verso, 2013.

Freeman, Elizabeth. *Time Binds: Queer Temporalities, Queer Histories.* Durham, NC: Duke University Press, 2010.

Friedman, Marilyn. "Beyond Caring: The De-moralization of Gender." *Canadian Journal of Philosophy* 17 (1987): 87–110.

Fullick, Melonie. "'My Grief Lies All Within': PhD Students, Depression & Attrition." *University Affairs* (14 December 2011), http://www.universityaffairs.ca/opinion/speculative-diction/my-grief-lies-all-within-phd-students-depression-attrition.

Garland-Thomson, Rosemarie. *Extraordinary Bodies: Figuring Physical Disability in American Culture and Literature.* New York: Columbia University Press, 1996.

Garland-Thomson, Rosemarie. "Human Biodiversity Conservation: A Consensual Ethical Principle." *American Journal of Bioethics* 15 (2015): 13–15.

Garland-Thomson, Rosemarie. "The Story of My Work: How I Became Disabled." *Disability Studies Quarterly* 34 (2014), http://dsq-sds.org/article/view/4254/3594.

Garrett, Charles Hiroshi. "Enterprising Students and the Future of the American Musicological Society." In *AMS at 75*, edited by Jane Bernstein, 33–37. Brunswick, ME: American Musicological Society, 2011.

Gaudio, Rudolf P. "Sounding Gay: Pitch Properties in the Speech of Gay and Straight Men." *American Speech* 69 (1994): 30–57.

Gawande, Atul. *Being Mortal: Illness, Medicine, and What Matters in the End.* London: Profile Books, 2014.

Gawande, Atul. *Complications: A Surgeon's Notes on an Imperfect Science.* New York: Picador, 2002.

Geertz, Clifford. "Thick Description: Toward an Interpretive Theory of Culture." In *The Interpretation of Cultures: Selected Essays*, 3–30. New York: Basic Books, 1973.

Gentry, Phil. "The Polite Musicologist." *2'23"* (4 April 2009), http://blog.pmgentry.net/2009/04/polite-musicologist.html.

Gilligan, Carol. *In a Different Voice: Psychological Theory and Women's Development.* Cambridge, MA: Harvard University Press, 1982.

Gleditsch, Nils Petter, ed., with Steven Pinker, Bradley A. Thayer, Jack S. Levy, and William R. Thompson. "The Decline of War." *International Studies Review* 15 (2013): 396–419.

Goffman, Erving. "Embarrassment and Social Organization." *American Journal of Sociology* 62 (1956): 264–71.

Goffman, Erving. *The Presentation of Self in Everyday Life.* Garden City, NY: Doubleday, 1959.

Goines, Lisa. "Noise Pollution: A Modern Plague." *Southern Medical Journal* 100 (2007): 287–94.

Goodman, Steve. *Sonic Warfare: Sound, Affect, and the Ecology of Fear.* Cambridge, MA: MIT Press, 2010.

Gopinath, Sumanth, and Jason Stanyek, eds. *The Oxford Handbook of Mobile Music Studies.* Vol. 1. New York: Oxford University Press, 2014.

Gordon, Bonnie. "The UVA Gang Rape Allegations Are Awful, Horrifying, and Not

Shocking at All." *Slate* (25 November 2014), http://www.slate.com/blogs/xx_factor/2014/11/25/uva_gang_rape_allegations_in_rolling_stone_not_surprising_to_one_associate.html.

Gordon, Bonnie. "Why We Matter." *Women & Music* 19 (2015): 116–24.

Gottschall, Jonathan. *The Professor in the Cage: Why Men Fight and Why We Like to Watch.* New York: Penguin, 2015.

Grant, Morag Josephine. "Pathways to Music Torture." *Transposition* 4 (2014): 54 paragraphs.

Grant, Roger Mathew. "The Queen of Music Theory Goes to Milwaukee City, or, Yes I Am a Music Theory Queen." Paper presented at AMS/SMT joint meeting in Milwaukee, WI (7 November 2014).

Grant, Roger Mathew. "Review of *À l'écoute* by Jean-Luc Nancy, Charlotte Mandell." *Journal of the American Musicological Society* 62 (2009): 748–52.

Green, Myra. "Thanks for Listening." *Chronicle of Higher Education* (19 October 2015), http://chronicle.com/article/Thanks-for-Listening/233825.

Greif, Mark. "What's Wrong with Public Intellectuals?" *Chronicle Review* (13 February 2015), http://chronicle.com/article/Whats-Wrong-With-Public/189921.

Grzanka, Patrick R., and Emily S. Mann. "Queer Youth Suicide and the Psychopolitics of 'It Gets Better.'" *Sexualities* 17 (2014): 369–93.

"Guidelines for Ethical Conduct." *American Musicological Society 2015 Directory* (2015), http://www.ams-net.org/administration/ethics.php.

Hackman, Rose. "'Women Are Just Better at This Stuff': Is Emotional Labor Feminism's Next Frontier?" *Guardian* (8 November 2015), http://www.theguardian.com/world/2015/nov/08/women-gender-roles-sexism-emotional-labor-feminism?CMP=share_btn_fb.

Hadlock, Heather. "'How to Sound Gay' at the AMS 2013 Meeting in Pittsburgh." *Still a Musicologist* (12 November 2013), http://amsfellowtraveler.wordpress.com/2013/11/12/how-to-sound-gay-at-the-ams-2013-meeting-in-pittsburgh.

Hadlock, Heather. "How to Sound Gay—Discipline (and Punish)?" *Still a Musicologist* (20 November 2013), http://amsfellowtraveler.wordpress.com/2013/11.

Hagberg, Garry L. "Jazz Improvisation and Ethical Interaction: A Sketch of the Connections." In *Art and Ethical Criticism*, edited by Garry L. Hagberg, 259–85. Malden, MA: Blackwell, 2008.

Hahn, Tomie. *Sensational Knowledge: Embodying Culture through Japanese Dance*. Middletown, CT: Wesleyan University Press, 2007.

Halberstam, (Judith) Jack. *Gaga Feminism: Sex, Gender, and the End of Normal*. Boston: Beacon Press, 2012.

Halberstam, (Judith) Jack. *In a Queer Time and Place: Transgender Bodies, Subcultural Lives*. New York: New York University Press, 2005.

Halberstam, (Judith) Jack. "It Gets Worse. . . ." *Social Text* (20 November 2010), http://socialtextjournal.org/periscope_article/it_gets_worse.

Halberstam, (Judith) Jack. *The Queer Art of Failure*. Durham, NC: Duke University Press, 2011.

Halberstam, (Judith) Jack. "You Are Triggering Me! The Neo-liberal Rhetoric of Harm, Danger and Trauma." *Bully Bloggers* (5 July 2014), http://bullybloggers.wordpress.com/2014/07/05/you-are-triggering-me-the-neo-liberal-rhetoric-of-harm-danger-and-trauma.

Hall, Kim Q. "No Failure: Climate Change, Radical Hope, and Queer Crip Feminist Eco-futures." *Radical Philosophy Review* 17 (2014): 203–25.

Halperin, David M. *How to Be Gay*. Cambridge, MA: Belknap Press of Harvard University Press, 2012.

Halperin, David M., and Valerie Traub, eds. *Gay Shame*. Chicago: University of Chicago Press, 2009.

Hamessley, Lydia. "How Did This All Start? Toward a History of the Feminist Theory and Music Phenomenon" (2009, revised 2015), http://www.femtheorymusic.org/ftm-history.

Hammel, Alice M., and Ryan M. Hourigan. *Teaching Music to Students with Autism*. New York: Oxford University Press, 2013.

Hanson, Ellis. "The Future's Eve: Reparative Reading after Sedgwick." *South Atlantic Quarterly* 110 (2011): 101–19.

Haraway, Donna. "Situated Knowledges: The Science Question in Feminism and the Privilege of Partial Perspective." *Feminist Studies* 14 (1988): 575–99.

Harpham, Geoffrey Galt. "Elaine Scarry and the Dream of Pain." *Salmagundi* 130–31 (2001): 202–34.

Harrington, Mona. *Care and Equality: Inventing a New Family Politics*. New York: Knopf, 1999.

Harris, George W. *Dignity and Vulnerability: Strength and Quality of Character*. Berkeley: University of California Press, 1997.

Hartman, Yvonne, and Sandy Darab. "A Call for Slow Scholarship: A Case Study on the Intensification of Academic Life and Its Implications for Pedagogy." *Review of Education, Pedagogy, and Cultural Studies* 34 (2012): 49–60.

Hegarty, Paul. *Noise/Music: A History*. New York: Continuum, 2007.

Heideman, Elizabeth. "'Inspiration Porn Is Not Okay': Disability Activists Are Not Impressed with Feel-Good Super Bowl Ads." *Salon* (2 February 2015), http://www.salon.com/writer/elizabeth_heideman.

Held, Virginia. *The Ethics of Care: Personal, Political, and Global*. New York: Oxford University Press, 2006.

Heller, Michael C. "Between Silence and Pain: Loudness and the Affective Encounter." *Sound Studies: An Interdisciplinary Journal* 1 (2015): 40–58.

Heller, Sharon. *Too Loud, Too Bright, Too Fast, Too Tight: What to Do If You Are Sensory Defensive in an Overstimulating World*. New York: Harper Perennial, 2003.

Henderson, Lisa. *Love and Money: Queers, Class, and Cultural Production*. New York: New York University Press, 2013.

Hern, Alex. "*Grand Theft Auto V* under Fire for Graphic Torture Scene." *Guardian* (18 September 2013), http://www.theguardian.com/technology/2013/sep/18/grand-theft-auto-5-under-fire-for-graphic-torture-scene.

Hess, Carol. "'De aspecto inglés pero de alma española': Gilbert Chase, Spain, and Musicology in the United States." *Revista de Musicología* 35 (2012): 263–96.

Hess, Carol. "Public Musicology . . . 1939." *Musicology Now* (15 November 2013), http://musicologynow.ams-net.org/2013/11/public-musicology-1939.html

Hirsch, Lily E. *Music in American Crime Prevention and Punishment*. Ann Arbor: University of Michigan Press, 2012.

Hitchcock, Peter. *Oscillate Wildly: Space, Body, and Spirit of Millennial Materialism*. Minneapolis: University of Minnesota Press, 1999.

Hofstadter, Richard. *Anti-intellectualism in American Life*. New York: Knopf, 1963.

Honoré, Carl. *In Praise of Slowness: Challenging the Cult of Speed*. San Francisco: HarperSanFrancisco, 2004.

House, Ernest R. "Origins of the Ideas in *Evaluating with Validity*." *New Directions for Evaluation* 142 (2014): 9–15.

"How to Sound Gay: David M. Halperin in Conversation with Ryan Dohoney." *AMS Pittsburgh 2013 (7–10 November) Program & Abstracts* (2013), http://www.ams-net.org/pittsburgh/abstracts.pdf.

Howe, Blake, Stephanie Jensen-Moulton, Neil Lerner, and Joseph Straus, eds. *The Oxford Handbook of Music and Disability Studies*. New York: Oxford University Press, 2015.

Howell, Alison. "The Demise of PTSD: From Governing through Trauma to Governing Resilience." *Alternatives: Global, Local, Political* 37 (2012): 214–26.

Hubbs, Nadine. "Homophobia in Twentieth-Century Music: The Crucible of America's Sound." *Daedalus* 142 (2013): 45–50.

Hubbs, Nadine. *The Queer Composition of America's Sound: Gay Modernists, American Music, and National Identity*. Berkeley: University of California Press, 2004.

Hutcheon, Emily, and Bonnie Lashewicz. "Theorizing Resilience: Critiquing and Unbounding a Marginalizing Concept." *Disability & Society* 29 (2014): 1383–97.

Hutchinson, Brian. "UBC Student Writes 52,438-Word Architecture Dissertation with No Punctuation—Not Everyone Loved It." *National Post* (8 May 2015), http://news.nationalpost.com/news/canada/ubc-student-writes-52438-word-architecture-dissertation-with-no-punctuation-not-everyone-loved-it.

Jackson, Jake. "On Critical Abyss-Gazing: Depression & Academic Philosophy." *PhDisabled* (19 August 2014), http://phdisabled.wordpress.com/2014/08/19/on-critical-abyss-gazing-depression-academic-philosophy.

Jackson Jr., John L. *Thin Description: Ethnography and the African Hebrew Israelites of Jerusalem*. Cambridge, MA: Harvard University Press, 2013.

Jackson, Timothy. *Tchaikovsky: Symphony No. 6 (Pathétique)*. Cambridge: Cambridge University Press, 1999.

Jankélévitch, Vladimir. *Music and the Ineffable*. Translated by Carolyn Abbate. Princeton, NJ: Princeton University Press, 2003.

Jenzen, Olu. "Revolting Doubles: Radical Narcissism and the Trope of Lesbian Doppelgangers." *Journal of Lesbian Studies* 17 (2013): 344–64.

Johnson, Bruce, and Martin Cloonan. *Dark Side of the Tune: Popular Music and Violence*. Burlington, VT: Ashgate, 2009.

Johnson, Carol. "The Politics of Affective Citizenship: From Blair to Obama." *Citizenship Studies* 14 (2010): 495–509.

Johnson, DMan. "The Role of Communication in Thought." *Disability Studies Quarterly* 31 (2011), http://dsq-sds.org/article/view/1717/1765.

Johnson Jr., Michael. "The It Gets Better Project: A Study in (and of) Whiteness in LGBT Youth and Media Cultures." In *Queer Youth and Media Cultures*, edited by Christopher Pullen, 278–91. New York: Palgrave Macmillan, 2014.

Joseph, Jonathan. "Resilience as Embedded Neoliberalism: A Governmentality Approach." *Resilience* 1 (2013): 38–52.

Jurecic, Ann. "Empathy and the Critic." *College English* 74 (2011): 10–27.

Jurecic, Ann. *Illness as Narrative*. Pittsburgh: University of Pittsburgh Press, 2012.

Kain, Erik. "*Grand Theft Auto V* Torture Scene Is Satire." *Forbes* (21 September 2013), http://www.forbes.com/sites/erikkain/2013/09/21/grand-theft-auto-v-torture-scene-is-satire.

Kane, Brian. "Jean-Luc Nancy and the Listening Subject." *Contemporary Music Review* 31 (2012): 439–47.

Kassabian, Anahid. *Ubiquitous Listening: Affect, Attention, and Distributed Subjectivity.* Berkeley: University of California Press, 2013.

Katz, Jack. *How Emotions Work.* Chicago: University of Chicago Press, 1999.

Kay, Taylan. "Description: Auti-Sim." *Game Jolt* (26 February 2013), http://gamejolt. com/games/auti-sim/12761.

Kennaway, James. *Bad Vibrations: The History of the Idea of Music as Cause of Disease.* Burlington, VT: Ashgate, 2012.

Kerman, Joseph. *Contemplating Music: Challenges to Musicology.* Cambridge, MA: Harvard University Press, 1985.

Kerschbaum, Stephanie L. "On Rhetorical Agency and Disclosing Disability in Academic Writing." *Rhetoric Review* 33 (2014): 55–71.

Keyes, Ralph. *The Quote Verifier: Who Said What, Where, and When.* New York: St. Martin's Press, 2006.

Killam, Rosemary. "Response to Professor Morse's Open Letter." *Music Theory Online* 3 (1997), http://www.mtosmt.org/issues/mto.97.3.4/mto.97.3.4.killam.html, 16 paragraphs.

Kim, Cynthia. *Nerdy, Shy, and Socially Inappropriate: A User Guide to an Asperger Life.* Philadelphia: Jessica Kingsley, 2015.

Kittay, Eva Feder. "At the Margins of Moral Personhood." *Ethics* 116 (2005): 100–31.

Kittay, Eva Feder. *Love's Labor: Essays on Women, Equality, and Dependency.* New York: Routledge, 1999.

Kittay, Eva Feder. "When Caring Is Just and Justice Is Caring: Justice and Mental Retardation." *Public Culture* 13 (2001): 557–80.

Kittay, Eva Feder, and Licia Carlson, eds. *Cognitive Disability and Its Challenge to Moral Philosophy.* Malden, MA: Wiley-Blackwell, 2010.

Koestenbaum, Wayne. *The Queen's Throat: Opera, Homosexuality, and the Mystery of Desire.* New York: Poseidon Press, 1993.

Korsyn, Kevin. *Decentering Music: A Critique of Contemporary Musical Research.* New York: Oxford University Press, 2003.

Kranowitz, Carol Stock. *The Out-of-Sync Child: Recognizing and Coping with Sensory Processing Disorder.* New York: Berkley Publishing Group, 2005.

Kristeva, Julia. "Women's Time." Translated by Alice Jardine and Harry Blake. *Signs* 7 (1981): 13–35.

Kuzniar, Alice A. "Sublime Shame (Review)." *GLQ: A Journal of Lesbian and Gay Studies* 15 (2009): 499–512.

Laqueur, Walter. *Optimism in Politics: Reflections on Contemporary History.* New Brunswick, NJ: Transaction Publishers, 2014.

Latour, Bruno. *Reassembling the Social: An Introduction to Actor-Network Theory.* New York: Oxford University Press, 2005.

Latour, Bruno. *We Have Never Been Modern.* Translated by Catherine Porter. Cambridge, MA: Harvard University Press, 1993.

Latour, Bruno. "Why Has Critique Run out of Steam? From Matters of Fact to Matters of Concern." *Critical Inquiry* 30 (2004): 225–48.

Leigh, Irene W., Donna A. Morere, and Caroline Kobek Pezzarossi. "Deaf Gain: Beyond Deaf Culture." In *Deaf Gain: Raising the Stakes for Human Diversity,* edited by H-Dirksen L. Bauman and Joseph J. Murray, 356–71. Minneapolis: University of Minnesota Press, 2014.

Leiter, Brian. "The Hermeneutics of Suspicion: Recovering Marx, Nietzsche, and

Freud." In *The Future for Philosophy*, edited by Brian Leiter, 74–105. New York: Oxford University Press, 2004.

Leppert, Richard. "Music 'Pushed to the Edge of Existence' (Adorno, Listening, and the Question of Hope)." *Cultural Critique* 60 (2005): 92–133.

Lester, David. "The Relationship between Paranoid Delusions and Homosexuality." *Archives of Sexual Behavior* 4 (1975): 285–94.

Levitt, Steven D., and Stephen J. Dubner. *Think Like a Freak*. New York: HarperCollins, 2014.

Levy, Gideon. "Demons in the Skies of the Gaza Strip." *Haaretz*, available at *Lebanon Wire* (6 November 2005), http://www.lebanonwire.com/1105/05110601HZ.asp.

Likierman, Meira. *Melanie Klein: Her Work in Context*. London: Continuum, 2002.

Lindsetmo, Rolv-Ole, and Jonah Stulberg. "Chronic Abdominal Wall Pain—a Diagnostic Challenge for the Surgeon." *American Journal of Surgery* 198 (2009): 129–34.

Lipman, Joanne. "Is Music the Key to Success?" *New York Times* (12 October 2013), http://www.nytimes.com/2013/10/13/opinion/sunday/is-music-the-key-to-success.html?_r=0.

Liu, Catherine. *American Idyll: Academic Antielitism as Cultural Critique*. Iowa City: University of Iowa Press, 2011.

Livio, Mario. *The Golden Ratio: The Story of Phi, the World's Most Astonishing Number*. New York: Broadway Books, 2002.

Livio, Mario. *Is God a Mathematician?* New York: Simon & Schuster, 2009.

Lorde, Audre. "The Uses of Anger." In *Sister Outsider: Essays and Speeches*, 124–33. Berkeley, CA: Crossing Press, 2007.

Love, Heather. "Close Reading and Thin Description." *Public Culture* 25 (2013): 401–34.

Love, Heather. "Doing Being Deviant: Deviance Studies, Description, and the Queer Ordinary." *differences* 26 (2015): 74–95.

Love, Heather. *Feeling Backward: Loss and the Politics of Queer History*. Cambridge, MA: Harvard University Press, 2007.

Love, Heather. "Truth and Consequences: On Paranoid Reading and Reparative Reading." *Criticism* 52 (2010): 235–41.

LRAD Corporation. "Extended Range & EOF Communication." *LRAD* (n.d.), http://www.lradx.com/application/defense.

LRAD Corporation. "LRAD Corporation Reports Fiscal Year 2014 Financial Results." *LRAD* (2014), http://www.lradx.com/press_release/lrad-corporation-reports-fiscal-third-quarter-2014-financial-results.

LRAD Corporation. "Safeguarding the Public & Protecting the Officers." *LRAD* (n.d.), http://www.lradx.com/application/law-enforcement.

LRAD Corporation. "Winter 2015 Newsletter." *LRAD* (2015), http://www.lradx.com/investors/newsroom/press-releases/lrad-newsletter.

"LRAD—Long Range Acoustic Hailing Devices." *AOL/YouTube* (14 September 2012), http://www.youtube.com/watch?v=1P3FsLMKwJE.

Ltlmason. "Can You Survive 10 Minutes of Barney Saying 'I Love You'?" *YouTube* (7 February 2012), http://www.youtube.com/watch?v=KOmVMWMyTBE.

Ma, Bob. "A Trip into the Controversy: A Study of Slum Tourism Travel Motivations." *Penn Humanities Forum on Connections* (2010), http://repository.upenn.edu/cgi/viewcontent.cgi?article=1011&context=uhf_2010.

Macarthur, Sally. "Music and Violence." *Musicology Australia* 34 (2012): 101–10.

Maggio, J. "'Can the Subaltern Be Heard?': Political Theory, Translation, Representation, and Gayatri Chakravorty Spivak." *Alternatives: Global, Local, Political* 32 (2007): 419–43.

Mangan, Katherine. "1 in 4 Female Undergrads Experienced Sex Assault or Misconduct, AAU Survey Finds." *Chronicle of Higher Education* (21 September 2015), http://chronicle.com/article/1-in-4-Female-Undergrads/233281.

Manne, Kate. "Why I Use Trigger Warnings." *New York Times* (19 September 2015), http://www.nytimes.com/2015/09/20/opinion/sunday/why-i-use-trigger-warnings.html?_r=1&pagewanted=all.

Manne, Kate, and Jason Stanley. "When Free Speech Becomes a Political Weapon." *Chronicle Review* (13 November 2015), http://chronicle.com/article/When-Free-Speech-Becomes-a/234207.

Manning, Catherine, et al. "Enhanced Integration of Motion Information in Children with Autism." *Journal of Neuroscience* 35 (2015): 6979–86.

Martell, Luke. "The Slow University: Inequality, Power and Alternatives." *Forum: Qualitative Social Research* 15 (2014), http://www.qualitative-research.net/index.php/fqs/article/view/2223/3693.

Martin, Kingsley. "Winston Churchill Interviewed in 1939." *New Statesman* (6 January 2014), http://www.newstatesman.com/archive/2013/12/british-people-would-rather-go-down-fighting.

Mathew, Nicholas, and Mary Ann Smart. "Elephants in the Music Room: The Future of Quirk Historicism." *Representations* 132 (2015): 61–78.

Maus, Fred Everett. "Masculine Discourse in Music Theory." *Perspectives of New Music* 31 (1993): 264–93.

McClary, Susan. "Constructions of Subjectivity in Schubert's Music." In *Queering the Pitch: The New Gay and Lesbian Musicology*, 2nd ed., edited by Philip Brett, Elizabeth Wood, and Gary C. Thomas, 205–33. New York: Routledge, 2006.

McClary, Susan. *Feminine Endings: Music, Gender, and Sexuality*. Minneapolis: University of Minnesota Press, 1991.

McClary, Susan. "Feminine Endings at Twenty." *TRANS: Revista Transcultural de Música* 15 (2011), http://www.sibetrans.com/trans/public/docs/trans_15_02_McClary.pdf.

McClary, Susan. "The Making of a Feminist Musicologist." In *True Confessions: Feminist Professors Tell Stories out of School*, edited by Susan Gubar, 301–10. New York: W. W. Norton, 2011.

McCreless, Patrick. "Review of *Decentering Music*." *Theory and Practice* 29 (2004): 252–66.

McDonnell, Cari E. "Parenting a Special-Needs Child in Academe: Should I Stay or Should I Go?" Paper presented at AMS meeting in Louisville, KY (13 November 2015).

Mercier, Hugo, and Dan Sperber. "Why Do Humans Reason? Arguments for an Argumentative Theory." *Behavioral and Brain Sciences* 34 (2011): 57–111.

Michaels, Sean. "Industrial Band Skinny Puppy Demand $666,000 after Music Is Used in Guantánamo Torture." *Guardian* (7 February 2014), http://www.theguardian.com/music/2014/feb/07/skinny-puppy-payment-guantanamo.

Michaels, Walter Benn. *The Trouble with Diversity: How We Learned to Love Identity and Ignore Inequality*. New York: Metropolitan Books, 2006.

Mills, Nicolaus. "Television and the Politics of Humiliation." *Dissent* 51 (2004): 79–81.

Miyakawa, Felicia. "Going Rogue: On Leaving the Academy and Taking Risks" (1 February 2015), http://fmmiyakawa.com/2015/02/01/on-being-brave-publicmusi-cology.

Morris, Mitchell. "Musical Virtues." In *Beyond Structural Listening? Postmodern Modes of Hearing*, edited by Andrew Dell'Antonio, 44–69. Berkeley: University of California Press, 2004.

Moscovici, Serge, Gabriel Mugny, and Eddy Van Avermaet, eds. *Perspectives on Minority Influence*. Cambridge: Cambridge University Press, 1985.

Mountz, Alison, et al. "For Slow Scholarship: A Feminist Politics of Resistance through Collective Action in the Neoliberal University." *ACME: An International E-Journal for Critical Geographies* 14 (2015): 1235–59.

Muñoz, José Esteban. *Cruising Utopia: The Then and There of Queer Futurity*. New York: New York University Press, 2009.

Munson, Benjamin, et al. "The Acoustic and Perceptual Bases of Judgments of Women and Men's Sexual Orientation from Read Speech." *Journal of Phonetics* 34 (2006): 202–40.

Nagel, Thomas. *The View from Nowhere*. New York: Oxford University Press, 1986.

Nancy, Jean-Luc. *À l'écoute*. Paris: Galilée, 2002.

Nancy, Jean-Luc. *Listening*. Translated by Charlotte Mandell. New York: Fordham University Press, 2007.

Newman, Lily Hay. "This Is the Sound Cannon Used against Protesters in Ferguson." *Slate* (14 August 2014), http://www.slate.com/blogs/future_tense/2014/08/14/lrad_long_range_acoustic_device_sound_cannons_were_used_for_crowd_control.html.

Ngai, Sianne. *Our Aesthetic Categories: Zany, Cute, Interesting*. Cambridge, MA: Harvard University Press, 2012.

Nishida, Akemi. "Neoliberal Academia and a Critique from Disability Studies." In *Occupying Disability: Critical Approaches to Community, Justice, and Decolonizing Disability*, edited by Pamela Block, Devva Kasnitz, Akemi Nishida, and Nick Pollard, 145–57. New York: Springer, 2015.

Noddings, Nel. *Caring: A Feminine Approach to Ethics and Moral Education*. Berkeley: University of California Press, 1982.

Nussbaum, Martha. *The Fragility of Goodness: Luck and Ethics in Greek Tragedy and Philosophy*. Rev. ed. Cambridge: Cambridge University Press, 2001.

Nussbaum, Martha. "The Future of Feminist Liberalism." In *The Subject of Care: Feminist Perspectives on Dependency*, edited by Eva Feder Kittay and Ellen K. Feder, 186–214. Lanham, MD: Rowman & Littlefield, 2002.

Nussbaum, Martha. *Not for Profit: Why Democracy Needs the Humanities*. Princeton, NJ: Princeton University Press, 2010.

Nussbaum, Martha. *Political Emotions: Why Love Matters for Justice*. Cambridge, MA: Harvard University Press, 2013.

Nussbaum, Martha. *Upheavals of Thought: The Intelligence of Emotions*. Cambridge: Cambridge University Press, 2003.

Nyong'o, Tavia. "School Daze." *Bully Bloggers* (30 September 2010), http://bullyblog-gers.wordpress.com/2010/09/30/school-daze.

Nyong'o, Tavia. "The Student Demand." *Bully Bloggers* (17 November 2015), http://bullybloggers.wordpress.com/2015/11/17/the-student-demand.

Oliver, Gideon Orion. "The NYPD's Use of Long Range Acoustic Devices for Crowd Control." *Scribd* (12 December 2014), http://www.scribd.com/doc/250122281/The-NYPD-s-Use-of-Long-Range-Acoustic-Devices-for-Crowd-Control.

Orue, Alex R. "The Person Worth Fighting For Is You." In *It Gets Better: Coming Out, Overcoming Bullying, and Creating a Life Worth Living*, edited by Dan Savage and Terry Miller, 35–37. New York: Dutton, 2011.

Paddison, Max. "Music as Ideal: The Aesthetics of Autonomy." In *The Cambridge History of Nineteenth-Century Music*, edited by Jim Samson, 318–42. Cambridge: Cambridge University Press, 2001.

Patton, Cindy. "Love without the Obligation to Love." *Criticism* 52 (2010): 215–24.

Pellegrinelli, Lara. "Scholarly Discord." *Chronicle of Higher Education* (8 May 2009), http://www.chroniclecareers.com/article/Scholarly-Discord/44312.

Peraino, Judith. "On Phone Theory." Paper presented at AMS/SMT joint meeting in Milwaukee, WI (7 November 2014).

Peraino, Judith. "The Same, but Different: Sexuality and Musicology, Then and Now." *Journal of the American Musicological Society* 66 (2013): 825–31.

Piekut, Benjamin. "Actor-Networks in Music History: Clarifications and Critiques." *Twentieth-Century Music* 11 (2014): 191–215.

Pieslak, Jonathan. "Review of *Decentering Music*." *Music Theory Online* 14 (2008), http://www.mtosmt.org/issues/mto.08.14.1/mto.08.14.1.pieslak.html.

Pieslak, Jonathan. *Sound Targets: American Soldiers and Music in the Iraq War*. Bloomington: Indiana University Press, 2009.

Pigeonhammer. "Why the Torture Scene in GTA V Made Me Quit Playing." *IGN* (24 September 2013), http://www.ign.com/blogs/pigeonhammer/2013/09/24/why-the-torture-scene-in-gta-v-made-me-quit-playing.

Pinch, Trevor, and Karin Bijsterveld, eds. *The Oxford Handbook of Sound Studies*. New York: Oxford University Press, 2012.

Pinker, Steven. *The Better Angels of Our Nature: Why Violence Has Declined*. New York: Viking, 2011.

Pinker, Steven. "Why Academics Stink at Writing." *Chronicle of Higher Education* (26 September 2014), http://chronicle.com/article/Why-Academics-Writing-Stinks/148989.

Pinto, Nick. "NYC Cops Are Blithely Firing a Potentially Deafening Sound Cannon at Peaceful Protesters." *Gothamist* (13 December 2014), http://gothamist.com/2014/12/13/lrad_nypd_protests_sound.php.

Prashad, Vijay. "Teaching by Candlelight." In *The Imperial University: Academic Repression and Scholarly Dissent*, edited by Piya Chatterjee and Sunaina Maira, 281–97. Minneapolis: University of Minnesota Press, 2014.

Price, Margaret. *Mad at School: Rhetorics of Mental Disability and Academic Life*. Ann Arbor: University of Michigan Press, 2011.

Prochnik, George. *In Pursuit of Silence: Listening for Meaning in a World of Noise*. New York: Doubleday, 2010.

Puar, Jasbir. "The Cost of Getting Better: Suicide, Sensation, Switchpoints." *GLQ: A Journal of Lesbian and Gay Studies* 18 (2012): 149–58.

Puar, Jasbir. "In the Wake of It Gets Better." *Guardian* (16 November 2010), http://www.theguardian.com/commentisfree/cifamerica/2010/nov/16/wake-it-gets-better-campaign.

Puar, Jasbir. *Terrorist Assemblages: Homonationalism in Queer Times*. Durham, NC: Duke University Press, 2007.

Puri, Michael J. "Dandy, Interrupted: Sublimation, Repression, and Self-Portraiture in Maurice Ravel's *Daphnis et Chloé* (1909–1912)." *Journal of the American Musicological Society* 60 (2007): 317–72.

Railton, Peter. "Innocent Abroad: Rupture, Liberation, and Solidarity." Dewey Lecture, APA-Central (February 2015), http://www.lsa.umich.edu/UMICH/philosophy/Home/News/Railton%20Dewey%20Lecture%20Central%20APA%202015%20revised.pdf.

Ramirez, Mark. "An Identity Unfolded." In *It Gets Better: Coming Out, Overcoming Bullying, and Creating a Life Worth Living*, edited by Dan Savage and Terry Miller, 99–101. New York: Dutton, 2011.

Rawls, John. *A Theory of Justice*. Rev. ed. Cambridge, MA: Belknap Press of Harvard University Press, 1999.

Rehding, Alexander. "Of Sirens Old and New." In *The Oxford Handbook of Mobile Music Studies*, vol. 2, edited by Sumanth Gopinath and Jason Stanyek, 77–106. New York: Oxford University Press, 2014.

Reiheld, Alison. "Just Caring for Caregivers: What Society and the State Owe to Those Who Render Care." *Feminist Philosophy Quarterly* 1 (2015), http://ir.lib.uwo.ca/fpq/vol1/iss2/1.

Rice, Tom. "Sounding Bodies: Medical Students and the Acquisition of Stethoscopic Perspectives." In *The Oxford Handbook of Sound Studies*, edited by Trevor Pinch and Karin Bijsterveld, 298–319. New York: Oxford University Press, 2012.

Richards, David. *Resisting Injustice and the Feminist Ethics of Care in the Age of Obama*. New York: Routledge, 2013.

Ricoeur, Paul. *Freud and Philosophy: An Essay on Interpretation*. Translated by Denis Savage. New Haven: Yale University Press, 1970.

Rivera, Gabrielle. "Getting Stronger and Staying Alive." In *It Gets Better: Coming Out, Overcoming Bullying, and Creating a Life Worth Living*, edited by Dan Savage and Terry Miller, 45–47. New York: Dutton, 2011.

Robbins, Hollis. "The Emperor's New Critique." *New Literary History* 34 (2003): 659–75.

Robinson, Fiona. *The Ethics of Care: A Feminist Approach to Human Security*. Philadelphia: Temple University Press, 2011.

Rorty, Richard. "The Pragmatist's Progress." In *Interpretation and Overinterpretation*, edited by Stefan Collini, 89–108. Cambridge: Cambridge University Press, 1992.

Ross, Andrew. *No Respect: Intellectuals and Popular Culture*. New York: Routledge, 1989.

Rousso, Harilyn. *Don't Call Me Inspirational: A Disabled Feminist Talks Back*. Philadelphia: Temple University Press, 2013.

Ruark, Jennifer. "In Academic Culture, Mental-Health Problems Are Hard to Recognize and Hard to Treat." *Chronicle of Higher Education* (16 February 2010), http://chronicle.com/article/In-Academe-Mental-Health/64246.

Ruddick, Sara. *Maternal Thinking: Toward a Politics of Peace*. Boston: Beacon Press, 1989.

Sacks, Harvey. "On Doing 'Being Ordinary.'" In *Structures of Social Action: Studies in Conversation Analysis*, edited by J. Maxwell Atkinson and John Heritage, 413–29. Cambridge: Cambridge University Press, 1985.

Salen, Katie, and Eric Zimmerman. *Rules of Play: Game Design Fundamentals*. Cambridge, MA: MIT Press, 2004.

Samuels, Ellen. "My Body, My Closet: Invisible Disability and the Limits of Coming-Out Discourse." *GLQ: A Journal of Lesbian and Gay Studies* 9 (2003): 233–55.

Sandel, Michael. *The Case against Perfection: Ethics in the Age of Genetic Engineering*. Cambridge, MA: Belknap Press of Harvard University Press, 2007.

Savage, Roger. *Hermeneutics and Music Criticism*. New York: Routledge, 2010.

Scarry, Elaine. "Beauty and the Scholar's Duty to Justice." *Profession* (2000): 21–31.

Scarry, Elaine. *The Body in Pain: The Making and Unmaking of the World.* New York: Oxford University Press, 1985.

Scarry, Elaine. "The Difficulty of Imagining Other Persons." In *Human Rights in Political Transitions: Gettysburg to Bosnia,* edited by Carla Hesse and Robert Post, 277–309. New York: Zone Books, 1999.

Scarry, Elaine. "Five Errors in the Reasoning of Alan Dershowitz." In *Torture: A Collection,* rev. ed., edited by Sanford Levinson, 281–90. New York: Oxford University Press, 2004.

Scarry, Elaine *On Beauty and Being Just.* Princeton, NJ: Princeton University Press, 1999.

Scarry, Elaine. "Poetry, Injury, and the Ethics of Reading." In *The Humanities and Public Life,* edited by Peter Brooks with Hilary Jewett, 41–48. New York: Fordham University Press, 2014.

Scarry, Elaine. *Rule of Law, Misrule of Men.* Cambridge, MA: MIT Press, 2010.

Scarry, Elaine. *Thermonuclear Monarchy: Choosing between Democracy and Doom.* New York: W. W. Norton, 2014.

Scarry, Elaine. *Who Defended the Country?* Boston: Beacon Press, 2003.

Schatzman, Morton. "Paranoia or Persecution: The Case of Schreber." *Salmagundi* 19 (1972): 38–65.

Schauer, Frederick. "The Phenomenology of Speech and Harm." *Ethics* 103 (1993): 635–53.

Scherzinger, Martin. "Review of *Decentering Music.*" *Journal of the American Musicological Society* 59 (2006): 777–85.

Schwartz, Marie Jenkins. *Birthing a Slave: Motherhood and Medicine in the Antebellum South.* Cambridge, MA: Harvard University Press, 2006.

Scott, Marvin B., and Stanford M. Lyman. "Paranoia, Homosexuality and Game Theory." *Journal of Health and Social Behavior* 9 (1968): 179–87.

Scott-Baumann, Alison. *Ricoeur and the Hermeneutics of Suspicion.* London: Continuum, 2009.

Sedgwick, Eve Kosofsky. *A Dialogue on Love.* Boston: Beacon Press, 1999.

Sedgwick, Eve Kosofsky. *Epistemology of the Closet.* Berkeley: University of California Press, 1990.

Sedgwick, Eve Kosofsky. "Melanie Klein and the Difference Affect Makes." *South Atlantic Quarterly* 106 (2007): 625–42.

Sedgwick, Eve Kosofsky. "Paranoid Reading and Reparative Reading, or, You're So Paranoid, You Probably Think This Essay Is about You." In *Touching Feeling: Affect, Pedagogy, Performativity,* 123–51. Durham, NC: Duke University Press, 2003.

Sen, Amartya. *The Idea of Justice.* Cambridge, MA: Belknap Press of Harvard University Press, 2009.

Sen, Amartya. *Identity and Violence: The Illusion of Destiny.* New York: W. W. Norton, 2006.

Senate Committee on Intelligence. "Unclassified: Committee Study of the Central Intelligence Agency's Detention and Interrogation Program," released to the public on 9 December 2014, http://www.nytimes.com/interactive/2014/12/09/world/cia-torture-report-document.html?_r=0.

Sequenzia, Amy, and Elizabeth J. Grace, eds. *Typed Words, Loud Voices.* Fort Worth, TX: Autonomous Press, 2015.

"*Sesame Street* Music Torture." *Young Turks* (3 June 2012), http://www.youtube.com/watch?v=IJOc0bOycf8.

Shapiro, Michael J. *Studies in Trans-disciplinary Method: After the Aesthetic Turn*. New York: Routledge, 2013.

Shaw, Claire, and Lucy Ward. "Dark Thoughts: Why Mental Illness Is on the Rise in Academia." *Guardian* (6 March 2014), http://www.theguardian.com/higher-education-network/2014/mar/06/mental-health-academics-growing-problem-pressure-university?CMP=share_btn_fb.

Shelemay, Kay Kaufman. "The Impact and Ethics of Musical Scholarship." In *Rethinking Music*, edited by Nicholas Cook and Mark Everist, 531–44. New York: Oxford University Press, 2001.

Siebers, Tobin. *Disability Theory*. Ann Arbor: University of Michigan Press, 2008.

Silberman, Steve. *NeuroTribes: The Legacy of Autism and the Future of Neurodiversity*. New York: Avery, 2015.

Simonson, Mary. *Body Knowledge: Performance, Intermediality, and American Entertainment at the Turn of the Twentieth Century*. New York: Oxford University Press, 2013.

Slote, Michael. *The Ethics of Care and Empathy*. New York: Routledge, 2007.

Smith, Phil, ed. *Both Sides of the Table: Autoethnographies of Educators Learning and Teaching with/in [Dis]ability*. New York: Peter Lang, 2013.

Snediker, Michael. *Queer Optimism: Lyric Personhood and Other Felicitous Persuasions*. Minneapolis: University of Minnesota Press, 2009.

Snyder, Sharon L., and David T. Mitchell. "Introduction: Ablenationalism and the Geo-politics of Disability." *Journal of Literary and Cultural Disability Studies* 4 (2010): 113–25.

Society for American Music. "Resolutions Introduced at the SAM Business Meeting" (3 March 2007), http://www.american-music.org/organization/tick_resolution.php.

Sokal, Alan D. *Intellectual Impostures: Postmodern Philosophers' Abuse of Science*. London: Profile Books, 1998.

Solie, Ruth A. "Introduction: On 'Difference.'" In *Musicology and Difference: Gender and Sexuality in Music Scholarship*, edited by Ruth A. Solie, 1–20. Berkeley: University of California Press, 1993.

Solie, Ruth A. "Review of *Decentering Music*." *Music and Letters* 85 (2004): 418–23.

Solie, Ruth A. "What Do Feminists Want? A Reply to Pieter van den Toorn." *Journal of Musicology* 9 (1991): 399–410.

Solomon, Maynard. "Franz Schubert and the Peacocks of Benvenuto Cellini." *19th-Century Music* 12 (1989): 193–206.

Sontag, Susan. *Against Interpretation and Other Essays*. New York: Farrar, Straus & Giroux, 1966.

Sontag, Susan. *Regarding the Pain of Others*. New York: Farrar, Straus & Giroux, 2003.

Spelman, Elizabeth V. *Repair: The Impulse to Restore in a Fragile World*. Boston: Beacon Press, 2002.

Sperber, Dan, et al. "Epistemic Vigilance." *Mind & Language* 25 (2010): 359–93.

Spinelli, Frank. *Pee-Shy*. New York: Kensington, 2014.

Springer, Mike. "Noam Chomsky Slams Žižek and Lacan: Empty Posturing." *Open Culture* (28 June 2013), http://www.openculture.com/2013/06/noam_chomsky_slams_zizek_and_lacan_empty_posturing.html.

Srinivasan, Radhika, et al. "Chronic Abdominal Wall Pain: A Frequently Overlooked Problem." *American Journal of Gastroenterology* 97 (2002): 824–30.

Stansfeld, Stephen A., and Mark P. Matheson. "Noise Pollution: Non-auditory Effects on Health." *British Medical Bulletin* 68 (2003): 243–57.

Steblin, Rita. "The Peacock's Tale: Schubert's Sexuality Reconsidered." *19th-Century Music* 17 (1993): 5–33.

Sterne, Jonathan. *The Audible Past: Cultural Origins of Sound Reproduction.* Durham, NC: Duke University Press, 2003.

Sterne, Jonathan. "Mediate Auscultation, the Stethoscope, and the 'Autopsy of the Living': Medicine's Acoustic Culture." *Journal of Medical Humanities* 22 (2001): 115–36.

Sterne, Jonathan, ed. *The Sound Studies Reader.* New York: Routledge, 2012.

Stevenson, Bryan. *Just Mercy: A Story of Justice and Redemption.* New York: Spiegel & Grau, 2014.

Stewart, Kathleen. *Ordinary Affects.* Durham, NC: Duke University Press, 2007.

Stockton, Kathryn Bond. *Beautiful Bottom, Beautiful Shame: Where "Black" Meets "Queer."* Durham, NC: Duke University Press, 2006.

Stockton, Kathryn Bond. *The Queer Child, or Growing Sideways in the Twentieth Century.* Durham, NC: Duke University Press, 2009.

Stone, Alex. "Why Waiting Is Torture." *New York Times* (18 August 2012), http://www.nytimes.com/2012/08/19/opinion/sunday/why-waiting-in-line-is-torture.html?_r=0.

Straus, Joseph. "Idiots Savants, Retarded Savants, Talented Aments, Mono-Savants, Autistic Savants, Just Plain Savants, People with Savant Syndrome, and Autistic People Who Are Good at Things: A View from Disability Studies." *Disability Studies Quarterly* 34 (2014), http://dsq-sds.org/article/view/3407/3640.

Stuckey, Zosha. *A Rhetoric of Remnants: Idiots, Half-Wits, and Other State-Sponsored Inventions.* Albany: SUNY Press, 2014.

Sue, Derald Wing. *Microaggressions in Everyday Life: Race, Gender, and Sexual Orientation.* Hoboken, NJ: Wiley, 2010.

Suk, Jeannie. "Laws of Trauma." In *Knowing the Suffering of Others: Legal Perspectives on Pain and Its Meanings,* edited by Austin Sarat, 212–35. Tuscaloosa: University of Alabama Press, 2014.

Sunderland, Naomi, Tara Catalano, and Elizabeth Kendall. "Missing Discourses: Concepts of Joy and Happiness in Disability." *Disability & Society* 24 (2009): 703–14.

Sutton-Smith, Brian, John Gerstmyer, and Alice Meckley. "Playfighting as Folkplay amongst Preschool Children." *Western Folklore* 47 (1988): 161–76.

Swayne, Steve. "Music Is Power: Michael Dunn, Jordan Davis, and How We Respond When People Turn up the Volume." *Pacific Standard* (5 March 2014), http://www.psmag.com/navigation/books-and-culture/music-power-volume-sound-michael-dunn-jordan-davis-75929.

Tan, Amy. "Mother Tongue." *Threepenny Review* 43 (1990): 7–8.

Tannen, Deborah. "Agonism in Academic Discourse." *Journal of Pragmatics* 34 (2002): 1651–69.

Tannen, Deborah. *The Argument Culture: Stopping America's War on Words.* New York: Random House, 1998.

Taruskin, Richard. "Agents and Causes and Ends, Oh My." *Journal of Musicology* 31 (2014): 272–93.

Taruskin, Richard. "Is There a Baby in the Bathwater? (Part I)." *Archiv für Musikwissenschaft* 63 (2006): 163–85.

Taruskin, Richard. "Is There a Baby in the Bathwater? (Part II)." *Archiv für Musikwissenschaft* 63 (2006): 309–27.

Thomas, Gary C. "'Was George Frideric Handel Gay?': On Closet Questions and Cultural Politics." In *Queering the Pitch: The New Gay and Lesbian Musicology*, 2nd ed., edited by Philip Brett, Elizabeth Wood, and Gary C. Thomas, 155–203. New York: Routledge, 2006.

Thompson, Marie Suzanne. "Beyond Unwanted Sound: Noise, Affect and Aesthetic Moralism." Ph.D. dissertation, Newcastle University (2014).

Thoreau, Henry David. *The Journal, 1837–1861*, edited by Damion Searls. New York: New York Review Books, 2009.

Titchkosky, Tanya. "Coming Out Disabled: The Politics of Understanding." *Disability Studies Quarterly* 21 (2001): 131–39.

Tomkins, Silvan S. *Affect, Imagery, Consciousness*. Vol. 2, *The Negative Affects*. New York: Springer, 1963.

Topol, Eric. *The Patient Will See You Now: The Future of Medicine Is in Your Hands*. New York: Basic Books, 2015.

Tracey, Emma. "Not Just a Game: Is It Right to 'Recreate' Disability?" *BBC* (11 June 2014), http://www.bbc.com/news/blogs-ouch-27763085.

Tracy, Erik C., et al. "Judgments of Self-Identified Gay and Heterosexual Male Speakers: Which Phonemes Are Most Salient in Determining Sexual Orientation?" *Journal of Phonetics* 52 (2015): 13–25.

Tronto, Joan. *Moral Boundaries: A Political Argument for an Ethic of Care*. New York: Routledge, 1994.

Tune, Rev. Romal J. "Bullying Starts at Home." *Huffington Post* (21 May 2012), http://www.huffingtonpost.com/rev-romal-j-tune/bullying-starts-at-home_1_b_1528898.html.

Tyler, Carole-Ann. "Passing: Narcissism, Identity and Difference." In *Feminism Meets Queer Theory*, edited by Elizabeth Weed and Naomi Schor, 227–65. Bloomington: Indiana University Press, 1997.

Van den Toorn, Pieter. "Politics, Feminism, and Contemporary Music Theory." *Journal of Musicology* 9 (1991): 275–99.

Volcler, Juliette. *Extremely Loud: Sound as a Weapon*. Translated by Carol Volk. New York: New Press, 2013.

Vorwaller, Scheridan. "The Marching Band Agreed to Yield." Student paper (12 May 2015).

Walczak, Witold J., et al. "Karen L. Piper vs. City of Pittsburgh et al." Full claim available at http://www.aclupa.org/download_file/view_inline/791/486.

Waldron, Jeremy. *The Harm in Hate Speech*. Cambridge, MA: Harvard University Press, 2012.

Walters, Shannon. "Unruly Rhetorics: Disability, Animality, and New Kinship Compositions." *PMLA* 129 (2014): 471–77.

Walton, Benjamin. "Quirk Shame." *Representations* 132 (2015): 121–29.

Warner, Michael. "Queer and Then." *Chronicle of Higher Education* (1 January 2012), http://chronicle.com/article/QueerThen-/130161.

Warren, Jeff R. *Music and Ethical Responsibility*. Cambridge: Cambridge University Press, 2014.

White, Khadija. "Considering Sound: Reflecting on the Language, Meaning and Entailments of Noise." In *Reverberations: The Philosophy, Aesthetics and Politics of Noise*, edited by Michael Goddard, Benjamin Halligan, and Paul Hegarty, 233–43. New York: Continuum, 2012.

Wiegman, Robyn. *Object Lessons*. Durham, NC: Duke University Press, 2012.

Wiegman, Robyn, and Elizabeth A. Wilson. "Introduction: Antinormativity's Queer Conventions." *differences* 26 (2015): 1–25.

Wilbourne, Emily. "On a Lesbian Relationship with Musicology: Suzanne G. Cusick, Sound Effects." *Women & Music* 19 (2015): 3–14.

Wills, David. *Prosthesis*. Stanford, CA: Stanford University Press, 1995.

Wilton, Robert, and Stephanie Schuer. "Towards Socio-spatial Inclusion? Disabled People, Neoliberalism and the Contemporary Labour Market." *Area* 38 (2006): 186–95.

Winslow, Luke. "The Undeserving Professor: Neoliberalism and the Reinvention of Higher Education." *Rhetoric & Public Affairs* 18 (2015): 201–46.

Worthington, Andy. "Hit Me Baby One More Time." *Counterpunch* (15 December 2008), http://www.counterpunch.org/2008/12/15/hit-me-baby-one-more-time.

Wu, Cynthia. "Tenured and Happy." *Inside Higher Ed* (30 March 2015), http://www.insidehighered.com/advice/2015/03/30/essay-earning-tenure-and-considering-responsibilities-faculty-life.

Yablo, Stephen. *Aboutness*. Princeton, NJ: Princeton University Press, 2014.

Yates, Scott. "Neoliberalism and Disability: The Possibilities and Limitations of a Foucauldian Critique." *Foucault Studies* 19 (2015): 84–107.

Yekami, Elahe Haschemi, Eveline Kilian, and Beatrice Michaelis. "Introducing Queer Futures." In *Queer Futures: Reconsidering Ethics, Activism, and the Political*, 1–15. Burlington, VT: Ashgate, 2012.

Yoffe, Emily. "The Problem with Campus Sexual Assault Surveys." *Slate* (24 September 2015), http://www.slate.com/articles/double_x/doublex/2015/09/aau_campus_sexual_assault_survey_why_such_surveys_don_t_paint_an_accurate.html.

Zola, Irving Kenneth. "Self, Identity and the Naming Question: Reflections on the Language of Disability." *Social Science and Medicine* 36 (1993): 167–73.

Zuazu, María Edurne. "Loud but Non-lethal: Acoustic Stagings and State-Sponsored Violence." *Women & Music* 19 (2015): 151–59.

Index

✦ ✦ ✦